Theory and Decision Library consists of special publications in connection with *Theory and Decision*, independently edited by invited guest editors of high standing in their respective fields, and covering subjects of recent topical interest and worthy of a deeper and more multifaceted investigation than they normally receive in isolated articles and monographs. These special publications appear outside the running numeration of *Theory and Decision* issues and are obtainable independently through bookstores or from the publisher.

The goal of the Library is to augment the journal's regular program covering (1) methodology and philosophy of social sciences (2) formal analysis of empirical and normative models of society and (3) interdisciplinary communication. Particular emphasis will be laid on the possibility of realizing theoretical or normative models in practice, and of evaluating the contents of differing ideologies by formal analysis.

THE METHODOLOGICAL UNITY OF SCIENCE

THEORY AND DECISION LIBRARY

AN INTERNATIONAL SERIES
IN THE PHILOSOPHY AND METHODOLOGY OF THE
SOCIAL AND BEHAVIORAL SCIENCES

Editors:

GERALD EBERLEIN, *Universität des Saarlandes*

WERNER LEINFELLNER, *University of Nebraska*

Editorial Advisory Board:

VOLUME 3

THE METHODOLOGICAL UNITY
OF SCIENCE

Edited by

MARIO BUNGE

Foundations and Philosophy of Science Unit, McGill University, Montreal

D. REIDEL PUBLISHING COMPANY

DORDRECHT-HOLLAND / BOSTON-U.S.A.

Library of Congress Catalog Card Number 73–83554

ISBN 90 277 0354 X

Published by D. Reidel Publishing Company,
P.O. Box 17, Dordrecht, Holland

Sold and distributed in the U.S.A., Canada and Mexico
by D. Reidel Publishing Company, Inc.
306 Dartmouth Street, Boston,
Mass. 02116, U.S.A.

CONTENTS

PREFACE

The present volume collects some of the talks given at the Bertrand Russell Colloquium on Exact Philosophy, attached to the McGill University Foundations and Philosophy of Science Unit. It also includes a paper, on Bertrand Russell's method of philosophizing, read at the memorial symposium held at Sir Gorge Williams University shortly after the philosopher's death. All the papers appear here for the first time.

Unlike many a philosophy of science anthology, this one is not centered on the philosophy of physics. In fact the papers deal with conceptual and, in particular, philosophical problems that pop up in almost every one of the provinces of the vast territory constituted by the foundations, methodology and philosophy of science. A couple of border territories which are in the process of being infiltrated have been added for good measure.

The inclusion of papers in the philosophy of formal science and in the philosophies of physics and of biology, in a volume belonging to a series devoted to the philosophy and methodology of the social and behavioral sciences, should raise no eyebrows. Because the sciences of man make use of logic and mathematics, they are interested in questions such as whether the formal sciences have anything to do with reality (rather than with our theories about reality) and whether or not logic has kept up with the practice of mathematicians. These two problems are tackled in Part II, on the philosophy of formal science.

As to physics and biology, since they are the oldest members of the family of sciences, every worker in the contemporary sciences of man and in its philosophy has sought inspiration in the former. And rightly so, because in spite of the obvious differences in subject matter and in special techniques, theory construction and theory testing proceed essentially in the same way regardless of the particular sector of reality concerned. Besides, many of the special problems that were born in physics or in biology are also appearing in the sciences of man. For example, theoretical psychologists and sociologists have sometimes wondered about the possible forms of their laws, i.e. about the constraints that could be imposed upon the possible hypotheses in order to shrink their bewildering number or ensure their objectivity (subject independence). This problem is the theme of Part III, on the philosophy of physics.

Part IV, on the philosophy of biology, handles two other problems of interest to the sciences of man. One is the organ-function relation, which also appears in anthropology and sociology in relation with the dispute over functionalism (Does every institution perform a useful function?) and the claims of structuralism (Are societies structures or are they concrete systems endowed with a structure – just like any other systems?). The second question faced in this part is that of the proper way of axiomatizing a scientific theory and using it to clarify conceptual muddles and even solve substantive problems.

The last two papers, too, are germane to the philosophy of the sciences of man. The eleventh, belonging to ethics, is actually concerned with social behavior norms – and, as we know, such norms have to be reckoned with when passing from the behavior of wild animals to that of domesticated animals such as humans. And the twelfth paper, by facing the question of determinism, is relevant to social science, particularly since in mathematical sociology laws of two kinds, deterministic and stochastic, coexist without much trouble.

In conclusion, the papers in this volume, though thematically disparate, are methodologically akin: they deal with problems that, in one guise or another, appear in every corner of the sciences of man. Such a ubiquity speaks in favor of keeping the methodology and philosophy of the sciences of man close to those of the other sciences. After all, it is men who build the sciences and all of these are concerned with understanding concrete systems.

It is a pleasant duty to thank the Canada Council for supporting our Colloquium on Exact Philosophy. It is also a pleasure to record my appreciation to Professors Werner Leinfellner and Gerald Eberlein for inviting me to prepare this anthology.

PART I

INTRODUCTION

MARIO BUNGE

BERTRAND RUSSELL'S *REGULAE PHILOSOPHANDI*

ABSTRACT. Bertrand Russell is presented as the first philosopher who attempted to be both exact and in tune with the science of his day. Certain rules of philosophical method are ferreted out of his writings. These rules can be summarized in the slogan: "To philosophize is to apply the scientific method to the study of human knowledge." Russell's failures may be construed as occasional unfaithfulnesses to his own *regulae*. And these lapses may be explained as the price paid for his attachment to two mutually incompatible philosophical traditions: those of British empiricism and Platonism.

It is well known that Bertrand Russell was not a single person but a whole sequence of scholars. Every one of them was eminent in at least one field and all of them were responsible, deep and clear thinkers as well as superb writers and outspoken men. Every one of the Russells had some fault to find with the writings of his predecessors, and so there is no question of a monolithic Russellian philosophy. There could be none, for every Russell was a truth-seeker, none was a knight intent on propagating and defending a philosophical faith. To criticize any of those Russells because he did not stick to the views of his predecessors is therefore to ignore the basic and unique fact that Bertrand Russell's brain was the abode of at least half a dozen eminent philosophers.

For all their diversity of interests or rather of emphasis, the Russells did share some family traits: a relentless searching for truth and clarity, an unusual readiness to change their minds when presented with evidence unfavorable to any of their views, an undying interest in human knowledge, and a precise way of going about posing and solving philosophical problems. These traits are patent in every one of the members of the Russell family: the young Hegelian, the slightly older Kantian, the mature empiricist, the phenomenalist and the neutral monist, the more mature semi-materialist and the ageless Platonist. While all of them wrestled with important problems and had interesting things to say, what attracts me most about them is the method they share. This, which may be called *Russell's method of philosophizing*, is the invariant of all the philosophical mutations we have mentioned. It should be worth our while to examine it.

M. Bunge (ed.), The Methodological Unity of Science, 3–12. All Rights Reserved.
Copyright © 1973 by D. Reidel Publishing Company, Dordrecht-Holland.

Russell's way of handling philosophical problems, as I see it, is a sequence with the following steps:

(1) discovering a genuine problem – not a puzzle but a problem the solution to which is likely to teach us something new;

(2) studying the context of the problem, i.e. the body of knowledge from which it raises its head; this involves getting hold of a stock of examples to be taken into account for the rest of the investigation;

(3) starting some sparks in the midst of this background knowledge, that might give rise to a suitable solution; that is, trying to produce some conjectures;

(4) stating the conjectures as clearly as possible and working them out to discover what they commit us to;

(5) to put the proposed solutions to the test, i.e. to criticize them and choose the best among them.

Russell's method of philosophizing is thus none other than the method of science applied to philosophical problems. The specific difference is that, in the case of philosophy, logical rigor in the formulations, analyses and inferences is emphasized at the expense of considerations of empirical validation. Let us take a closer look at this procedure.

Russell starts by realizing or choosing some genuine philosophical problem. He disdains miniproblems such as verbal questions: to him language is a tool for expressing ideas, not the primary object of philosophical research – and it must be admitted that he handles both ordinary language and the language of mathematics with more dexterity and elegance than any of the linguistic philosophers. He felt these people were "occupied solely with trivialities"[1] and could not understand why they practised the "cult of common usage" rather than devoting themselves to authentic problems. He blamed this on the later Wittgenstein who, unlike the earlier one, "seems to have grown tired of serious thinking and to have invented a doctrine which would make such an activity unnecessary. I do not for a moment believe that the doctrine which has these lazy consequences is true. I realize, however, that I have an overpoweringly strong bias against it, for, if it is true, philosophy is, at best, a slight help to lexicographers, and at worst, an idle tea-table amusement."[2] Russell, in short, is interested in philosophical problems, not in word games. "In common with all philosophers before W II [the second Wittgenstein], my fundamental aim has been to understand the world as well as may be, and to separate what may count as knowledge from what must be rejected as unfounded opinion."[3]

Once he has chosen the problem Russell tries to find out what he can learn from others about it: in particular what science can teach him. He is therefore constantly learning new facts, not just new words. Thus he teaches himself the most novel and difficult scientific theories of his time, like relativity, quantum theory and Pavlovian learning theory. He must have felt that it is preposterous and even dishonest to propound views on human knowledge without knowing anything. For example, when dealing with perception he did not make an effort to ignore whatever physics, physiology and psychology had to say about it. He did not handle it as a linguistic exercise: he did not ask what the common usages of the verbs 'to see', 'to hear', and so on happened to be in the Oxford colleges during his time. He analyzed specific cases of perception and he propounded a causal theory of perception that makes sense to the physiologist even though it may leave the lexicographer quite cold. In sum, he opposed the tendency to sever the relationships between philosophy and science: "A philosophy which is to have any value should be built upon a wide and firm foundation of knowledge that is not specifically philosophical. Such knowledge is the soil from which the tree of philosophy derives its vigour. Philosophy which does not draw nourishment from this soil will soon wither and cease to grow."[4]

The same research that uncovered the context of the problem may spark some hints as to its possible solution. Only research can fill the gaps it creates. There is no other way of expanding one's mind than expanding one's knowledge. In the field of philosophy, 'LSD' stands for "Learn, Solve problems, Discuss." In short: investigate. It is in the course of an investigation, though often spontaneously rather than as a result of putting on a thinking cap, that new ideas pop up. They are born embryonic, often obscure, and sometimes so quickly that it is hardly possible to keep track of them all. Some of them may constitute the clue for solving the problem; most are bound to be inadequate. But how shall we find out which ones are correct and which are not if we hasten to throw them at the faithful, the commentators and the popularizers? A responsible thinker is not one who fails to have intellectual intuitions but one who controls them, for he knows that initial conjectures are sometimes confused, at other times clear but false, always sketchy. Which will lead Russell, or any other responsible thinker, to the fourth stage.

This fourth stage is the one of clarifying the possible conjectures and of exploring their logical consequences, in order to be able to put them to the test. This analysis has to be supplemented by a sort of reverse deduction, whereby the founding premises are disclosed. It is important to find them because they may already be known as true, or as false, and because if they were not known before they may supply the basis for a new theory. And this, a theory, is of course the ultimate desideratum of philosophical research: like every other great philosopher before him, Russell regarded analysis as a tool rather than as an end in itself. In any case, this phase of logical elaboration is where Russell excelled. At times he got carried away by his enthusiasm for logic: he went as far as to claim that "all philosophy is logic."[5] But this was more apparent than real: I believe it was a reaction against intuitionism and irrationalism, rather than a faithful image of his own philosophy. For the same book where that panlogicist statement occurs is devoted to expounding the epistemological and metaphysical theories he held at the time. Be that as it may, if Russell finds his conclusions and their premises unsatisfactory, he says so. If he finds them satisfactory, he terminates *pro tempore* his research and jumps over to some other problem. He has got a theory that his admirers and critics will repeat, belabor, or criticize for a number of years. He could not care less for any such development.

Satisfaction with a theory, if attained at all, is ephemerous unless one stops thinking about the problems the theory is supposed to solve. Sooner or later the fifth stage, theory evaluation, will have to set in. During this stage Russell will criticize his own theory with all candour: he will show its limitations, or its inconsistency with what he has learned since proposing the theory. He may go as far as proposing not just counter-examples but a whole new theory – a theory produced by a new Russell, one who has been able not only to discover past mistakes but to find alternative solutions and sometimes alternative approaches. But the new Russell will use again the same method I have sketched above. This is why it is always worth our while to reread Russell: to learn to philosophize the exact and scientific way.

One may disagree with many or even all of the results of this way of philosophizing, just as one may disagree with many outcomes of scientific research while adhering to the scientific method. The reason is simply this:

a philosophical view is not an isolated item but an outcome of a process that starts out with a body of knowledge, or of opinion, that contains more than one false assumption. If one accepts a Platonist assumption one will not be able to avoid ending up with a doctrine containing Platonist elements; if one subscribes to the phenomenalist thesis one will end up by construing every empirical concept as a sort of collection of subjective experiences, and so on. That mixed body of knowledge and opinion, so important in the genesis of every problem, is not entirely above suspicion in the case of philosophy. So, even an exact and scientific philosopher like Russell has often been unwittingly dragged by historical currents which, on closer examination, he would eventually repudiate. One can imagine the liberating effect that the writing of his *History of Western Philosophy* exerted on him: it must have helped him getting rid of some tenets and improving consistency.

We have time to consider but two points in Russell's philosophy that seem unsatisfactory to me: one of his theories of proper names and his treatment of simplicity.

At one point[6] Russell proposes to eliminate particulars, replacing them by logical constructions in which only universals may occur. Thus this particular podium should be regarded as a bundle of co-present qualities. Consequently instead of referring to the podium by its name or by a definite description, like "the podium in the classroom," we must refer to it as to a certain collection of properties, among them the spatial and temporal location. In other words, things and events are replaced by a set of properties and, consequently, the singular concept is analyzed into a bundle of universals. This view seems to have had two independent sources: one is Platonism, the other is phenomenalism of the Berkeley-Mach kind. But the manifest origin mentioned by Russell looks neutral, namely that we seem to have experience of qualities but not of the subject in which those qualities inhere. Yet this again is a version of the polemics of Locke against the idea of substance.

Whatever its historical sources, Russell's proposal is untenable, and he himself seems to have abandoned it. *Prima facie* there are two possibilities: either Russell's analysis of particulars is valid but lacks the ontological significance he attributes to it, or it is invalid. Assume first the analysis is valid. It does not follow that the singular and concrete has been eliminated in favor of the universal and abstract: conceptual analysis has no causal efficacy. But the analysis cannot be valid: properties hanging in mid-air are no more real than substrates without properties. Both in experience and in scientific theory we are given objects that can be analyzed in various ways, none of which consists in the elimination of particulars. Thus the fact expressed by the sentence 'That kettle is boiling' may be construed as "k is a B", where 'k' names that particular kettle, or as "The temperature of k equals 100°C". Moreover, upon analyzing the temperature concept we find that it is a certain function on the set of all possible particular bodies. In either case we cannot dispense with proper names. Besides, if we were to eliminate proper names in favor of logical constructions of the Platonic kind, we would violate the empiricist principle that commands that we analyze everything in terms of experiences. Moreover, something as simple as a proper name, which is after all a conventional tag, becomes a huge logical construction involving countless bits of information. In other words, one cannot be a Platonist and an empiricist at the same time – unless one happens to be B.R. But quite apart from the inadequacy of this view, it constitutes a typical example of the Russellian mode of philosophizing, in the sense that it brings together metaphysics, epistemology, and logic. To him these were not separate disciplines but aspects of a whole. It is possible to emphasize one of them at a time but it is impossible to separate them.

The second difficulty I wish to mention is this: Russell, alongside the conventionalists and the logical empiricists, has defended simplicism and at the same time validation by empirical confirmation, even though he came to the conclusion that science employs the hypothetico-deductive method rather than the inductive one.[7] Take any so called empirical curve, or set of points on a plane, each representing the outcome of the measurement of two correlated quantities. Given any set of such experimental points there are infinitely many curves passing through them or close to them. If the criterion of truth is maximal confirmation, then we must choose the most complex of the hypotheses involved, i.e. the most wavy of the curves. In this way there will be no anomalous data, i.e. points far from the proposed curve. And the chances are that any new datum will confirm this complex hypothesis, while the simplest hypothesis is the most exposed of all. That was not Russell's recommendation: he proposed choosing the simplest hypothesis, which is the riskier one, without abandoning the desideratum of maximal confirmation. However, it is clear that these two desiderata, maximal confirmation and maximal simplicity, are mutually inconsistent.[8]

This leads us to another trait of Russell's: he was a skeptic in search of certainty – not the simple minded certainty of a Santayana or the slightly more sophisticated one of Dewey to be sure, but certainty at last. He wants analysis itself to serve this purpose: he asserts once and again that the aim of logical analysis is to restrict the number of elements and of hypotheses with the final aim of decreasing uncertainty: "you diminish the risk of error with every diminution of entities and premisses. When I spoke about the desk and said I was not going to assume the existence of a persistent substance underlying its appearances, it is an example of the case in point. You have anyhow the successive appearances, and if you can get on without assuming the metaphysical and constant desk, you have a smaller risk of error than you had before. You would not necessarily have a smaller risk of error if you were tied down to *denying* the metaphysical desk. That is the advantage of Occam's Razor, that it diminishes your risk of error."[9]

Russell was of course right in claiming that, upon decreasing the number of hypothesized entities, one decreases the possibility of error. He might as well have taken this point to its logical consequence, namely that the risk of error is altogether eliminated upon keeping quiet. But then this is not the goal of science but rather an aim of mystics. Scientists multiply hypotheses and complicate them, even at the risk of error, because they are after the truth – and experience has taught them that truth is usually complex rather than simple. Russell, the philosopher of science, knows this and is eager to exploit every new scientific complication; Russell, the rationalist, dislikes complexity in science even though he himself has contributed to increasing the complexity (the richness) of mathematics.

Let this suffice as a sample of the many disputed questions one finds on rereading Russell – a fascinating experience that is never repeated, because one finds every time thought provoking hypotheses one had overlooked before.

What was Russell's final philosophy? I think it can be found in his beautiful book *My Philosophical Development* and in remarks scattered along the three volumes of his revealing *Autobiography*. Let me mention just a few of the theses, or rather hypotheses, that Russell seems to have arrived at towards the end of his philosophical career. They are all taken from the above mentioned books.

(1) All events are physical; those which are only physical are known by inference.

(2) The mind has emerged in an evolutionary process that has proceeded according to laws in which the mental has had no role.

(3) The way the brain converts a light signal into a light sensation is not more mysterious than the way a radio-set transforms electromagnetic waves into sounds.

(4) Strictly speaking we observe only that which happens within our skulls. When we observe another brain, what we see belongs to our private world. This does not mean that the other brain is a creation of ours: we infer its existence and do not doubt it.

(5) The problems of language do not constitute an autonomous realm, because what is essential to language is that it has meaning, that is, that it is related to something which, as a rule, is extra-linguistic.

(6) Factual truth is a certain causal relation between a belief and a fact.

(7) The structure of our discourse must be somehow related to the structure of facts, whence the study of syntax must supply some knowledge about the world.

(8) Whatever can be said about a complex system may also be said, without mentioning the system, about its parts and their mutual relations.

(9) Analysis supplies new knowledge without destroying the starting point, which is usually vague; and philosophical research starts from what is vague and often enigmatic, attaining clarity through analysis.

(10) "One very general conclusion to which I have been led by reading Professor Ryle's book [*The Concept of Mind*] is that philosophy cannot be fruitful if divorced from empirical science. And by this I do not mean only that the philosopher should 'get up' some sciences as a holiday task. I mean something much more intimate: that his imagination should be

impregnated with the scientific outlook and that he should feel that science has presented us with a new world, new concepts and new methods, not known in earlier times, but proved by experience to be fruitful where the older concepts and methods proved barren."[10]

Russell's pleas for the adoption of a scientific outlook in philosophy have fallen mostly on barren soil: most contemporary philosophers find little if any use for Russell's writings: they hardly read and discuss them. This they do at their own risk – at the risk of being unable to produce any piece of interesting and exact philosophy. (Note the conjunction: exactness is compatible with hollowness, and interesting ideas come often expressed in inarticulate ways.) Moreover, those philosophers who afford ignoring Russell deprive themselves of the almost sensual pleasure of reading his terse and witty prose, to my taste the best philosophical literature since Lucretius.

On the other hand, because of his confidence in science and because of his preoccupation with the logical, epistemological, semantical, metaphysical and even ethical and social problems generated by scientific research, Bertrand Russell is, of all contemporary philosophers, the most widely read by practising scientists. Not that his ideas are all acceptable to a scientist: the secret of his success is that his books deal with problems that catch the interest of the scientist, and he handles them in a way that looks familiar to the scientist.

Bertrand Russell has not left us a theory that puts an end to philosophical research. He has bequeathed upon us something much more valuable than any allegedly final system, namely a swarm of epistemological and metaphysical problems which he clarified and related to problems in science and in logic. And, above all, he has left us an exemplary attitude: the attitude of respect for scientific knowledge and for the scientific method as well as the rationalist attitude of analyzing carefully not only other people's views but also and primarily one's own, and of doing it with maximal integrity. This, the *Russell attitude*, is scientific, hence intellectually honest. And, as he showed himself, it can be, nay it must be adopted in all fields, from mathematical logic to politics, through science and philosophy, if we are to perpetuate the species called *Homo sapiens*.[11]

Foundations and Philosophy of Science Unit
McGill University

NOTES

[1] *The Autobiography of Bertrand Russell*, Vol. III, George Allen and Unwin, London, 1969, p. 37.
[2] *My Philosophical Development*, George Allen and Unwin, London, 1959, p. 217.
[3] *Ibid.*
[4] *Loc. cit.*, p. 230.
[5] *Our Knowledge of the External World* [1914], George Allen and Unwin, London, 1949, p. 42.
[6] *An Inquiry into Meaning and Truth*, George Allen and Unwin, London, 1940, Chap. VI.
[7] *Human Knowledge: Its Scope and Limits*, George Allen and Unwin, London, 1948, *passim*. He conceives of induction as "an application of mathematical probability to premisses arrived at independently of induction" (p. 451).
[8] See my book *The Myth of Simplicity*, Prentice-Hall, Englewood Cliffs, N.J., 1963.
[9] *The Philosophy of Logical Atomism*, Lecture VIII, repr. in *Logic and Knowledge* (ed. by R. C. Marsh), George Allen and Unwin, London, 1956, p. 280.
[10] *My Philosophical Development*, p. 254.
[11] For a discussion of the applicability of this method in philosophy, social science, and biology, see my book *Method, Model and Matter*, Reidel, Dordrecht, 1973.

PART II

FORMAL SCIENCE

CHARLES CASTONGUAY

MATHEMATICS AND ONTOLOGY

ABSTRACT. The Platonist attitude towards mathematical existence, though heuristically fruitful, remains epistemologically obscure. Heuristics is in fact the proper sphere in which to entertain ontological talk in mathematics, where objectivity rests rather on proof than on reference to purported objects, and where anontological heuristic strategies, or styles, have also proven powerful. From this perspective, Quine's applications to mathematics of his notions of ontological commitment and reduction unduly emphasize set-theoretic semantics as supplying ontologies for mathematical theories, and heuristic cross-fertilization, more than reduction, is seen to be the significant outcome of the formal comparison of mathematical theories.

The mathematician deals with his subject with a degree of assurance which the philosopher often envies. But when questioned on the ontological nature of the objects of his study, the mathematician more often than not adopts one of two attitudes: he either flatly denies any validity to the question, or – perhaps to the questioner's secret glee – displays a definite uneasiness in attempting a satisfactory reply. I will try here to reconcile these divergent reactions. In combining the opinions of several active mathematicians, an answer may be offered to the question of mathematical existence. This not too uneasy answer will still not enjoy the sharpness of W. V. Quine's applications to mathematics of his ontological notions, which I shall object to, however, as inappropriate for mathematics.

1. Proof and Objectivity

Evidently the verification of his theoretical findings against some parcel of physical reality is not in the mathematician's habits. Unlike any of the natural sciences, assurance of truth in mathematics derives entirely from the testing of proofs of statements against a common logical code and a minimal common understanding of basic concepts.

Thus Goodstein (1969) asserts that in mathematics, truth reduces to proof, Benacerraf (1965) finds that the mathematician's interest properly stops at the level of structure, Robinson (1966) holds that mathematical meaning is to be sought in the logical development of a theory and not in the determination of a denotation for its individual terms, and Quine himself (1969, p. 44) attests that numbers and sets are known only through their laws. Kreisel (1958) proposes, indeed, that the entire question of mathematical existence would best be discarded in favour of that of mathematical objectivity.

The gruff shrugging off of ontological questions by some mathematicians (Y. Bar-Hillel is notoriously one such shrugger) is consequently to be expected. Yet it is just as sharply felt by the practicing mathematician that he is not pursuing purely conventional games, either. There is more to mathematical proof than rigid deduction: a 'good' proof should enhance the understanding of the concepts at play in the statement of the theorem. Conviction does not follow simply from strictly formal manipulation, at least not the kind of conviction which leads to further results.

It is this elusive quality in mathematical activity which brings other mathematicians to hesitatingly attempt a positive answer to existence questions. Ranking among the better such efforts are the themes of a "mathematical community of understanding" (Myhill, 1951), that of a "mathematical factuality" (Bernays, 1950), and that of "informal rigour" (Kreisel, 1967a). Each of these themes entertains a kind of mathematical objectivity which does not derive solely from formal deduction, and from which inspiration for further deductions may proceed. In the eyes of many mathematicians, various parts of mathematics, such as analysis or set theory, appear to have a factual 'hard core', the possible articulations of which it is the mathematician's task to examine.

I have emphasized elsewhere (1972) the unnecessary risk of neo-Platonism accompanying such conceptions of mathematical objectivity, which I find to be misleadingly static. I would prefer to avoid this risk, and, at the same time, try to do justice to the dynamism characteristic of mathematical activity, as follows.

2. HEURISTICS AND THE MATHEMATICAL OBJECT

In seeking to lay bare new interrelations between mathematical objects and to devise proof of these relations, the mathematician may well resort to Platonist fictions, and clothe his conceptions in striking garb the better to excite his imagination; to such an extent that Beth finds evidence of a "pre-established harmony" between pure mathematical thought, the deductive method, and Platonism (Beth and Piaget, 1966, pp. 101ff.). Examples of Platonist heuristic tactics are the prodigiously fruitful fiction of the infinitesimal, the equally suggestive make-believe of the actual infinite, or the Cantorian vision of the set concept.

But these successes do not prohibit the securing of similar results from other heuristic grounds, be it through the re-working of the calculus from the limit standpoint, by the intuitionist development of analysis, or with the predicativist approach to set theory. And in the process, the supposedly stable mathematical 'object' may lose old properties, or gain new ones, according to the perspective from which it is observed.

Ultimately, what perception of the object is to be retained as the 'correct' one depends on the use to which the mathematician would put it – not excluding its eventual use as an instrument with which to observe, in turn, other objects, as the notion of set, for example, may serve to explain that of number, following one of the familiar 'reductions' of numbers to sets. Hence how the object is seen, how the notion is grasped, is contingent upon the aim of the mathematician, upon those properties of the object which he would emphasize in striving towards certain new applications, new results, or, at times, in reformulating old ones.

Just as the representation of the complex numbers as vectors strongly suggests their addition laws, while their representation as operators on vectors does likewise for their multiplication, so will different mathematical properties 'behave' more or less well, or seem more or less 'natural', under the action of different stylistic approaches to them. What conceptual framework, e.g., what version of set theory, works out as a "comfortable home for our intellect," as Bernays (1967) puts it, depends on the mathematician's experience and the applications he has in view.

More strongly than in the natural sciences, then, in mathematics the representation of the object dominates the object itself. An emerging mathematical structure exists much more as a perspective on an object than as an object proper, the expression of this perspective being a particular unity in the orientation of research moves, a particular heuristic strategy before the developing theory. Epistemologically, I find it more rewarding and more appropriate to thus regard mathematics as process rather than as a static accumulation of finished products, and consequently to stress mathematical construction over acquired mathematical structures.

Under such a constructivist bias, heuristics holds primacy over the object. I find little more than formal pleasure, in particular, in considering set-theoretic models of a mathematical theory as constituting the 'semantics' of the theory, or as providing an 'ontology' for the theory. While satisfaction for the natural scientist essentially derives from a more apt description of reality borne out by physical experimentation, that of the mathematician resides mainly in the success of definite heuristic moves, or stylistic posits, in formulating fresh conjectures concerning his relatively free constructions. The mathematical object earns its keep, I propose, only insofar as it is heuristically productive.

In this light I can appreciate today a talk on mathematical existence given by Hans Zassenhaus some years ago at the University of Montreal. Rather than come to grips directly with mathematical objects, Zassenhaus insisted instead on the pleasure experienced by mathematicians in pursuing their activities, and, to the confusion and disappointment of many of the philosophers in attendance, presented the mathematician's happiness in manipulating his creations as measure and gage of their existence. That this way of grounding objectivity on heuristic pleasure and success did not overly dismay several of the active mathematicians present bears out, perhaps, the aptness of only visualizing the mathematical object in such a heuristic context.

3. Ontological commitment?

Talk of set-theoretic 'semantics' for mathematics is itself acceptable to me, therefore, only as an expression of a possible style, a style which undeniably can prove epistemologically fruitful (in obtaining or explaining, say, the completeness and incompleteness results in logic, or non-standard analysis, etc.) but which it is not proper to accept as absolute, as the proper way to deal with reference in mathematics. Whatever arguments are brought forth for or against Quine's holding that the existential interpretation of the quantifiers is the key idiom of ontology (e.g. Parsons, 1971), I cannot approve as entirely fitting his claim that mathematics is "up to its neck in commitments to an ontology of abstract entities" (1953, p. 13). However heavily the heuristic components of some mathematical theories, e.g., number theory or Cantorist set theory, may be keyed to the entertainment of beings-in-the-abstract, there are means of bringing such theories into play, for instance through a category-theoretic formulation, which seriously deflates such commitment.

Following the reduction of several branches of mathematics to set theory, it was surprising to discover that such apparently disparate concepts as triangles and numbers were all recognizable as set-theoretic constructs. The unification of mathematics brought about by these reductions certainly proved heuristically stimulating, but talk of the supposed accompanying 'ontological' reduction of, for example, numbers to sets, leaves most mathematicians indifferent – and some irate. The heuristic 'ontologies' of the theories in play in such reduction situations have never lost their autonomous vitality for the working mathematician.

It is noteworthy here that W. Lawvere's category-theoretic foundations for mathematics, set theory included, provides a conceptual basis for mathematics which brings to the fore the constructive aspect of mathematical activity, through the emphasis which it puts on morphisms (functions, transformations) and the natural setting which it provides for the hierarchical manipulation of mathematical constructs: the same basic categorial concepts suffice to transparently describe the relevant mathematical features encountered throughout successive levels of abstraction (cf. MacLane, 1972). In contrast to the usual set-theoretic interpretations, which focus on the notion of object, or element, one of the effects of this categorial style is to play down the role of the notion of mathematical object in favour of a direct approach to structural phenomena. The mathematical objects become known and identified solely through the recognition of the structural features which characterize them. Such categorial interpretations of mathematical activity quite faithfully render the ontological apathy of a growing number of mathematicians.

While Quine opines that there is a continuum of gradations within natural science running from statements of observations to statements of theory, and that "statements of ontology or even of mathematics and logic form a continuation of this continuum... the differences here... [being] in my view differences only in degree and not in kind" (1951, p. 134), I feel that such extension of the referential interpretation to also cover mathematical discourse runs against the fact that in mathematics relevant ontological discussion goes on beyond the theoretic-heuristic line, however vague that line may be. An objective analysis of the mathematician's ontological commitment by means of set-theoretic interpretations or 'semantics' strikes me as a perversion of the properly heuristic nature of ontological considerations in the mathematical enterprise.

4. ONTOLOGICAL REDUCTION?

Entertainment of ontological reductions amongst mathematical theories presupposes a clear idea of the ontologies of these theories. As I hold that the significant sense of ontological questions in mathematics is primarily heuristic, I cannot agree with Quine that the arithmetization of syntax through Gödel numbering is a notable ontological reduction of strings of signs to numbers (1969), nor that the Frege interpretation of numbers as sets ontologically reduces numbers to sets (1966).

Talk of the ontology of a mathematical theory results, in my view, from a carry-over of our means of perception and description of physical phenomena (from which a first elaboration of a mathematical theory frequently enough derives) to the mathematical sphere. The ontological quality which runs through the heuristic component of many a mathematical theory is vividly acknowledged even by the supposedly frigid formalist, Bourbaki: "The mathematician does not work mechanically, like a worker on an assembly line; one cannot insist enough on the fundamental role played, in a mathematician's research, by a particular kind of *intuition*, not a common sensory intuition, but rather a kind of direct divination (preceding all reasoning) of the normal behavior which he seems justified to expect of mathematical entities with which he has, through long experience, become almost as familiar as with beings of the real world. Each structure brings with it its own proper language, all laden with special intuitive resonances..." (1962, p. 45).

Such words pay tribute to the heuristic specificity of developing mathematical theories. Recognition of this specificity runs against the notion of reduction, making questionable the validity of speaking of reducing one theory to another. As I have tried to substantiate at length elsewhere (1972), the mathematically important end result of inter-theoretic comparisons and correspondences is not the possibility of reducing or eliminating one theory in favour of another, but rather the stimulating effect which the juxtaposition of the 'proper languages' of the theories involved has on their mutual development, in suggesting fresh conjectures, new directions in which their deductive investigation may evolve. Colourful expression of a similar opinion may be found in Kreisel (1967b, p. 214), Thom, (1970, p. 236), or Wang: "There is no reason to suppose that numbers evaporate but classes are rocks" (1966, p. 341).

For mathematical theories, then, I hold that the worthwhile concept – indeed, phenomenon – is ontological, or heuristic, cross-fertilization, not reduction. The well-known definition of ontological reduction given by Quine (1966, p. 205) simply fits more correctly into the category of inter-theoretic correspondences where the *intensional*, that is to say deductive, components of meanings (cf. Castonguay, 1972) are preserved, correspondences which are commonly called translations, interpretations, or iso-morphisms. As does Tharp (1971), even from the examples of ontological reduction given by Quine himself (none of which are heuristically trivial) I can only conclude that for mathematical theories, ontological entertain-ment – and theoretical advancement – is more properly found in the in-teresting clashes and cross-fertilizations of heuristic components than in formal, pseudo-referential correspondences.

There is little epistemological gain in over-extending the referential way of speaking from the natural sciences into the mathematical context, or in assuming a greater assurance before ontological questions in mathe-matics than the mathematician sees fit to adopt himself. I am afraid that my difficulties with Quine's vocabulary is not a basic controversy over ontology of the sort which can be docilely "translated upward into a se-mantical controversy about words and what to do with them" (1953, p. 16).

Department of Mathematics,
University of Ottawa

BIBLIOGRAPHY

Benacerraf, P.: 1965, 'What Numbers Could Not Be', *Phil. Rev.* **74**, 47–73.
Bernays, P.: 1950, 'Mathematische Existenz und Widerspruchsfreiheit', in *Études de Philosophie des sciences en hommage à F. Gonseth*, Griffon, Neuchâtel, pp. 11–25.
Bernays, P.: 1967, 'What Do Some Recent Results in Set Theory Suggest?', in I. Lakatos (ed.), *Problems in the Philosophy of Mathematics*, North Holland Publ. Co., Amsterdam, pp. 109–112.
Beth, E. W. and Piaget, J.: 1966, *Mathematical Epistemology and Psychology*, Gordon and Breach, N.Y.
Bourbaki, N.: 1962, 'L'architecture des mathématiques', in F. Le Lionnais (ed.), *Les grands courants de la pensée mathématique*, 2nd ed., Blanchard, Paris, pp. 35–47.
Castonguay, C.: 1972, *Meaning and Existence in Mathematics*, Springer-Verlag, N.Y.-Wien.
Goodstein, R. L.: 1969, 'Empiricism in Mathematics', *Dialectica* **23**, 50–57.
Kreisel, G.: 1958, 'Wittgenstein's Remarks on the Foundations of Mathematics', *Brit. J. Phil. Sci.* **9**, 135–158.
Kreisel, G.: 1967a, 'Informal Rigour and Completeness Proofs', in I. Lakatos (ed.),

Problems in the Philosophy of Mathematics, North Holland Publ. Co., Amsterdam, pp. 138–186.

Kreisel, G.: 1967b, 'Mathematical Logic: What Has It Done for the Philosophy of Mathematics?', in R. Schoenman (ed.), *Bertrand Russell: Philosopher of the Century*, George Allen and Unwin, London, pp. 201–272.

MacLane, S.: 1972, *Categories for the Working Mathematician*, Springer-Verlag, N.Y.-Heidelberg-Berlin.

Myhill, J.: 1951, 'On the Ontological Significance of the Löwenheim-Skolem Theorem', in I. M. Copi and J. A. Gould (eds.), *Contemporary Readings in Logical Theory*, MacMillan, N.Y., pp. 40–51.

Parsons, C.: 1971, 'A Plea For Substitutional Quantification', *J. Phil.* **68**, 231–237.

Quine, W. V.: 1951, 'On Carnap's Views on Ontology', in *The Ways of Paradox*, Random House, N.Y., 1966, pp. 126–134.

Quine, W. V.: 1953, *From a Logical Point of View*, Harper and Row, N.Y.

Quine, W. V.: 1966, 'Ontological Reduction', in *The Ways of Paradox*, Random House, N.Y., 1966, pp. 199–207.

Quine, W. V.: 1969, 'Ontological Relativity', in *Ontological Relativity and Other Essays*, Columbia Univ. Press, N.Y., pp. 26–68.

Robinson, A.: 1966, 'Formalism 64', in Y. Bar-Hillel (ed.), *Logic, Methodology, and Philosophy of Science*, North Holland Publishing Co., Amsterdam, pp. 228–246.

Tharp, L.: 1971, 'Ontological Reduction', *J. Phil.* **68**, 151–164.

Thom, R.: 1970, 'Les mathématiques 'modernes': une erreur pédagogique et philosophique?', *L'Age de la science* 3, 225–242.

Wang, H.: 1966, 'Process and Existence in Mathematics', in Y. Bar-Hillel *et al.* (eds.), *Essays in the Foundations of Mathematics*, Hebrew Univ. Press, Jerusalem, pp. 328–351.

JOHN CORCORAN

GAPS BETWEEN LOGICAL THEORY
AND MATHEMATICAL PRACTICE

ABSTRACT. Mathematical practice seems to presuppose what Church has called an underlying logic. Mathematical logic proceeds in strict analogy with mathematical physics where mathematical models of physical systems are constructed and studied. Mathematical logic constructs models of underlying logics. This paper focuses on mismatches between currently accepted models and the underlying logics.

By a proof, I understand a section of a mathematical text.... . Proofs, however, had to exist before the structure of a proof could be logically analyzed; and this analysis... must have rested... on a large body of mathematical writings. In other words, logic, so far as we mathematicians are concerned, is no more and no less than the grammar of the language which we use, a language which had to exist before the grammar could be constructed.... The primary task of the logician is thus the analysis of the body of mathematical texts....
                                                                N. Bourbaki, 1949

In order to approach a topic of this kind, it is useful to adopt an attitude concerning the respective natures of logic and mathematics and to delimit the border between them. Clearly, different attitudes and different borders yield different judgments concerning what is and what is not a gap. The most useful attitude/border complex would maximize content and minimize grounds for philosophic disagreement. My framework may not be optimal but I think that many people will find it useful. I do not subscribe to every particular of it myself but, needless to say, I find it very attractive. At the least it is a useful myth, a Wittgensteinian ladder.

1. MATHEMATICAL PRACTICE
AND ITS LOGICAL PRESUPPOSITIONS

But it should be pointed out that this Platonism is already inherent in classical mathematics generally, and it is not made more acute or more doubtful, but only more conspicuous, by its application to theoretical syntax....
                                                                Alonzo Church, 1956

The view of mathematics adopted here can be called neutral platonism. It understands mathematics to be a class of sciences each having its own subject-matter or universe of discourse. Set theory is a science of objects called sets. Number theory is about the natural numbers. Geometry pre-

M. Bunge (ed.), The Methodological Unity of Science, 23–50. All Rights Reserved.
Copyright © 1973 by D. Reidel Publishing Company, Dordrecht-Holland.

supposes three universes of objects: points, lines and planes. String theory or *Semiotik* is about strings of ciphers (digits or characters). Group theory presupposes the existence of complex objects called groups.

Following Bourbaki, Church, Hardy, Gödel and many other mathematicians, it holds that these objects exist and that they are independent of the human mind in the sense that

(1) their properties are fixed and not subject to alteration and

(2) they are not created by any act of will.

In a word: mathematical truth is discovered, not invented; mathematical objects are apprehended, not created.

According to this view the unsettled propositions of mathematics (Goldbach's problem, the twin prime problem, the continuum problem and the like) are each definitely true or definitely false and when their truth-values are derived it will be by discovery and not by *con*vention and not by *in*vention.

Foundations of mathematics is usually discussed in a metalanguage of mathematical languages, as has been the case here. Platonism, purely and simply, makes in the metalanguage the presuppositions that mathematicians make in their object languages. What the mathematician lets his object language variables range over the platonist lets *his* metalanguage variables range over. The neutral platonist differs from the platonist by distinguishing the foundations of the *foundations* of mathematics from the foundations of mathematics. With regard to foundations, simply, the neutral platonist is a platonist, simply. With regard to the foundations of the foundations the neutral platonist is neutral. Using the metalanguage the neutral platonist agrees that numbers exist but adds, using the meta-meta-language, that he does not know how such assertions should be *ultimately* understood. The question of the existence of mathematical objects is answered affirmatively but the question of the ultimate nature of that existence is not answered at all. To the neutral platonist the various philosophies of mathematics which have been offered are all considered as interesting hypotheses concerning foundations of foundations each of which may be true, false or meaningless – indeed the neutral platonist admits that foundations of foundations may be meaningless. Contrast neutral platonism with extreme formalism. The extreme formalist claims that foundations of mathematics is contentful but that mathematics itself is meaningless. The neutral platonist claims that both foundations and mathematics are meaningful but offers no view on foundations of foundations.

To revert to the first metalanguage of mathematics, then, we have various mathematical sciences each with its own universe of discourse, and each with its own vocabulary of content words which determines its own topical sublanguage. The language of number theory, the language of set theory, the language of string theory – these and the others are what we call topical sublanguages.

In the typical case one organizes a mathematical science axiomatically by taking certain known truths of the science *ab initio* and then *recovering* the other known truths by a combination of definition and logical deduction. Within the compass of axiomatic activity the capacity to reason logically is presupposed, not explicitly asserted. Neither Euclid, nor Hilbert, nor Veblen said anything about the exact nature of the logical deductions which appear in their treatises on geometry. Their axioms and definitions are explicitly stated in more or less clear language but there is not a word about what should or should not count as a deduction. The theorems are said to be obtained from explicitly stated axioms by means of logical deductions but the nature of the deductions is merely presupposed.

In this connection Church had the following to say concerning the period before 1925 (personal communication), "It is hard to comprehend now, but the implicit position of mathematicians of the day was that 'mathematical' theorems require proof, but logic is to be taken for granted."

It is to be noted that the process of logical deduction was supposed to apply equally well to any set of statements, not just to the axioms. Given P, any set of sentences, and c, any sentence, one established that c is a logical consequence of P by producing a logical deduction of c from P. Moreover, as was not explicitly noticed by Euclid but much heralded by Hilbert, the soundness of the deductions was regarded as completely independent of the actual interpretation of the language – any interpretation of the language which satisfied the premises of a sound deduction was to satisfy its conclusion. This too was presupposed and without this presupposition there would have been no point in seeking proofs.

The just-mentioned process of giving a deduction of c from P was taken to establish that c indeed follows from P. A process for establishing that c does *not* follow from P was also present and the process involved consideration of *alternative interpretations* of the language (Church, 1956, p.

328). To show that *c* does not follow from *P* one produces an interpretation of the language which satisfies *P* and falsifies *c*. The works of Hilbert and Veblen contain many applications of this process in showing the logical independence of their axioms.

If we use the term intuition to indicate the source of our knowledge of those mathematical truths which we do not logically deduce from others, then the process of axiomatization can be seen as an attempt to factor a mathematical science into its intuitive component and its logical component. The axioms of a science are often intended to represent a concentration or distillation of the intuitive component while the process of deduction is used to reconstitute the whole science from its concentrate. It may be a largely unexamined dogma of traditional mathematics that a science can always be divided into intuitive and logical components and then reconstituted without loss by recombination. Beth has referred to this view as one of Aristotle's most important discoveries.

Although the distinction between intuitive or contentful mathematics, on one hand, and logic, on the other, is very old, the exact border is problematic. This manifests itself in debates over whether second-order logic is best thought of as mathematics or as logic. It also manifests itself in debates concerning the nature and extent of logical constants. For example, some authors go to great lengths to argue that identity should not be taken as a logical concept. Furthermore, it may well be the case that one basic issue among logicism, platonism and intuitionism turns on drawing the border between mathematics and logic. Logicism would hold that the border does not exist, that all mathematics is logic. Some intuitionists (certainly not all) would also hold that the border does not exist, but would add that no mathematics is logic, i.e., that all mathematical inferences are intuitive or contentful. Platonism would hold an intermediate view that some of mathematics is contentful and that some is derived by logic.

Most mathematicians, even those who do not regard themselves as platonists, take an intermediate view. The fact that logically true sentences are not written as proper axioms of mathematical theories is some evidence of this. Similar evidence derives from the fact that a non-independent set of axioms is regarded as redundant. An axiom deducible from the others is only redundant if one presupposes that what is obtained by logic is somehow obtained free of charge. The usual view that proper mathematical axioms are paid for by intuition (or postulation) while the consequences come for free entails that logic is presupposed in mathematics and that there is a substantive border to be drawn.

2. THE MATHEMATICAL CHARACTER OF LOGIC

Now we are ready to give our view of the nature of logic. As just indicated, the axiomatic development of a science presupposes, apart from those things involved in the actual subject matter, three other things: (1) a language, (2) a system of deductions, and (3) a system of interpretations. This three-part structure has been called the underlying logic of the science. In my view the aim of the science of logic is the understanding both of underlying logics and of theories which presuppose them. Logic is the science of axiomatic sciences. Logic must produce theories of 'propositional forms' to account for the 'linguistic' phenomena. It must produce theories of deduction to account for the phenomenon of deduction and it must produce theories of semantics to account for the phenomenon of reinterpreting languages and satisfying or falsifying sentences. [The term 'underlying logic' is probably due to Church (e.g. 1956, p. 58).]

The mathematical character of the science of logic is as well-established as that of physics; and the general mode of procedure seems the same. The experimental physicist studies actual physical phenomena and conveys his results to the mathematical physicist who constructs mathematical models in order to get a useful and faithful analogue of the physical system under consideration. Once the mathematical model is constructed it is studied within mathematics and its properties are obtained in the same way that the properties of any other mathematical object are – viz. by logical deductions from the basic laws of the relevant branch of mathematics augmented by the definition of the model. Given the purely mathematical results about the model, the experimental physicist returns to the laboratory to determine the faithfulness of the model to the physical system that it is designed to mirror.

One hardly ever expects to get a faithful model on the first try. Usually deliberate oversimplifications are made in order to get experience and in order to develop a feel for the relevant questions. In a sense there are no perfect gases, no adiabatic processes, no rigid bodies, no frictionless pulleys, no physical systems composed of point-masses, etc. In the same sense there are no propositional logics, no axiomatic deductive systems and no set-theoretic semantic systems. Literally, all of the things just mentioned exist – but not, as is often said, 'in physical reality' and not, as we now say, 'in logical reality'. All of the above mentioned 'things' are really mathematical models designed in analogy with various physical systems, on one hand, and with underlying logics, on the other.

Just as one constructs a mathematical model of a solar system in order to account for which events can and cannot happen, so one constructs mathematical models of an underlying logic to account for which logical phenomena can and cannot occur. For example, a mathematical model of the underlying logic of Hilbert's geometry gives us an account of which sentences can or cannot be deduced from his axioms, which sentences follow and which do not, whether all logical consequences can be deduced, and so on.

The models of logical systems under current investigation generally have three parts: a grammar, a deductive system and a semantics. Their respective roles are clear enough from what has been said above. It is always the case that the grammar is defined first because the deductive system and the semantics are defined relative to the grammar. The order in which the other two are defined is immaterial because they are not interrelated definitionally.

Let $ML = \langle G, D, S \rangle$ be a mathematical logic with G for grammar, D for deductive system and S for semantics. The grammar G is often studied separately from D and S and purely *grammatical theorems* are proved – e.g., that every sentence is uniquely decomposable according to a certain mode of decomposition, that sentencehood in G is decidable and so on. When the deductive system D is studied apart from the semantics one gets purely *proof-theoretic* results – e.g., that every deduction is equivalent to a deduction which does not use a given rule of inference, that not all sentences are provable, and so on. When the semantics S is studied apart from the deductive system, one gets purely *model-theoretic* or *semantic* results – e.g., that every infinite interpretation is equivalent to a countable one, that certain sets of sentences are or are not satisfiable, that all interpretations satisfying a given set of sentences are isomorphic and so on. Results which relate the deductive system to the semantics have been called *bridge results* by some of the members of the Berkeley School (but this terminology has not caught on). Examples of bridge results are completeness and soundness theorems. A deductive system can only be complete or sound relative to a semantics. It is only a logic as a whole that can be complete or sound.

Typical Grammatical Results
Decidability of sentencehood
Unique decomposability
Equivalence of different grammars

Typical Proof-Theoretic Results
Normal Form Theorems
Derivability of Rules
Consistency Theorems
Decidability of Theoremhood
Theory-Completeness
Interpolation Theorems

Typical Semantic Results
Compactness (every unsatisfiable set has a finite unsatisfiable subset)
Skolem-Löwenheim (every interpretation is equivalent to a countable one)
Tarski-Vaught (every infinite interpretation has an equivalent countable submodel)
Functional Completeness of Sentential Logic
Representation Theorems

Typical Bridge Results
Logic-Completeness
Soundness
Logic-Incompleteness
Axiomatizability of Semantically Defined Theories

In an experimental spirit one often compares two logics which differ only in deductive system or which differ only in semantics. For philosophical reasons which need not be explored here the term syntax has been applied to the complex of G and D when contrasted with S. This has its merits but it does not permit ready discussion of two logics that differ only in deductive system.

The traditional logical investigations of Aristotle, Leibniz, Boole and the others have the same aim as modern logic – viz., the understanding of the underlying logic or logics of standard mathematical practice. Modern logic differs from traditional logic most conspicuously in scope but most importantly in method. Instead of aiming to characterize the properties of the underlying logic directly as did earlier logicians, modern logic constructs mathematical models as an intermediate step. The construction of mathematical models not only increases clarity and precision but it also relieves two pressures – the pressure to be right in every detail and the pressure to give an account of the ontological status of the subject. Today the value of idealized models is widely accepted and hardly any of the current logicians feel pressure to decide the relation between the logical and the mental, to give an account of propositions, to explicate the ground of logical consequence, etc.

Incidentally, with the possible exception of modal logics, hardly any worthwhile logical doctrines seem to have started from any analysis of ordinary language or from analysis of reasoning outside of mathematics and science. The reason is not hard to find: if one wants to study a certain phenomenon then one seeks places where the phenomenon occurs repeatedly and clearly. The reasoning which occurs in mathematics and science is frequently free of the emotionalism and sectarianism which infects other areas.

3. CLASSIFICATION OF GAPS

For purposes of discussion let us imagine that every systematic deductive discourse presupposes an underlying logic (but certainly not that every two distinct discourses need presuppose two distinct logics). Then we are imagining a logic of Euclid's geometry, a logic of Hilbert's geometry, a logic of Veblen's geometry, a logic of Dedekind's number theory, etc. Moreover, in certain cases we have a choice whether to regard a given discourse as embodying an underlying logic or as describing a mathematical model of an underlying logic. For example, do we regard *Principia Mathematica* as a basically object-language treatise developing a branch of mathematics or do we regard it as a meta-language treatise aiming at construction of a mathematical model of the underlying logic of some other discourse? I would suggest that both points of view be followed through, perhaps one will recommend itself more persuasively than the other, perhaps not. In either case some interesting ideas are likely to emerge.

We take the class of underlying logics to represent the logical component of mathematical practice. The business of the science of logic is to understand them, and the *modus operandi* is construction of mathematical models for them and comparison of the models with them.

It may be preferable to broaden this viewpoint at the cost of multiplying activities. Here we imagine three kinds of activity: the object-language activity of the mathematician as such, the metalanguage activity of the logician trying to develop theories of the logic presupposed by the mathematician, and the metalanguage activity of the 'metalogician' who constructs mathematical models – not only of the actual underlying logics of the mathematician but also of the putative underlying logics embodied in the logician's theory. This enables us to understand as logic the reconstructions related to various logical theories even though the systems envisaged by those theories do not represent actual underlying logics. For example no one actually reasoned in accord with Aristotle's rules. The logic that Aristotle imputed to the mathematicians of his time was just too simple to be able to account for much at all. Likewise for Stoic logic, although in this case, too, we want to construct mathematical models of the logic envisaged by the Stoics.

Thus we have broadened our framework. Instead of modeling just the actual underlying logics, we see the science of logic as constructing models for putative logics – i.e., for logics which are envisaged by various theories of logic but which do not necessarily correspond in any very faithful way to actual underlying logics. We use the term 'putative' without prejudice, i.e., we do not take it as necessarily implying non-correspondence with an actual underlying logic.

Given this framework there are three broad categories of gaps between mathematical practice, real and merely putative, and the science of logic. In the first place there are underlying logics which have never been modeled at all or else so inadequately that the existing models are almost useless. Examples of underlying logics which have yet to be modeled are the following: Stoic logic, Leibniz's logic of the *Monadology*, Frege's logic of the *Begriffsschrift* and the logic underlying Russell's deduction of his paradox. In regard to the paradox, Russell wanted to show that type restrictions were necessary. To this end he produced a piece of reasoning which neglected type distinctions and ended in a contradiction. If type distinctions are really necessary then the reasoning he offered was incoherent and no contradiction was actually derived. If the reasoning is coherent then type distinctions are not necessary though the premises he started with are jointly contradictory. Cocchiarella is currently trying to reconstruct the underlying logic of Russell's argument taking as a hypothesis that Russell's reasoning is coherent.

In the second place there are underlying logics which have been modeled but only inadequately. Of course, the difference between these gaps and some of those previously mentioned is only one of degree. Here we are thinking of the deficiencies which can be overcome by making only minor alterations to existing models. These will be discussed in detail below.

In the third place there are logical concepts and distinctions which arise in underlying logics but for which no accounts have been given within mathematical logic. For example, we often want to ask whether one theory is simpler than another, but there is yet no reasonable mathematical explication of the concept of simplicity. Another such example involves a problem which Kreisel has described (Kreisel, 1970; cf. Corcoran, forthcoming). One observes here that it is normal mathematical practice to distinguish derivations from proofs in analogy with the distinction between sentences and propositions. A derivation of a theorem from axioms is thought of as expressing a proof of the theorem from the axioms. Derivations are thought to be inherently finite, linguistic objects whereas proofs are non-linguistic and may even be infinite: derivations can be said to be finite encodings of proofs. In normal mathematics we often say that two distinct derivations express the same proof. In addition we often look for a new proof of a known theorem, and in such cases we are not merely seeking a different derivation. In any case practically nothing has been done on the general problem of constructing mathematical models for proofs in order to obtain results about the relation between proofs and derivations. One might add, by the way, that construction of mathematical analogues for propositions has been attempted by Scott and others. But some logicians will want to count as open the problem of accounting for the distinction between propositions and sentences in the context of mathematical logic. Other elusive phenomena will be treated below.

There is another class of phenomena which may be called gaps by some but which we do not regard as such. Recall that in constructing mathematical models one not only tries to model existing phenomena but one also alters more or less adequate models in an experimental spirit just to see what would happen. For example, one wonders what the solar system would be like were the inverse-square force law replaced by an inverse-cube law. To answer this question one constructs a deliberately fictional model and deduces the properties. Similarly, in logic one might wonder what would happen were infinite sentences or infinite deductions available.

The main thrust of the present discussion is not toward underlying logics which have not been modeled but rather toward underlying logics which have been only inadequately modeled. Many mathematicians, Bourbaki for example, take the idea of an underlying logic very seriously and talk as if there were one logic underlying all branches of mathematics. We interpret such remarks to mean that the similarities among the underlying logics are so great that it is better to regard them as variants of one logic.

It is interesting to note that Bourbaki regarded Aristotle's theory as adequate. Of course, Bourbaki did not actually read the Aristotelian corpus and compare the 'model' therein described with the underlying logic of his own work. Had he done that, he would have seen several gaps between the model and the logic. In the first place there are *grammatical deficiencies* in the Aristotelian language. In the second place there are *deductive deficiencies* in Aristotle's model; *modus ponens*, conditionalization, generalization, reductio and other familiar inference rules are absent from his system. Likewise the semantics for connectives, function symbols, etc. is absent, so there are *semantic deficiencies* as well. In this case the deductive and semantic deficiencies are engendered by the grammatical deficiencies but this is generally not true, i.e., generally deductive and semantic deficiencies are not predicated on grammatical deficiencies. It should be clear that grammatical deficiencies are often not purely grammatical – they are called grammatical because they can be thought of as 'originating' in the grammar but they are usually recognized as a mismatch between the expressive power of the underlying logic and that of the model. For example, Russell's type distinctions were designed to overcome a grammatical deficiency in Frege's model.

We have just indicated three locations of gaps between an underlying logic and mathematical logic (regarded as a model of the underlying logic). Since logic models not only the underlying logic but also the mathematical and scientific theories which presuppose it, there is a fourth potential source of gaps. We use the terms 'postulational gap' to indicate a mis-

match between the possible theories (in underlying logic) and their possible analogues (in a mathematical logic).

In each class of deficiencies there are two subclasses – defects in the
model and excesses in the model. A defect results from the model lacking
analogues of components of the underlying logic. An excess results from
the model containing components which do not correspond to anything
in the underlying logic. Lack of identity in Aristotle's model results in a
grammatical defect. Sentences in violation of type distinctions in Frege's
system result in a grammatical excess; that is, Frege's language contained
expressions, viz. those involving type violations, which do not correspond
to anything in normal mathematics (assuming that the underlying logic of
normal mathematics does have type restrictions). Likewise there are defects
and excesses in the realms of deduction, semantics and postulate systems.

The following list summarizes our classification of gaps between mathematical practice (real and putative) and existing mathematically defined
logics.

I.   Existence of underlying logics not yet modeled
II. Inadequate models of underlying logics
        Kinds of inadequacies: Excesses
                                Defects
        Locations of inadequacies: Grammar
                                   Deductive System
                                   Semantics
                                   Postulate Systems
III. Existence of Phenomena not yet treated mathematically
IV. Purely Experimental Models

The balance of this article handles these four areas as follows. For
reasons of space the first and last are not treated any further. Section 4
treats inadequate models of underlying logics focusing on gaps between
standard mathematical practice and standard logic. Section 5 treats elusive phenomena.

4. Gaps between standard logic and standard practice

For purposes of discussion we take Kleene's first-order logics (Kleene,
1952, p. 81ff) with identity and operation symbols as standard logic, and

as mathematical practice we take the grammatical, deductive and semantic constructions presupposed in current mathematics texts including Kleene's. In fact many of the claims we want to make about standard mathematical practice are actually exemplified in Kleene's *Introduction to Metamathematics*.

Kleene presents branches of mathematics in what Tarski (1953, p. 5ff) calls "standard formalization". Each branch has its own vocabulary of non-logical constants which are either individual constants, operation (function) constants, or predicate (relation) constants. The logical constants of the languages are conjunction, disjunction, 'implication', negation, the two quantifiers and identity. There are only individual variables and the usual formation rules are used.

4.1. *Gaps Relative to Presuppositions*

Widespread adoption of standard first-order logic indicates a willingness to accept certain basic semantic presuppositions: that every sentence is true or false, that every proper name denotes an object, that universes of discourse are non-empty, that predicates are everywhere applicable, that functions are everywhere defined. In the present subsection we do not question these presuppositions. Here we are concerned with gaps which exist relative to the correctness of the presuppositions.

4.1.1. *Grammatical defects.* (i) Logical Constant: In ordinary mathematical practice one finds other binary connectives used as primitives: neither-nor, the biconditional and the converse conditional. To notice that the latter is used just notice that we often find it natural to indicate the consequent before the antecedent. For example, an instance of mathematical induction is commonly stated: P holds of all numbers if P holds of zero and P holds of the successor of any number it holds of.

$$\forall n P n \subset (Po \ \& \ \forall m (Pm + 1 \subset Pm))$$

In addition there are connectives which occur not as binaries but as multinaries. We do not say 'A and, B and C' but rather 'A, B and C'. The same with disjunction and the biconditional. This would involve adding rules of formation, e.g. if $A_1, A_2, \ldots$ and An are formulas then so is $(A_1 A_2 \ldots \ \& \ An)$. In addition, given n formulas as above we say 'At most

one of the following: $A_1, A_2, ..., An$', 'At least one of the following: etc.'
and 'Exactly one of the following: etc.'. This gives three new multinary
connectives. A multinary connective can be defined as one which applies
to an arbitrary number of formulas (usually two or more) and combines
them into one formula. (Apparently all of the multinary connectives actually occurring in normal mathematics are permutable, i.e., their arguments commute pairwise.)

Obviously all of the above can be handled by means of metalinguistic
definitions. The point is *not* that they cannot be handled in the present
framework but rather that they occur as primitives in normal mathematics.
Obvious modifications to standard logical grammar would close these
gaps.

The situation is similar in respect to quantifiers. Numerical quantifiers
are common in normal mathematics: we say 'there are at least n objects
such that...', 'there are at most n objects such that...' and 'there are exactly n objects such that...' (for each fixed finite n). Sometimes we even
say 'there are infinitely many objects such that...'. Except for the last,
these can also be handled by metalinguistic definition. Also missing is the
null quantifier 'No objects are such that...' and the multinary quantifiers
'For all $x_1, x_2, ... x_n$,–', and 'For some $x_1, x_2, ..., x_n$–'.

Again a similar situation arises in regard to identity. Identity is generally used as a multinary relation, not simply as binary. Moreover, non-
identity (distinctness) often occurs as a primitive logical relation.

(ii) Non-logical Constants: In addition to the individual constants,
function constants and relation constants which occur in standard logic,
mathematical practice uses several other kinds of descriptive constants.
The most obvious type missing includes minimalization in arithmetic,
abstraction in set theory and the definite description operator. These constants apply to a formula with at least one free variable and produce a
term having one more bound variable than the formula and one fewer
free variable. For example,

$$(mx)(x^2 > 5)$$

denotes the minimum of the numbers whose squares exceed 5, viz. 3.

The next omission to be noticed concerns operators like iterated summation and iterated product which apply to terms to produce new terms

by binding some free variables of the operand and introducing new free variables. For example, in

$$\forall xy\left(x < y \supset \left(\sum_{z=x}^{y}(2z+1) = (y^2 - x^2 + 2x + 1)\right)\right)$$

the left most term indicates the sum of the odd numbers between $2x+1$ and $2y+1$ and thus the occurrence of z is bound.

Also lacking in standard logic is the lambda operator which forms function symbols from terms and the pi operator which forms predicates from formulas. The addition of the former seems necessary for a natural treatment of calculus. Instructors in this subject frequently warn about the ambiguity of terms because, where they need to speak both of the quantity of x^2 and of the function of x^2, $(\Lambda x : x^2)$, they have notation only for the former.

Once that deficiency is noted we see the lack of constants for operators, such as integration and differentiation, which apply to functions and yield function symbols. Using I for integration and D for differentiation we would have, for example

$$\forall y([I(\Lambda x : 2x)]\, y = (\Lambda x : x^2)\, y)$$
$$\forall z([D(\Lambda x : x^2)]\, z = (\Lambda y : 2y)\, z)$$

instead of the usual expressions

$$\int 2x\, dx = x^2$$
$$\frac{d(x^2)}{dx} = 2x$$

which utterly obscure the logical form of the statements. Defects of the present kind have been treated by Kalish and Montague (1964) and, more recently, by Corcoran and Herring (1971).

The above defects can be regarded with some confidence as genuine failures of standard logic to represent faithfully the logical forms of mathematical statements, but the following 'defect' may not be genuine. To see this point recall that when we want to indicate that subsequent members of a finite sequence are related by a given relation we simply interpose the relation symbol between subsequent symbols for the members.

$$1 < 2 < 3 < 4 < 5$$
$$((x + y) + z) = (z + (x + y)) = ((z + x) + y) = (y + (z + x))$$

If this indicates a "primitive sentence forming operation" then we have another gap to be filled by changing the rules of formation to allow for 'quasi-atomic' formulas obtained by iterating partial atomic formulas.

4.1.2. *Grammatical excesses.* Not only does standard logical grammar fail to mirror expressions found in standard practice; it also includes expressions which lack analogues in practice. The most obvious excess here involves the existence of the so-called vacuous quantifiers. The following is a sentence in Kleene's grammar but one which would never 'be said' by a mathematician.

$$\exists y \exists z \exists x \, (0 = 0)$$

4.1.3. *Deductive defects.* (i) Expressive Defects: When comparing actual deductions as found in mathematical texts with those generated by the rules given in Kleene (1952), one is struck by the fact that although deductions in Kleene are sequences of formulas of the declarative language, actual deductions are sequences of sentences some of which contain concepts beyond those involved in statement of mathematical truth or falsehood. In a mathematical deduction the main premises are marked as such by use of a phrase such as 'take the following as axioms'. We also find sentences beginning with 'for purposes of reasoning suppose that'. Here suppositions other than axioms are being introduced not as main premises but merely to begin a subsidiary deduction. The term 'define' is also used and this does not occur in the expressive language. Furthermore, we find symbols, e.g. x_0, y_0, etc. used as individual constants which are not among the constants of the declarative language. There are a few other defects of the same sort. We find also that the expression 'a contradiction' is used as a sentential constant although no such constant occurs in the declarative part of mathematical language. Finally, notice that deductions are self-referential in that a given deduction may contain expressions which explicitly refer to previous expressions in the same deduction.

A deduction conveys information of a radically different kind from that conveyed by a mathematical statement. Roughly speaking a deduction gives directions for tracing a logical path from axioms to their consequences, and no such directions can be given in a declarative mathematical statement. The myth that a proof is simply a sequence of (declarative) formulas has its usefulness but truth cannot be claimed for it. This has been treated in some detail in Corcoran (1971a).

(ii) Inferential Defects: The most obvious group of inferential defects of standard logic is implicitly indicated in Kleene. Several pages after presenting the standard system of twelve logical axioms and three rules of inference, Kleene gives a list of twelve derived rules. It so happens that all twelve derived rules correspond to primitive rules in actual practice.

It is also the case that none of the standard primitive axioms correspond to primitive axioms used in practice. One of Kleene's three rules corresponds to a primitive rule of normal practice. Thus, standard logic is standard practice turned topsy-turvy. Loosely speaking, what is primitive in practice is derived in logic and what is derived in practice is primitive in logic.

From the time of Frege until the mid-twenties there had been no systematic comparison of the standard systems of deduction with deduction as found in practice. In the twenties Jaskowski began work on the question of whether deductive practice could be described with the same degree of mathematical rigor as the standard systems. Fitch (1952) is largely responsible for dissemination of Jaskowski's ideas in this country. Although Jaskowski's work was an important and large step toward codification of normal deductive practice, the full details are yet unknown. To many logicians the remaining questions may seem unimportant but it is possible that further research will unearth results which will have far reaching consequences in applied areas such as linguistics and pedagogy (cf. Corcoran, 1971a).

It should be clear that we are not claiming the existence of implications which can be derived in actual practice but which cannot be derived in standard logic. By the Gödel completeness theorem we know that if A is a set of first-order sentences and t is a first-order consequence of A then t can be formally derived from A in standard logic. The point is that the methods of getting from A to t in standard logic are not the methods actually used in practice. As Kreisel has pointed out more than once, that one can ride to work on a camel or a donkey does not imply that a camel is a donkey.

It is interesting to note that many standard systems have at most three

kinds of rules: nullary, unary and binary. A rule is called n-ary if it produces a 'conclusion' on the basis of n premises. Nullary rules are simply
axiom schemes. This system of classification applies only to *immediate*
inference rules, i.e., rules whose applications are determined by consideration of a fixed number of lines in a deduction. In addition to the immediate
rules normal practice admits of several further kinds of rules. In the first
place there are global rules whose applications in a deduction depend on
the character of the entire deduction down to the point of application.
Generalization is an example: we infer $\forall xPx$ as the next line of a deduction in which Px_0 has been proved and in which x_0 is arbitrary. The determination of whether x_0 is arbitrary in a deduction requires scanning of
the entire deduction. Secondly, there are subordinate deduction rules
which correspond to inference of a conclusion not on the basis of a fixed
number of previously proved lines but rather on the basis of a previously
carried out pattern of reasoning. Reductio is an example: we infer C on
the basis of a subordinate deduction beginning with the supposition of
not-C and ending with a contradiction. Combinations of the three basic
properties (immediate, subordinate and global) also occur.

Since normal mathematical deductions include the introduction of definitions, absence of rules of definition constitutes another defect in standard logic. Moreover definition is usually not treated as a deductive phenomenon but rather as a method for extending theories. In order to build
a logic capable of handling definitions, non-logical vocabularies need be
divided into two parts: descriptive terms and auxiliary terms. Although
the descriptive terms need be finite in number (to be realistic), there must
be countably many auxiliary terms of each grammatical kind. Then rules
must be formulated:

(1) which prohibit introduction of an auxiliary term by definition more
than once in a deduction,

(2) which limit the forms of definitions relative to contexts so that 'creative definitions' are avoided and

(3) which regard definitions as suppositions which begin subordinate
proofs on the basis of which the last line can be inferred provided that it
lacks the defined term.

These alterations can, of course, be made in otherwise standard systems.
If this is done then, since the standard systems are complete, no conclu-

sions will be deducible which were not already deducible *but* many deductions will be considerably shortened. It may be interesting to compute some measure of relative efficiency between a system with definition and the same system without. Indication of the efficacy of definitions was got by Maloney (1969), who showed that in second-order logic the rule of definition is equivalent to Church's formula substitution rule.

4.1.4. *Deductive excesses.*

It has already been noted that many standard formulations of first-order logic include many axioms and rules which are not found in normal practice. This means that many of the deductions countenanced by standard systems do not correspond to normal deductions. For example, Kleene gives a 17 line deduction of $a=a$, a triviality to which normal practice would grant a single line, or two at most.

Apparently, normal practice admits of only two axiom schemes, the so-called laws of identity and excluded middle, and it is ironic that often both of these are absent from standard deductive systems.

4.1.5. *Postulational gaps.*

In standard logic an analogue of an axiomatized branch of mathematics is obtained as follows. First a formal language is constructed having as descriptive constants a set of symbols of the same grammatical type as the content words of the branch in question. A language for Veblen's geometry will have one ternary relation symbol. A language for Peano's arithmetic will have one individual constant and one unary function symbol. Relative to the language, standard logic determines a system of deductions and a system of interpretations. Then as proper axioms one takes formal analogues of the postulates of the science in question. This results in a *standard formalization of the theory*. A formal theorem is defined as a sentence obtainable as the last line of deduction whose proper premises all come from the set of axioms.

In certain cases this process seems to go through without a hitch. For example, we could give formalization of the theory of the ordering of the rationals by choosing the first order language whose only descriptive constant is < (analogue of 'less than') and write down axioms asserting 'no terminal elements', transitivity, strict trichotomy and density.

However, when we try this method on Peano arithmetic we are blocked because we cannot state mathematical induction in a first-order language. The usual way around this is to take all instances of mathematical induction as axioms, i.e., to take a scheme which is really an infinite number of axioms. This move has been felt to be unsatisfactory for two reasons. In the first place the resulting infinite set of axioms is still not equivalent to mathematical induction. In the second place, one feels that there is something illegitimate about taking an infinite number of sentences as axioms.

The only condition that standard logic places on a set of axioms is that it be recursive, i.e., that it admit of a mechanical decision procedure. From an epistemological consideration of the notion of an axiomatized science it is clear that decidability is a necessary condition but it is not at all clear that decidability should be regarded as sufficient also. This situation is especially suspicious when one realizes that the infinite axioms sets in current formalizations all resulted from a reluctance to accept second-order logic as logic. The feeling that second-order logic is really set theory in disguise loses some of its force when one reflects that if it *is* set theory then it is far weaker than any theory that has ever been advanced as a theory of sets (second-order logic presupposes at worst only sets of rank one and it does not even presuppose the axiom of choice for those sets).

From the above and similar situations we can identify as a possible postulational excess the fact that standard logic admits of infinite axiom sets. In addition, some mathematicians regard mathematical induction as a non-logical rule of inference, not as a scheme or second-order sentence. Since non-logical rules are not admitted in standard formulations, we can identify their absence as a possible postulational defect.

There is a simple way of eliminating the above gaps in some settings. By (1) allowing 'auxiliary predicates' as required by a rule of definition and (2) formulating mathematical induction as a non-logical rule of inference which applies to auxiliary predicates, we can produce a categorical 'first-order' axiomatization of arithmetic. The new style of formalization envisaged here codifies a theory by giving a finite set of axioms and a finite set of (schematic) rules. The result is still much weaker than the genuinely second-order formalizations (in regard to theorems it is equivalent to first-order). The new formalizations would define a theory as a set of finitary rules closed under derivability. A model of a theory would be an interpretation which satisfies the theorems and whose assignments all satisfy the rules. The principal change can be seen to be the addition of the auxiliary predicates. However, the new formalization is able to accommodate much clearer versions of set theory than are possible in standard formalization.

4.2. *Absolute Gaps: Free Logics*

It is axiomatic in empiricist epistemology that one cannot prove existential statements by logic alone (Kneale and Kneale, 1964, p. 707) and yet the following is a logical truth in standard logic.

$$\exists x\,(x = x)$$

This reflects the fact that standard semantics presupposes non-null universes of discourse. Empiricists can be ignored in the present context but mathematical practice cannot and the fact that mathematicians feel the need to explicitly assume non-emptiness of universes (Halmos, 1963 and Huntington, 1917) indicates that this presupposition is not made in practice.

To see the next point it is necessary to notice that there are predicates which are true of some things, false of others and not applicable to still others. For example, the predicate 'prime' is true of two, false of four and not applicable to pi. This means that each predicate has a range of applicability within which it holds true or false and outside of which it does not hold at all. Thus a sentence can fail to be true without being false and it can fail to be false without being true. Yet the following is logically true in standard logic.

$$\forall x\,(Px \lor \sim Px)$$

This reflects the fact that standard semantics presupposes universal ranges of applicability for all predicates.

A mathematician feels that he is saying something contentful when he asserts that aleph-two exists and yet

$$\exists x\,(x = a)$$

is logically true in standard logic. This points to the fact that standard logic presupposes that every individual constant denotes and it points to the absence of a means of expression of genuine existence. The myth that existential statements assert existence is hard to deflate until one realizes that such statements merely affirm that objects whose existence has been presupposed satisfy certain conditions. To be able to make existence assertions we need a logical predicate E which holds true if its argument denotes and which holds false otherwise.

Finally note that the following statement in analysis is undefined.

$$\exists x \left(x = \frac{1}{0} \right)$$

However, it follows by standard logic from the following sentence which is logically true in standard logic.

$$\forall y \exists x \left(x = \frac{1}{y} \right)$$

This points to two facts: first, that standard logic presupposes that each function is total and, second, that standard practice makes no such presupposition.

Use of partial functions in mathematics is fairly widespread. Boole, for example, defined 'union' in such a way that $x+y$ is meaningful only when x and y are disjoint and his relative complementation is defined only when the second argument is a subset of the first (Kneale and Kneale, 1964, p. 410).

4.2.1. *The problem of free logics.* On the face of it, the problem of constructing a mathematical logic which is faithful to mathematical practice seems easy. The grammar of such a logic may seem to be an ordinary first-order language with the following modifications.

(1) E is taken as a logical constant
(2)   auxiliary symbols of all grammatical types are taken
(3)   vacuous quantification is eschewed
(4)   the non-logical (descriptive) constants include operators of appropriate kinds

The semantics seems equally straight forward. If L is a language with constants C, an interpretation of L is defined as a pair (U, m) where U is a set, possibly empty, and m is a meaning function defined on a subset of C so that

(1)   for an individual constant in the domain of m, mx is in U
(2)   for an n-ary function symbol x in the domain of m mx is a partial n-ary function $U^n \to U$

(3)   for an n-ary predicate symbol x in the domain of m, mx is a pair (D, T) of subsets of U^n with T a subset of D [D is the range of applicability and T is the 'truth-set']

(4)   for an operator x in the domain of m, mx is an appropriate partial function; e.g. if x forms a term from a formula binding a single variable then mx is a partial function from the power set of U into U.

To construct the deductive system it would seem to be sufficient to consult normal mathematical practice and then simply codify formal analogues of the inferences which are actually made.

Although the problem does not seem difficult, the fact that nearly one hundred papers have been written on the subject since 1950 indicates otherwise. It must be admitted however that many of the articles have been written by younger logicians who lack the experience which enables comprehensive formulation of problems. In this connection it is relevant to note that the first article concerned with properties of axiomatic theories formalized with a free underlying logic was published only quite recently (Ebbinghaus, 1969; cf. Eberle, 1969).

What are the difficulties? One annoying problem arises in the semantics. Although the nature of the interpretations themselves is clear, the correct definition of truth is quite problematic. In effect mathematical practice does not seem to indicate unambiguously how the logical constants are to be understood. For example, if P is true and Q is undefined do we take the disjunction to be true or to be undefined? One might think that the meaning of the conditional or if-then connective would be especially problematic but this problem seems to have received a definitive solution (Ebbinghaus, 1969). It may very well be the case that mathematical practice is itself vague on some of these points so that more or less arbitrary connectives will have to be adopted – but one should always be reluctant to accept that kind of a conclusion.

Another problem is to describe actual deductive practice. This will involve considerable study of mathematical discourses but, unfortunately, few logicians seem to have any interest in such studies.

The problem of free logics is clear. The difficulties involved in solving it do not seem severe and yet it has eluded definitive solution. It may well be the case that the difficulty is more with the logicians than with the logic. Blatantly aprioristic thought is widespread in this area. One logician has very carefully worked out the full details of a free logic which preserves all of the logical truths of standard logic. Another has claimed the existence of a kind of assertion which is 'correct' when what is asserted is not false. Another has developed a system whose if-then connective occurs only once in each formula. Generally, few of the logicians working on free logics have paid significant attention to actual practice.

4.2.2. *Many-sorted logics*. Standard logics can account only for theories which have a single universe of discourse; yet many branches of mathematics are naturally formulated in a manner that presupposes two or more domains. For example, Hilbert's geometry has three domains: points, lines and planes. Many-sorted logics, i.e., logics which admit of multiple domains, have been worked out, but all within the standard framework (non-empty universes, all terms denoting, etc.). However, even Hilbert's geometry presupposed a free many-sorted logic. It is not meaningful to say that a plane is on a point. However, there may be no serious difficulties in constructing a faithful many-sorted free logic once a faithful one-sorted free logic has been given.

5. Elusive phenomena

The modern history of logic can be seen as a progression which continually incorporates more and more logical concepts from standard mathematics into mathematical models. The idea of an ideal formal language was already implicit in the mathematical writings of Leibniz, Bolzano, Boole and others – but no precise mathematical analogue existed until the present century. The notion of truth was taken for granted until Tarski's work of the late twenties. A whole body of independence results in geometry and algebra had been accumulated long before logical consequence was defined relative to a mathematical logic. This later development made it possible to distinguish mathematically between deducibility and logical consequence – two notions which had been distinguished in practice by Veblen and others long before.

What we intend to do in this section is to highlight some deductive and definitional concepts which have currency in mathematics but which have not yet been incorporated into mathematical logics. In Section 3 above we mentioned the distinction between proofs and derivations that has been discussed by Kreisel. Kreisel seems to hold that each branch of mathematics has its own peculiar class of 'proof structures', but so far there seems to be no convincing model for proofs over and above formal derivations. Another problem already mentioned involves distinguishing mathematically between propositions and sentences. A problem of the same sort involves distinguishing algorithms (as abstract computational procedures) from programs (concrete instances of algorithms).

Two hundred years ago when there were but two branches of mathematics the common view was that some of the truths of mathematics are somehow immediately evident and that the rest should be proved as consequences. This view became unfashionable with the discovery of non-Euclidean geometry and the subsequent rise of formalism in philosophy and abstract algebra in mathematics. Recent mathematics books (e.g. Shoenfield, 1967) and articles (e.g. Kreisel, 1970) have revived the older view which, of course, was never abandoned by the working mathematicians. In any case, one may suspect that a 'concrete' mathematical structure (a particular interpretation of a formal language) naturally 'gives rise' to some of its truths. Obviously the particular set of 'natural axioms' is determined not only by the structure itself but also by how it is given. Of course, if the structure is 'given' by a set of axioms then the whole discussion is circular, so the above writers seem to presuppose some method of conceiving a structure apart from its own formal language. How this happens is more the concern of the epistemology of mathematics than of logic, properly so-called. However, it does seem within the realm of logic to ask whether there is any mathematically objective way of choosing basic axioms from among the truths of an (interpreted) theory.

Another elusive phenomenon arises in investigation of rules of inference. The problem is to give a mathematically precise definition of the notion of a rigorous (naturally primitive) rule of inference. It is already clear that in order to be taken as a rule of inference (relative to a given semantics) a rule must be sound and effective (Church, 1956). However, first, there are infinitely many rules which meet these two conditions but which would not be regarded as rigorous (see Corcoran, 1969) and, second, we seem to be able to make rather stable and uniform judgments concerning whether a given rule is naturally primitive or whether it should be derived on the basis of simpler rules. Myhill has given counter-examples to a previous conjecture on this point (Corcoran, 1969).

To the annoyance of formalists, mathematicians have stable criteria for distinguishing in a given deduction between important errors and inessential errors. Note that if formalism were true all errors would be on a par. In any case, there seems to be some global aspect of deductions which carries the essential information, and this has yet to be investigated.

An indication of the maturity of the field of logic might be found in the fact that logicians are increasingly willing to point to inadequacies in their own specialty. In addition to the logicians already mentioned in this connection, several others have written on elusive phenomena. Hasenjaeger (1972) has pointed out that the logics so far developed are capable of treating naturally only interpretations whose universes of discourse are composed of discrete objects and, consequently, that treatment of continuous domains always entails considerable logical difficulties. He suggests the need for a logic which involves a 'truly continuous ontology'. The fact that Hasenjaeger has not indicated in any detail what a continuous ontology is should be regarded more as an indication of the difficulty of the problem than as an inadequacy of his exposition. A somewhat similar situation is found in Scott (1970, p. 146) where the need for a 'general theory of contextual definitions' is discussed without including in any detail what such a theory should accomplish. In both cases, logicians have felt a lack of theory in a certain area without knowing in detail what the required theory should do. Dummett, de Jongh and others have become concerned with what they have called 'feasibility'. The idea seems to be that there is a sense in which the following sentence holds: 'A man who is not bald is still not bald when one hair is removed.' According to standard logic (and arithmetic) it would seem to follow that a person could not become bald by losing hairs one at a time. This problem seems similar to ones arising in several other areas. For example, in linguistics there is reluctance to recognize sentences of arbitrary length and yet there is reluctance to accept the existence of a longest sentence. More generally, vagueness seems to be an inherent property of many languages and yet there are no logics which handle vague concepts in a satisfactory way.

For reasons of space limitations the list of elusive phenomena is being ended here. Perhaps a more comprehensive and more sophisticated list would provide for future logicians the kind of impetus that Hilbert's problems provided for mathematicians.

ACKNOWLEDGMENTS

Previous versions of this paper were read during 1972 at McGill University, Ottawa University and the Pennsylvania Logic Colloquium. I am grateful to Prof. Mario Bunge of McGill for encouragement to undertake the project of formulating the paper. Many of the auditors of the readings contributed generously of their own ideas. Some of these ideas are in the present version of the paper but, for lack of space, many have been omitted. Special thanks to James Munz and George Weaver.

Department of Philosophy,
State University of New York at Buffalo

BIBLIOGRAPHY

Bourbaki, N.: 1949, 'Foundations of Mathematics for the Working Mathematician', *Journal of Symbolic Logic* **14**, 1–8.
Church, A.: 1956, *Introduction to Mathematical Logic*, Princeton.
Corcoran, J.: 1969, 'Three Logical Theories', *Philosophy of Science* **36**, 153–77.
Corcoran, J.: 1971a, 'Discourse Grammars and the Structure of Mathematical Reasoning I, II, III', *Journal of Structural Learning* 3, No. 1, 55–74; No. 2, 1–16; No. 3, 1–24.
Corcoran, J.: 1971b, 'Review of Eberle (1969)', *Mathematical Reviews* **42**, 31.
Corcoran, J.: 'Review of Kreisel (1968)', *Mathematical Reviews*, forthcoming.
Corcoran, J. and Herring, John: 1971, 'Notes on a Semantic Analysis of Variable Binding Term Operators', *Logique et Analyse* **55**, 644–57.
Corcoran, J. and Herring, John: 1972, 'Review of Ebbinghaus (1969)', *Journal of Symbolic Logic*, **37**, 617–8.
Ebbinghaus, H. D.: 1969, 'Über eine Prädikatenlogik mit partiell definierten Prädikaten und Functionen', *Archiv für mathematische Logik und Grundlagenforschung* **12**, 39–53.
Eberle, R.: 1969, 'Denotationless Terms and Predicates Expressive of Positive Qualities', *Theoria* **35**, 104–123.
Fitch, F.: 1952, *Symbolic Logic*, New York.
Halmos, P.: 1960, *Naive Set Theory*, Princeton.
Hasenjaeger, G.: 1972, *Introduction to Basic Concepts and Problems of Modern Logic*, Reidel, Dordrecht.
Huntington, E.: 1917, *The Continuum*, New York.
Jaskowski, S.: 1934, 'On the Rules of Supposition in Formal Logic', *Studia Logica* **1**.
Kalish, D. and Montague, R.: 1964, *Logic: Techniques of Formal Reasoning*, New York.
Kleene, S.: 1952, *Introduction to Metamathematics*, Princeton.
Kneale, W. & M.: 1964, *The Development of Logic*, Oxford.

Kreisel, G.: 1970, 'Principles of Proof and Ordinals Implicit in Given Concepts', in *Intuitionism and Proof Theory* (Proceedings of the Summer Conference at Buffalo, 1968) (ed. by Kino, Myhill and Vesley), Amsterdam.

Maloney, M.: 1969, *Logical and Axiomatic Foundations for the Study of Formal Languages and Symbolic Computation*, Dissertation, University of Pennsylvania.

Scott, D.: 1970, 'Advice on Modal Logic', in *Philosophical Problems in Logic*, (ed. by Karel Lambert), D. Reidel Publ. Co., Dordrecht-Holland, p. 143.

Shoenfield, J.: 1967, *Mathematical Logic*, Reading, Massachusetts.

Tarski, A.: 1953, *Undecidable Theories*, Amsterdam.

PART III

PHYSICS

ROGER B. ANGEL

RELATIVITY AND COVARIANCE

ABSTRACT. Following the inception of General Relativity, a dialogue ensued between A. Einstein and E. Kretschmann concerning the status of the Principle of General Covariance. Einstein supposed it to have physical content whereas Kretschmann proved that all lawlike statements of physics are expressible in generally covariant form. Einstein finally concurred with Kretschmann. Subsequently, M. Bunge argued that all covariance principles are metatheoretical, i.e. their referents are not physical patterns but theories. However, recently, J. L. Anderson argued that the imposition of covariance requirements restricts the possible forms of the laws of a given theory, indicating that they do have physical content. We show that there is an element of truth in both positions. However, the dispute has rested on a confusion between principles of covariance and principles of relativity, the former being formal and the latter being physical. We distinguish between the covariance group and the relativity group of several theories in support of our contention.

An interesting dispute has been simmering in philosophy of physics for the last fifty years concerning the semantic status of the covariance principles of physics. Recently, fresh attempts have been made to settle it. In his founding paper, Einstein (1916) gave the clear impression that the Principle of General Relativity led to new physics. Briefly, he argued that if we adopt this principle on independent epistemological grounds and require a field theory of gravitation to satisfy it, the resulting field equations will entail physical consequences which are significantly different from those of the classical theory of gravitation. The most striking example of the fecundity of this principle was the direct prediction of the precession of the perihelion of Mercury. Thus, it seemed clear that the Principle of General Relativity must have physical content, on the formal ground that in conjunction with certain physical assumptions it entails factual consequences which are not entailed by those assumptions alone.

However, shortly after the publication of Einstein's paper, an article appeared by Kretschmann (1917) which convincingly demonstrated that any putative law, e.g. Newton's laws of motion, could be formulated in a generally covariant way, thus satisfying the Principle of General Relativity. Einstein (1918) concurred with the view of Kretschmann, and since that time the bulk of orthodox opinion has followed a similar line.

M. Bunge (ed.), The Methodological Unity of Science, 53–68. All Rights Reserved.
Copyright © 1973 by D. Reidel Publishing Company, Dordrecht-Holland.

Bunge (e.g., 1961) has frequently argued in favour of the same view on independent logical grounds. Briefly, Bunge's position is to the effect that it is essential to distinguish between the axioms of a theory, e.g. its basic physical hypotheses, and those other lawlike principles which are to be associated with a theory but which actually belong to the corresponding metatheory. In particular, there are principles which he calls *laws of physical laws* or *metalaws* whose referents are not the objective patterns of nature but the lawlike descriptions of them. In short, metalaws are not statements about the world but statements about physical laws. According to Bunge, the Principle of General Covariance and, in fact, all covariance principles (Galilei, Lorentz, canonical, etc.) clearly belong to the class of metalaws. On this view, it would be patently absurd to assert that physical reality is generally covariant. Clearly, one should and would say that the basic laws of this or that theory are generally covariant.

A position diametrically opposed to that of Bunge has recently received an exposition by Anderson (1967) in a text-book on relativity physics. Anderson argues in considerable detail that the imposition of a covariance requirement (or of a related symmetry requirement) has definite physical consequences. Specifically, he claims to show that when a theoretical description of a physical system is required to admit a specific group of transformations, the choice of basic laws is severely delimited and, in certain cases, may even be uniquely determined.

Anderson disposes of Kretschmann's argument by toeing an empiricist line to the effect that any term which occurs in a physical formula must allow of a specific physical and observational interpretation. He argues that Kretschmann was able to render any arbitrary lawlike formula generally covariant by importing terms which model no aspect of the world. In other words, his criticism amounts to the charge that Kretschmann's argument depended on an ingenious but irrelevant 'cooking of the results'.

It is clear that the treatments of Bunge and Anderson have a much wider significance than those of Einstein and Kretschmann. Whereas the latter were concerned specifically with the status of general covariance, the former are directed at all covariance principles. Thus, what they have to say has implications for classical physics and Special Relativity physics as much as for the Theory of General Relativity.

A *prima facie* indication of the factual content of covariance principles is that the commonly accepted interpretation of the Principle of Special

Relativity is to the effect that the covariance group of electrodynamics must contain the invariant velocity c which is interpreted as the velocity of electromagnetic propagation. But since the only invariant velocity of the Galilei group is an infinite velocity, it is obvious, *on experimental grounds*, that electromagnetic theory is not Galilei covariant. Thus, it would *seem* that there may be at least indirect experimental confutation of a covariance principle. Of course, it is still logically possible to follow the line advocated by Bunge which would presumably consist in arguing that to say that Maxwell's theory is not Galilei covariant is obviously to say something about Maxwell's theory but to say nothing about the world. However, Maxwell's laws are not formulae that have been picked from a hat but purport to be reasonably accurate descriptions of *something* called the electromagnetic field. It might make a difference to say that a purportedly true description of reality is not Galilei covariant. Surely that would be to say something, at least indirectly, about the world. In any event, the invariance of c is surely a brute fact, and no theory which incorporates it in its fundamental laws can admit the Galilei group of transformations.

Finally, we may as well add that considerable *prima facie* evidence in support of the position that symmetry properties of theories have physical content has been well known to physicists for some time. However, with the exception of some discussion by Bunge, it has been ignored by writers who combine both technical awareness and philosophical perspective. In particular, every theoretical physicist should be aware of the celebrated theorem of Noether (1918) which showed that once a theory has been reduced to variational form, then from every symmetry property of that theory a corresponding conservation law is derivable. The best known and most perspicuous examples would be the derivation of the principle of conservation of linear momentum from translational symmetry, the conservation of angular momentum from rotational symmetry and the conservation of energy from temporal homogeneity. In addition, the incompatibility of certain experiments with the so-called conservation of parity may possibly suggest that the latter is a falsifiable and hence factual principle.

Actually, it is not the writer's intention to engage in polemics. On the contrary, the purpose of this paper is to argue for a middle ground between the two opposed viewpoints, each of which contains part of the truth. However, we do intend to show that the entire question of the status of covariance principles as factual or formal has rested on a fundamental confusion between covariance principles and relativity principles.

As we have already seen, Bunge's position is essentially to the effect that covariance principles are calculable metatheorems of pure mathematics. For example, the Lorentz covariance of the celebrated wave-front equation of optics is not determined by experiment but by an elementary mathematical computation. While it would be quite proper to subject this law of optics to experimental test, it would be absurd to contemplate the experimental testing of its Lorentz covariance, which would be akin to the experimental testing of an analytically true statement.

In the general literature of physics, covariance principles and relativity principles have been closely identified. The Principle of Classical Relativity has been taken to mean that Newton's laws of motion are covariant under the group of Galilean transformations. The Principle of Special Relativity has been understood to signify that the basic laws of physics, when properly formulated, are covariant under the group of Lorentz transformations and, in particular, that the Principle of General Relativity signifies that genuine basic laws of nature satisfy the Principle of General Covariance. That is to say that a fundamental law of nature must hold regardless of the coordinatization which we adopt to describe the physical system of interest. A physical theory should be as indifferent to the coordinate system in which it is expressed as it is to the language of its author. Accordingly, a well-formed basic law should retain its form under an extremely wide class of coordinate transformations. For obvious reasons, such transformations must be differentiable and with non-vanishing Jacobian. Apart from the latter requirements, they are quite arbitrary. We shall call this set of mathematically admissible coordinate transformations the general covariance group of transformations, although, strictly speaking they are the realization of a groupoid rather than of a group. The requirement that a theory be covariant under the general covariance group(oid) is the Principle of General Covariance in a nutshell.

While Bunge's interpretation of covariance principles as metatheoretical statements is logically incontrovertible, it may nevertheless lead to serious misunderstanding if one infers from it that the corresponding relativity principles are likewise metatheoretical. We shall now present a paradox which is an extreme example of the sort of difficulty which may arise when the two kinds of principle are confounded.

A sufficient condition for the general covariance of a physical law is that it be expressible in the form of a Riemannian tensor equation. That is to say, Riemannian tensors are a basis for the realization of the general covariance group. Given a tensorial law which has a certain form when expressed in terms of a set of coordinates x^i, it will retain that form under a transformation to any arbitrary set of coordinates y^i. To paraphrase Einstein, we say that a tensor equation is preserved under an arbitrary set of substitutions. It is well-known to mathematical physicists in general, and has been stressed by Post (1962, 1967) in particular, that Maxwell's laws of electrodynamics *naturally* lend themselves to such a generally covariant formulation. Accordingly, they must be covariant under any subgroup of the general group corresponding to the selection of a particular class of coordinates y^i. Now one such subgroup is the Galilei group. Hence, the basic laws of electrodynamics must be Galilei covariant which, as every physicist knows, is false. To complete our paradox, we need only add that another such subgroup is the Lorentz group. Consequently, Maxwell's laws must be both Galilei covariant and Lorentz covariant, which is not merely false but impossible. Clearly, an error has crept into our train of reasoning. In uncovering its source, we shall lay bare the distinction between a covariance principle and a relativity principle.

In the first place, it is necessary to remark that several ambiguities cloud the very notion of covariance. We shall here allude only to the most obvious ones. Firstly, it is meaningless to say of a physical law, *per se*, that its form is an invariant of a given group. One and the same theory may be formulated in a variety of ways, and the covariance group of the theory will depend on the choice of mathematical formalism. For example, in its elementary vectorial form, Newtonian Mechanics is covariant under the general inhomogeneous Galilean group. However, such a formulation presupposes a metrically connected manifold, more specifically a Euclidean manifold. What is less well-known is that the very same theory may be formulated on the much weaker geometrical presupposition of an affinely connected manifold, in which case the covariance group of the theory is the four parameter affine group. In short, the covariance group of a theory will depend on the geometrical objects at one's disposal for the expression of the basic laws of that theory. In the second place, it is always possible to enlarge the covariance group of a physical law by adding terms *ad libitum*. For example, it is a truism of physics that Newton's second law is not covariant under a transformation from an inertial frame of reference to one that is accelerating with respect to the inertial frame. However, by adding terms corresponding to the linear acceleration, the Coriolis force, the transverse force and the centrifugal force, there results a law which is covariant under a much more inclusive group, but which yields the very same computational results as the familiar $F = ma$, since, in the more specialized cases, the additional terms are simply equal to zero. Hence, the requirement of covariance must be restricted to fundamental laws or it is completely trivialized (cf. Bunge, 1967). However, the first difficulty is ineradicable and simply supports Bunge's contention concerning the metatheoretical status of covariance principles.

We now turn directly to the distinction between a covariance principle and a relativity principle. We have already remarked that many physicists tend to assimilate the two, and to speak indifferently of a theory as, for example, Lorentz relativistic or Lorentz covariant. The origin of the error appears to stem from the seemingly harmless solecism of using the concept of coordinate system interchangeably with that of reference frame. Again Bunge must be cited as the one philosopher who has pointed out this error on numerous occasions. However, we suspect that his protests have fallen on deaf ears, at least in scientific circles. Specifically, a coordinate system is a conceptual object of mathematics whereas a frame of reference is a physical object such as the earth, the sun, the galaxy, and so forth. A coordinate system may be employed as a mathematical model of a frame of reference, but a moment's reflection will assure one that to each frame of reference there corresponds a non-denumerable set of coordinate systems which could serve as its models. Yet physicists who would never dream of alluding to electrically charged numbers blithely speak of moving coordinate systems and inertial coordinate systems, both of which are equally barbaric. The final step on the path to philosophic perdition is then to assimilate the notions of coordinate transformation and frame transformation. Needless to say, when we perform frame transformations we employ coordinate transformations. That is to say, the first frame of reference is associated with a fixed set of coordinates x^i and the second frame of reference is associated with a fixed set of coordinates y^i. Then the equations which relate the x^i to the y^i model the laws which relate the two frames. But coordinate transformations have other uses which are quite unrelated to the carrying out of frame transformations, most notably to attain the optimum of mathematical tractability for discovering the solution of a physical problem. For example, we may transform the description of an electrostatic configuration from Cartesian to spherical coordinates to facilitate the solution of Poisson's equation.

In general, the mark of a physically significant frame transformation is the occurence of the time parameter in the coefficients of the coordinate transformation which is its model. Furthermore, it should be remarked that the coordinate transformations which model frame transformations are not given *a priori* since they express the kinematical relationships which exist between the physical coordinates of physical systems. If such frame transformations were *a priori* then the Galilean transformation would never have been superseded by the Lorentz transformation, since the former would have had the status of a law of arithmetic. In short, frame transformation equations belong to the *object language* of physics.

One final preliminary observation should be made. The primary concern of the physicist, as distinct from that of the mathematician, is not in the formal mathematical structure of a law but in its factual content. Physical laws purport to represent objective physical processes – that is their content. But one and the same factual law may be expressible in a variety of distinct mathematical forms. This fact has direct bearing on our interpretation of the various principles of relativity. A principle of relativity asserts that an objective physical process is indifferent with respect to an equivalence class of reference frames which are called inertial. The point of a relativity principle is not that the mathematical form of a law is unaffected when referred to different inertial frames but that its factual content is unaltered. However, it is easy to fall prey to confusion on this point since for purposes of convenience the physicist will select or possibly invent geometrical objects to express laws which are covariant with respect to the inertial frames of the theory of interest. An obvious case in point is that of the four-vector formalism invented by Minkowski. When the equations of electrodynamics are expressed in four-vector form, they are automatically covariant under transformations between the inertial frames of electrodynamics. But it would be quite erroneous to assert that Maxwell's laws satisfy the Principle of Special Relativity because they may be expressed in the four-vector formalism. On the contrary, they are expressible in the four-vector formalism because they satisfy the Principle of Special Relativity.

To codify our distinction between a principle of covariance and a principle of relativity, we propose to draw the distinction between the covariance group of a theory and its relativity group and, in particular, to show that the two do not coincide. We begin with a consideration of the elementary vectorial form of Newtonian Mechanics. It is easily shown that the covariance group of this theory is the direct product of three groups: $R_{i3} \times G_s \times T$, where R_{i3} is the inhomogeneous proper rotation group, G_s is the special Galilean group, and T is the group of time translations. The subgroup $R_{i3} \times T$ simply corresponds to alternative coordinatizations of one and the same physical system and has no physical significance. On the other hand, G_s is the symmetry group of the equivalence class of inertial frames of Newtonian Mechanics. That the inertial frames of Newtonian Mechanics are defined up to a special Galilean transformation is a testable hypothesis belonging to the object theory of Newtonian Mechanics. We may now attempt a precise formulation of the Principle of Classical Relativity. We employ $'=s.'$ to mean semantically equivalent or having the same factual content, and $'t(l)'$ to signify the transform of the law statement l under the element t of the group of transformations T.

> L is the set of basic laws of Newtonian Mechanics.
> K is the set of possible frames of reference.
> T is the set of possible frame transformations modelled by elements of the group G_s.

For any $l \in L$ and any $t \in T$, there exist at least two distinct k_i, $k_j \in K$, such that l wrt $k_i \in K \leftrightarrow t(l) = s.l'$ wrt $k_j \in K$.

The factual status of this principle may be verified immediately by deriving therefrom the Galilean law of the composition of velocities which satisfies a sufficient condition for factuality, namely that it is both logically consistent and false.

We now turn to the Principle of Special Relativity and its metatheoretic counterpart the Principle of Lorentz Covariance. The correct way to deal with this subject is via an analysis of Classical Electrodynamics. However, demands of brevity compel us to approach the subject by a more elementary route. We adopt the fundamental postulate that the velocity of light propagation *in vacuo* is equal to the universal constant c. From this postulate there follows the celebrated wave-front equation $x^2 + y^2 + z^2 = c^2 t^2$. It is easily shown that if we subject this equation to a Galilean transformation it turns out not to be Galilei covariant. On the other hand, it is easy to deduce a set of transformation equations under which the form of the wave-front equation is invariant, namely the group of general Lorentz transformations. It should be emphasized that we do not discover the Lorentz transformation empirically but calculate it. The Lorentz covariance of the wave-front equation is therefore metatheoretic. It follows that it is incorrect not only to regard the Principle of Lorentz Covariance and the Principle of Galilei Covariance as rival physical hypotheses but even to regard them as incompatible metatheorems. The one asserts that Classical Electrodynamics is Lorentz covariant while the other asserts that Newtonian Mechanics is Galilei covariant. Both assertions are analytically true. Virtually all authors of textbooks on relativity physics are guilty of the erroneous simplification of saying that since the Galilean transformation is false, it is necessary to modify the laws of mechanics to make them Lorentz covariant. Such a *non sequitur* precludes the necessity of including a serious analysis of the foundations of physics in a textbook, but at the price of gravely misleading the reader.

The covariance group of electrodynamics is the complete Lorentz group. One would suppose intuitively that the relativity group of which frame transformations are a realization would be the special homogeneous Lorentz group L_s, just as the relativity group of Newtonian Mechanics was found to be G_s. However, while L_s is a relativity subgroup, it is not the complete relativity group of Classical Electrodynamics. A special Galilean transformation has a different significance from that of a special Lorentz transformation. Specifically, while the special Galilean transformation is merely a formal simplification of the general Galilean transformation which is effected by a judicious choice of coordinate systems, the special Lorentz transformation represents the physically restricted case of reference frames with respect to which all velocity vectors are parallel. Thus, the composition of two arbitrary special Lorentz transformations is not generally equivalent to a third special Lorentz transformation. The relativity group of electrodynamics is the group of Lorentz transformations with rotation which is not identical with the direct product $R_{i3} \times L_s$. We shall simply call it L_r, and recall that L_s is a relativity subgroup. We may now formulate the Principle of Special Relativity.

L is the set of fundamental laws of a given theory.

K is the set of possible frames of reference.

T is the set of possible frame transformations modelled by elements of the transformation group L_r.

For any $l \in L$ and any $t \in T$, there exist at least two distinct $k_i, k_j \in K$ such that l wrt $k_i \in K \leftrightarrow t(l) = s \cdot l'$ wrt $k_j \in K$.

We shall offer but one piece of supporting evidence for the non-formal character of this principle. We choose this particular case since it has always been of particular interest to philosophers. One of the consequences of the relativistic invariance of electrodynamics is the so-called paradox of the spherical wave-front. Imagine two inertial frames of reference which are so coordinatized that at an arbitrary initial time t_0 the origins of the two systems coincide. At this moment a light pulse is emitted from the common origin. In accordance with the laws of optics, a wave front will expand uniformly from the origin of the first frame in the form of a sphere with the equation $x^2 + y^2 + z^2 = c^2 t^2$. Now since the second frame is *ex hypothesi* an inertial frame of electrodynamics, it follows that a spherical wave-front will be propagated with respect to that frame. Hence, at any later time t, one and the same wave-front will be a sphere centered at the origin of the second frame, even though these origins no longer coincide. Thus, we are presented with the mathematical impossibility of a sphere having two distinct centers. However, a careful analysis of the situation reveals the paradox to be only apparent. Specifically, the set of events which is singled out in one frame of reference as constituting the wave-front differs from the set which is singled out in the second frame. Now a formal coordinate transformation simply relabels the numerically identical set of events which constitute a physical system at a given time. However, a Lorentz frame transformation results in the selection of distinct events, which clearly distinguishes it from a formal coordinate transformation.

We now turn to the principles of General Covariance and General Relativity, which are so frequently identified in the literature of physics. Since a coordinate system is merely a mathematical device for labelling the points of a manifold unambiguously, it is obvious that the factual content of a law should be indifferent to an arbitrary choice of coordinates. Accordingly, it is desirable to express laws of nature in a formalism which is indifferent to an arbitrary coordinate transformation. It has already been noted that such a desideratum may be achieved when a law is expressed in the form of a tensor equation. That all fundamental laws be so expressible is the Principle of General Covariance. Clearly, if a law be indifferent to an arbitrary coordinate transformation, it must be indifferent to the proper subset of coordinate transformations which model arbitrary frame transformations. Hence, from the standpoint of general relativity all frames of reference are equivalent. A frame which is accelerating with respect to a Lorentz frame, i.e. an inertial frame of special relativity physics, will be just as 'inertial' from the standpoint of General Relativity as the Lorentz frame itself.

As we have just expressed it, the relationship between General Covariance and General Relativity appears to be that the former entails the latter. However, if our thesis is correct, such an entailment is impossible since the antecedent is metatheoretical while the consequent is factual. The one pertains to mathematics and the other to physics, and no physical hypothesis may be derived from a metamathematical theorem. By the same token, we would hold that the Principle of Galilei Covariance does not entail the Principle of Classical Relativity, and that the Principle of Lorentz Covariance does not entail the Principle of Special Relativity.

The specious justification for all such entailments is that if a law is covariant under a group of transformations G, it must be covariant under the subgroup of G corresponding to possible frame transformations. However, while the law of interest may be G-covariant, as stated, and therefore *suggest* the existence of a corresponding relativity principle, it may actually turn out that the elements which compose the formal expression of the law have been endowed with the incorrect geometrical properties. Thus, a quantity which has been treated as a scalar in pre-relativistic physics may turn out to be the component of a four-vector in relativity physics. Hence, one is not licensed to claim that given a law with certain covariance properties, it must necessarily satisfy an associated relativity principle. A relativity principle could only be entailed by a covariance principle if, *per impossibile*, the law of interest were absolutely incorrigible.

Before dealing directly with the matter in hand, we shall review some elementary aspects of manifold geometry. All of the readers will have heard talk of flat space and curved space. Moreover, they will be aware that ordinary Euclidean space is flat. One of the well-known properties of Euclidean 3-space, which is the standard geometrical background of Newtonian Mechanics, is that the Pythagorean theorem is satisfied. In differential form, this property may be expressed as:

$$(\mathrm{d}s)^2 = \delta_{ik}\, \mathrm{d}x^i\, \mathrm{d}x^k \quad (i, k = 1, 2, 3)$$

where δ_{ik} is the Kronecker symbol. The δ_{ik} are an array of metric coefficients which constitute a special form of what is called the *metric tensor*. When expanded, this expression assumes the familiar form:

$$(\mathrm{d}s)^2 = (\mathrm{d}x^1)^2 + (\mathrm{d}x^2)^2 + (\mathrm{d}x^3)^2 .$$

Now the square of the line element of Euclidean 3-space may be expressed in a more complicated form if, for example, we choose to employ spherical coordinates, in which case we have:

$$(\mathrm{d}s)^2 = (\mathrm{d}r)^2 + r^2(\mathrm{d}\theta)^2 + r^2 \sin^2\theta(\mathrm{d}\varphi)^2 .$$

However, we call the space flat if it is possible to find a single transformation which carries the second expression into the former one throughout the entire space or manifold. Now such a possibility does exist for ordinary Euclidean space. Since the metric coefficients are, in that case, $+1$, $+1$, $+1$, we say that ordinary Euclidean space is a flat space with signature $+3$. Now while the square of the spatial line element is not an invariant of the Lorentz transformation, there is another quantity called the space-time interval which is just such an invariant. It has the form:

$$(\mathrm{d}\sigma)^2 = (\mathrm{d}x^1)^2 + (\mathrm{d}x^2)^2 + (\mathrm{d}x^3)^2 - c^2(\mathrm{d}t)^2 .$$

It was shown by Minkowski that if one employs a four-dimensional Cartesian coordinate system in which $x^4 = \mathrm{i}ct$, then it is possible to express the metric of space-time in a form which is analogous to that of the standard Euclidean metric, namely:

$$(\mathrm{d}\sigma)^2 = \delta_{\mu\nu}\, \mathrm{d}x^\mu\, \mathrm{d}x^\nu \quad (\mu, \nu = 1, 2, 3, 4).$$

However, in expanded form, this becomes:

$$(\mathrm{d}\sigma)^2 = (\mathrm{d}x^1)^2 + (\mathrm{d}x^2)^2 + (\mathrm{d}x^3)^2 - (\mathrm{d}x^4)^2 .$$

Now when a space-time manifold has the property that regardless of the coordinatization a single transformation will carry the metric coefficients into the above canonical form, it is said to be a flat space-time manifold.

However, the signature of the four-dimensional manifold is now $+2$. Thus, the manifold of special relativity physics is a flat four-dimensional manifold of signature $+2$. We may now proceed to the generalization of the foregoing notions, namely to that of a Riemannian manifold. In place of the Kronecker symbol, the metric coefficients of the interval are given by g_{ik}, so that the expression for the interval becomes:

$$(\mathrm{d}r)^2 = g_{ik}\, \mathrm{d}x^i\, \mathrm{d}x^k \quad (i, k = 1, 2, ..., n).$$

The g_{ik} are arbitrary functions subject only to the condition that $(dr)^2$ be invariant. In general, a Riemannian manifold is not flat. That is to say, there will be no single transformation which carries the metric coefficients into canonical form. However, a property of Riemannian manifolds is that there exist transformations which will carry each infinitesimal region of the manifold into canonical form. Moreover, although such transformations vary from region to region, the canonical form will be unique for a given manifold. Thus, we may speak of a curved manifold of such and such signature. It is obvious that Euclidean space, Minkowski space and the various curved surfaces with which we are all familiar are special cases of Riemannian manifolds. Finally, it is to be noted that a sufficient condition for a Riemannian manifold to be flat may be expressed in the compact form:

$$R^i_{jkl} = 0$$

where R^i_{jkl}, called the Riemann-Christoffel tensor, is a function of the metric tensor and its first and second derivatives.

We now turn to physical matters. The physical significance of the vanishing of the Riemann-Christoffel tensor is that it is a system of differential equations all of whose solutions correspond to flat spaces. Now the space of Special Relativity, as we have seen, is one such flat space. On the hypothesis that Classical Electrodynamics is correct, it follows that its laws are valid for any frame of reference with respect to which the gravitational forces are zero. In short, if the world were devoid of gravitational fields, the laws of electrodynamics would hold rigorously, although perhaps vacuously. Accordingly, to be consistent with electrodynamics, the gravitational field equations must admit a flat space solution. However, the vanishing of the Riemann-Christoffel tensor is the mathematical model of a universe in which gravitational fields are never present, obviously far too stringent a condition for physical reality. However, this condition may be weakened by the tensor operation of contraction. The contraction of the Riemann-Christoffel tensor in the foregoing equation yields the further tensor equation:

$$R_{jl} = 0.$$

This equation is again compatible with a flat space but also admits curved space solutions which may be physically interpreted as gravitational potentials. Now it is obvious that the last equation is generally covariant. That is to say, it is form invariant under arbitrary coordinate transformations. Now we pose the question: Does the latter equation model a law of gravitation which is independent of any arbitrary reference system? The answer must be a resounding No! In the first place, while the indices j and l of our equation may run over any number from 1 to n, our physical law is specialized to a four-dimensional manifold. This is trivial in itself except that we are concerned specifically with a space-time manifold where x^4 is a distinguished coordinate. Moreover, while the formal tensor equation admits any flat space solution, we require the unique flat space solution of Special Relativity. That is to say, the signature of the manifold must be that of the Lorentz metric. Accordingly, severe restrictions are placed on the possible g_{ik}. Hence, while the form of the law is generally covariant, the law itself is not.

Confronted by a tensor equation of physics, the mathematician could subject it to transformations which would violate the most fundamental requirements of physical theories. Accordingly, since the permissible coordinate transformations of physics are not arbitrary, it is erroneous to speak of a law or theory of physics as generally covariant, even though the geometrical objects which we employ to express such laws may indeed constitute a basis for the realization of a generally covariant group of transformations. Thus, we hold the general covariance of physical laws to be a myth engendered by the confounding of mathematical theories with the physical theories which they are employed to represent. In particular, the tensor formalism which is so useful in enabling physicists to express frame independent laws is far too permissive in that it allows coordinate transformations which have no physically interpretable counterpart. However, when we place the necessary restrictions on the metric tensor to block such transformations, the physical laws cease to be generally covariant.

Accordingly, we are now in the position to assert that whatever General Relativity may mean, it does not have the same meaning as General Covariance.

What then is the meaning of General Relativity? To give a reasonably precise formulation of the Principle of General Relativity, we must first introduce the notion of a *physically realizable frame of reference*. Such a frame is one which while not necessarily rigid is such that no point of reference is travelling with a velocity greater than that of light with respect to any other reference point of the same frame (Møller, 1952). For example, the tangential velocity of a distant star may exceed the velocity of light with respect to the rotating earth, but the earth-star system does not constitute a frame of reference, although taken individually, each may serve as such a frame. We shall call any physically realizable frame of reference an *Einstein frame*. We now offer our formulation of the Principle of General Relativity.

> L is the set of fundamental laws of a given theory.
> K is the set of Einstein frames.
> T is the set of mathematically admissible coordinate transformations.

For any $l \in L$, any $t \in T$ and any $k_i, k_j \in K : l$ wrt $k_i \in K \leftrightarrow t(l) = s.l'$ wrt $k_j \in K$.

It is worthwhile to compare the foregoing with the formal statement of the Principle of Special Relativity. The following distinctions are to be noted. T is here restricted only by the weakest formal requirements on coordinate transformations in general. On the other hand, the denotation of K places definite limits on the $t_i \in t$ which would, in fact, be applicable. For example, Galilean transformations would be excluded which provides, for example, that Maxwell's laws would be Galilei covariant only under coordinate transformations between coordinate systems which model physically unrealizable frames of reference. The generality of the principle is reflected in its ranging over the entire set K as distinct from a proper subset of K, which was the case for both of the restricted principles. Finally, it is of interest to note that while the principle is testable it is as yet untested. The so-called tests of the Theory of General Relativity have only provided evidential support for the claim that Einstein's field equations hold in a particular Einstein frame, namely the solar system. Hence, another interesting consequence of our analysis is that one must distinguish between Einstein's generally covariant formulation of the theory of gravitation and the Principle of General Relativity itself.

In conclusion, we are now in the position to answer one of the most crucial questions concerning the foundations of relativistic theories: Do covariance principles have factual content? The answer is clearly negative. In this regard Bunge's position is clearly correct. However, in contrast to covariance principles, the various principles of relativity do have factual content. In brief, they are statements about the kinematical relations which hold between the inertial frames of the theory of interest. Moreover, what constitutes an inertial frame of a given theory is, contrary to some conventionalistic accounts, not a matter of definition but a subject for experimental investigation. A final moral to be drawn is that in any discussion of the relationship between geometry and physics, one must avoid the pitfall of confusing the mathematical theory, which is a matter of choice, with its physical interpretation which is a representation of the world. This again is a basic error in the conventionalistic interpretation of physical theories.

Department of Philosophy,
Sir George Williams University

BIBLIOGRAPHY

Anderson, J. L.: 1967, *Principles of Relativity Physics*, Academic Press, New York.
Bunge, M.: 1961, 'Laws of Physical Laws', *Am. J. Phys.* **29**, 518–524.
Bunge, M.: 1967, *Foundations of Physics*, Springer Verlag, New York.
Einstein, A.: 1916, 'Prinzipielles zur allgemeinen Relativitätstheorie', *Ann. der Phys.* **49**, 769–822.
Einstein, A.: 1918, 'Prinzipielles zur allgemeinen Relativitätstheorie', *Ann. der Phys.* **55**, 241–244.
Kretschmann, E.: 1917, 'Über den physikalischen Sinn der Relativitäts-Postulate', *Ann. der Phys.* **53**, 575–614.
Møller, C.: 1952, *The Theory of Relativity*, Clarendon Press, Oxford.
Noether, E.: 1918, 'Invariante Variationsprobleme', *Goett. Nachr.*, 235–257.
Post, E. J.: 1962, *Formal Structure of Electromagnetics*, North Holland Publ. Co., Amsterdam.
Post, E. J.: 1967, *General Covariance in Electromagnetism*, in M. Bunge (ed.), *Delaware Seminar in the Foundations of Physics*, Springer Verlag, New York.

PART IV

BIOLOGY

PAUL PIRLOT AND REJANE BERNIER

PRELIMINARY REMARKS ON
THE ORGAN-FUNCTION RELATION

ABSTRACT. The organ-function relation has been viewed in various ways in the course of history, starting with the teleological conception of Aristotle for whom the organ is made for the function, up to some XXth century biologists who look upon the relation as one of utility within the frame-work of adaptation-selection processes. The recent introduction of the word 'teleonomy' to characterize that relation seems to be quite unnecessary since, in practice, the new term does not add anything significant to the notion of adaptation and its implications in a Darwinian sense, as attached, according to us, to the relation. 'Adaptation' is a long-standing term and the one most in harmony with factual as opposed to intentional purposiveness or, in the jargon of molecular genetics, with the randomness-programmation context. Teleology has crept into bio-philosophy as a result of an unjustified, often unconscious, overuse of induction, the concept of function being shifted from the part played to the part to be played by an organ. Furthermore, the views proposed here regarding the organ-function relation are in agreement with up-to-date scientific ideas about normality and integration in the organism.

The purpose of the following remarks is to throw some light on the problem of the organ-function relation. That this problem is at the same time real and interesting is beyond doubt: both the past history and the present state of the question clearly show it.

We should like firstly to review some of the opinions expressed by naturalists on this topic since the dawn of biology. We will emphasize the ambiguity and uncertainty of the biologists' thinking on that subject, on the one hand, and the difficulties encountered by philosophers to delineate the problem, on the other hand. This is, in fact, a problem in biophilosophy. We feel that the border-line between a well-structured biophilosophy and a biology that reflects upon itself is not easy to draw. We realize, of course, that it is more difficult to reach a reasonable degree of accuracy of language in biology than in other natural sciences. Indeed, quantification and formalization have not been carried so far in biology as in physics. Attempts have been made in that direction but the results seem to be rather disappointing in the sense that little advance followed from them, as noted by Simpson [1]. Without engaging into formalization, we will nevertheless try and improve the approach and the expression of the problem.

1. FINALISM FROM ARISTOTLE TO JACOB AND MONOD

The pair of concepts under discussion here is 'organ-function'. In other studies, one finds 'form-function'. We consider the word 'organ' better defined, less vague and better suited than 'form' in the present instance: we shall indeed refer to morphologically well individualized organs. On the other hand, the term 'shape' is also found together with 'form', but this duality needs not be discussed here. (See Waddington [2] on that subject.)

Can one conceive of an organ without a function or a function without an organ? At first sight, the answer is no. We will come back to this problem further down. Let us simply remark that both terms are perhaps linked with one another to the point that each one really is implied in the very definition of the other one. Or, in other words, each one is almost defined by a reference to the other one: the eye is the organ of vision; vision is the function of the eye.

The link or relationship between the two terms being obligatory, our real problem probably is the nature and degree of the relation. Indeed, we enter here a field which the scientist considers as essentially qualitative but with a quantitative aspect, that of the intensity of the relation.

Avoiding a speech in abstracto, we will take a historical approach. As long as fixism was the only existing attitude in biology, the relation between organ and function was clearly finalistic. Function was, for Aristotle, the *final cause* of the organ. The latter is for the former: teeth have been made by nature in order to eat, horns in order to attack or defend. Aristotle has further a remarkably clear idea of the purposive subordination of organs to systems and of systems to organism, which in fact leads toward a rather modern concept of organismic integration. It seems that Aristotle refers to a natural non-conscious goal-directedness, not to a supranatural theistic finality.

Although static, the fixist biology of Aristotle takes into account the relationship between the organism and its environment. This relationship is conceived by him as harmonious to the point that the idea of improvement or progress does not really find its place. The adequation of the living being to the environment is established through the various vital functions: these are suitable, precisely because the organs are built *in order to* perform those functions. It seems that, for Aristotle, there is a dual determination of the organ by the function and of the function by the organ. He gives, as an illustration of this, the fact that the same function can be performed in different ways by different organs. For him, the ontological principle which is the cause at the same time of the structures and of the functions is *the form itself* of the living being. Organ and function are integrated into a living entity which stands in harmony with its environment, but neither the mutual adjustment of organ and function nor the adaptation of the living being to its environment are *caused by the living being itself.* The living being is born with its adaptation, its organs and functions and, in this totally fixist position, the organ does not form itself, does not create itself out of its own dynamism.

When Descartes came with his animal-machine, he did not touch explicitly the core of the problem. Function was for him a result of the structure and movement inherent in the forces of matter. However, purposiveness is implied in some places in his works; e.g. the nerves are conceived as tubes equipped with small valves the role of which is to prevent the back-flow of the animal spirits towards the brain. The valves are there *in order to* perform that function. Descartes does not really see any problem there: a fixed relation given at the start by nature exists between organ and function.

With the advent of transformism, the problem was bound to draw considerably more attention from both biologists and philosophers. Now, the organ is conceived as subject to important modifications or evolution. The first theory, that of Lamarck, insists on need as a basic factor and fundamental concept. The use and disuse of an organ are rooted to the need. So, function is the direct *answer* that the organ provides to need and therefore the *change in the function is the cause of the change of the organ.* In this view again, the function is the *goal* of the organ. This also implies for Lamarck that the modification of an organ is always advantageous and this holds for regressions or disappearance of structures as well as for the emergence of new parts.

Darwin takes a different stand in this respect. For him the variations are random, undirected, not brought about by specific needs. The only constancy or fixity of the relation between organ and function is that maintained by selection: i.e., selection preserves the structure the function of which is most appropriate under given circumstances. This is not a goal-directed action in the sense of the former finalists. The fittest occurs in a fortuitous way among many less fit or unfit living forms: it is not designed in advance as the fittest.

We may now mention the contribution of L. Cuénot, one of the sharpest thinkers of our century with regard to this problem [3]. Cuénot admits, in full agreement with Darwinism and mutationism, the primary importance of random mutations and he endorses the criticisms of the mechanicists against many naive finalistic explanations. But he maintains that not all the problems pertaining to the organ-function relation are thereby completely solved. He is impressed by certain well-known cases of very complex and sophisticated adaptations which he labels cases of finalism or purposiveness, being very cautious, however, to introduce here an important distinction. He sets aside the *finalité d'intention* (intentional purposiveness), which he considers characteristic of man exclusively. Along with the former, however, he recognizes a *finalité de fait* (factual purposiveness) [4]. He also calls it 'organic purposiveness'. What struck Cuénot's mind is the extraordinary similarity between the adjustment of certain living structures to precise vital functions, on the one hand, and the truly intentional act by which man makes *a tool* adapted to a definite task or work on the other hand. Ex.: parachutes of certain seeds, traps of carnivore plants, adaptation of the shape of pedicelles in sea urchins like sugar pincers, spider cobweb [5]. In a slightly different category of facts, Cuénot insists on the coaptations such as button and buttonhole on the wing of some insects.

Where, according to Cuénot, should the origin of those marvelous purposive arrangements be located? The author rejects providentialism. No intelligent God in the usual sense is introduced by him. But he expresses clearly the view that Nature is *teleological in itself*: she does whatever is necessary for the continuation of life, including the invention of clever weapons or tools. Cuénot thinks that an immanent force is at work in the germ-cells of a warthog to ensure that the animal will be at the same time endowed with the digging instinct by which it finds its food and equipped with the rough thickening of the skin on the carpal bones used for digging (such callosities appearing already before birth). So, something in the germ-cells is considered by him intelligent although all religious and mystical entities are firmly excluded. His view is in fact a kind of pantheism constituting for Cuénot a narrow escape from pure mechanism. He considers the introduction of such an immanent purposiveness into

Life or Nature as a necessary complement to mutation and selection [6].

We may now consider one of the best representatives of contemporary thought on evolution, G. G. Simpson, who has dealt in several chapters of his numerous books with the problem of finalism or purposiveness in organs and functions. He is well known as a tenant of materialistic and mechanistic views within the framework of the well-known synthetic theory of evolution. He writes: "Adaptation does exist and so does purpose in Nature if we define 'purpose' as the opposite of randomness, as a causal and not a merely accidental relationship between structure and function, without necessarily invoking a conscious purposeful agency" [7]. Elsewhere in the same book (p. 191), he accepts as a habit of speech and apparently approves of expressions such as gills are made "in order to breathe water" and wings are made "in order to fly". This naturally leads to the concept of utility which Simpson discusses at length.

"The organisation of organisms certainly has utility and the evolution leading to them has that utility as a goal in a sense. That sense is, however, quite special and does not at all correspond with teleology in the classic meaning of correspondance with a preordained plan, with divine providence or with purposes especially relevant to the human species" [8]. And the author writes a little further: "This is not to say that all features of all organisms are useful to them at every moment in time. Some features reflect a utility now passed, hence vestigial organs and many characteristics involved in transformations. The vast body of evidence for the irrevocability of evolution shows that the structures of organisms were not created or evolved, shiny and new, *for* the organism but were evolved *by* the organism from what history made available to them", and again a few lines further down: "It is still true... that utility in the teleonomic not teleological sense here given the word is the principle that makes evolution orderly to the extent that it is in fact orderly."

Simpson himself stresses the fact that such an order does not require any purpose external to the organism. He recognizes that there are goals peculiar to and arising within organisms, and he wonders whether such purposes must be concious and, if so, "how far does consciousness extend? Perhaps it is only a matter of definition", as he finally puts it [9]. Refusing to be a teleological finalist, Simpson may appear as a utilitarian finalist or, in his own words, as a supporter of a relatively recent teleonomic view.

What is, then, teleonomy? How is it distinguished from teleology and could this new concept express more adequately the relation between organ and function as well as the state of equilibrium of an organism within its environment? The word *teleonomy* was coined by Pittendrigh in 1958 "in order to emphasize that the recognition and description of end-directedness does not carry a commitment to Aristotelian teleology as an efficient causal principle" [10]. We doubt if this dispute over teleology and teleonomy really is as important and profound as Pittendrigh makes it. That author presents teleonomy as a great improvement over the word *adaptation* which has been, according to him, contaminated by Aristotelian teleology to the point that even the correct use of the term by Darwin in association with natural selection did not improve the situation sufficiently. Pittendrigh gives some examples showing different uses of the word 'adaptation' and says that all cases "connote that aura of design, purpose or end-directness which has, since Aristotle, seemed to characterize the living thing, to set it sharply aside from the non-living." This is, to say the least, a personal interpretation of Pittendrigh, who does not give a convincing justification for it. This quarrel over an old word is in fact of limited interest. It would have been more interesting to stress and discuss, from the point of view of finality, the much more important distinction between adaptation as a status and adaptation as a process.

We are here firstly concerned with adaptation as a status or permanent condition. It seems to us, that, if we say that an organ is adapted *to a certain function*, we express its end-directedness as correctly as with the word teleonomy. No more animism or intentionality or other metabiological element is implied in adaptation than in teleonomy. We doubt if the historical view of Pittendrigh is correct. To say that all usages of the word 'adaptation' before Darwin have been Aristotelian amounts to denying all value to the transformist thinking before 1859. It is true that, for Aristotle, adaptation was static, i.e., it was a given condition, inherent in the species which was for him eternal and fixed. But transformism was born long before Darwin.

The word 'teleonomy', however, has gained an additional favour since two Nobel laureates, Jacob and Monod, have used it in an attempt to give purposiveness a *statut légal*, a legal or lawful status in biology. These authors think that by simply saying that a function results from the genetic programming of the organ, purposiveness is legalized. The magic words are 'D.N.A.' and 'program'. Since the program is assumed to be a product of pure chance or randomness, there is, in their work, no objection to using the expression *fait pour* (made for), to characterize a particular organ.

We doubt that it is advisable to restore the terms *finalité* or 'purposiveness' even in the randomness-progammation context. It seems to us that those words carry an untimely implication of intentionality. If not the end-organ and the end-function, at least the program still appears to have been made for, designed for by a mysterious Intelligence hidden behind the program: this is certainly not what Jacob and Monod have in mind. We would criticize Jacob and Monod for satisfying themselves with the observation of a present day given fact: the structure of the mammalian eye, with all its complexity, *is determined by a genetic program which also determines its functions*. Those two authors did not scrutinize the problem of the genesis of the program itself; this would have led them to detecting the part played by the adaptation on the various phylogenetic levels. For us, adaptation and adapted are key concepts related to key events of the history of life and those words do not call for any finalistic interpretation. For this reason, we would banish 'teleonomical' as well as 'teleological'.

2. FINALITY AND INTEGRATION

Let us try and analyze now a little more deeply the idea of 'made for', *fait pour*. From our short historical review, we can already notice that, actually, the naturalists have done a very curious thing. They have gone from the observation of the activity of the organ to a finalistic interpretation of the part to be played by that organ. This is nothing but an abuse of induction. From the statistical or repeated observations of a given activity, they have gone to talking about an *essential* relation between an organ and a particular activity. A first step has been the passage from particular to general. Then, it was easy to go from the observation of a fact to the acceptance of a necessity or lawfulness to which the organ must conform itself, of a kind of duty which that organ had to fulfill. Unconsciously, biologists were led from the idea that the organ had a given activity to the idea that *it had to have it* and finally that it existed only *in order to* perform that activity. We may agree that the passage between step one and step two is simply the consequence of the establishment of a law, but it seems more difficult to accept step three whereby one goes from the formulation of a law to the assertion of finality. Through an anthropomorphic over-interpretation of the law, finality has been, in many cases, inserted into an inductive process. Nothing justifies such a teleological view of the organ-function couple. The result is that, through this shift from *the part played* to the *part to be played*, the word 'function' is often used to designate both the real activity of an organ and the activity that man thinks the organ must or can perform. In this sense, it is said that an organ without actual activity nevertheless has a function (embryonic lung or certain silent brain cells).

We could perhaps go a little further into our analysis. Could it not be that the deepest foundation of that finalism lies in the perception of the marvelous unity to be found in the great complexity of the living, especially in higher animals? Indeed, in these organisms the integration of the organs and of the functions is so obvious that it soon becomes impossible, in any serious study, to consider one organ or one function alone. Our knowledge of the living is firstly a total or holistic one although still relatively superficial. The living being shows itself at once as a unified entity that can be identified more or less easily. Only later, at a subsequent stage, can analysis begin and the separate organs and functions be distinguished. Owing to the reality of the distinction between organ and function, this analysis of the living being emphasizes either the morphology or the physiology of the organism. Later again, and at least as far as physiology is concerned, it is obvious from all historical accounts that a new holistic or synthetic stage follows the analytic one. Indeed, the physiologist seems to keep in mind, more easily than anybody else, the idea of integration, surely because the coordination of functions is so apparent.

At first sight, it may appear that the situation is different in morphology, i.e., that the structure could not be integrated to the same degree as the functions. However, if the functions, with all their diversity, can cooperate within the total organism, the organs which are their material basis should also constitute a unity on the morphological level. There is such a thing as a morphological integration. By this we mean that the various parts making up the morphology of the organisms must be well-fitted or well-adjusted to each other. This notion remains a little vague because the idea of a mutual adjustment is complex. It implies a number of adaptations or co-adaptations between separate elements each of which must occupy its proper location.

The concept of integration leads us to that of structure. No term, perhaps, is more fashionable nowadays and also subject to more fanciful semantic variations. In biology, a structure will appear as composed of interrelated sub-structures. What will be the interrelations of these sub-structures in a morphological integration? Since functional relations are here put aside, we are left with spatial or topographical relations. In other words, morphological integration demands a good spatial adjustment or arrangement. What do we mean by this? We could follow A. Dürer and give this expression a purely plastic and aesthetic sense, but this would not help us much in our particular problem.

When and how, then, can we say that an arrangement of parts is good, adequate, suitable? Do these terms indicate a condition of *harmony* and *equilibrium* within the living forms? We simply have here two more words to justify. It seems utopian and unrealistic to try and utilize all those concepts in an abstract way, without referring to concrete cases. In fact, we are forced to enter here the field of the *normalcy*. And immediately we see that we must not put too much confidence in the common notion of *normal* as a support for the idea of integrating arrangement. Indeed, teratology offers a large number of cases of living beings that constitute structures made up of sub-structures in unusual assemblages and lay-outs but that hold together and can be viable modes of morphological association and integration. What, then, is similar and what is dissimilar between two structures one of which is said to be normal and the other one monstrous? What they have in common is obviously the fact that both possess a large number of identical sub-structures, by virtue of their conspccificity, but also a few non-identical sub-structures which stand nevertheless in stable topographical interrelations. The stability of the connexions seems to be an essential element of morphological integration

The differences between the normal and the monstrous appear finally to be located at two distinct levels at least. In the first place, a teratological structure is so considered because it differs excessively from the one that can be observed in the group of individuals representing the species as a whole. We must refer here to a concept of norm which is not static, or absolute or independent of spatio-temporal coordinates but which, rather, designates what is most common, nearest to the mode or statistical maximal frequency. Such a norm cannot be static because it is shifted one way or the other as the species themselves change. For quantitative characters, the norm is obviously related to the mode and, in fact, morphological norms do vary a great deal as far as the dimensions of parts are concerned. Can they also vary in the spatial relations within parts, for example, as in the case of a mammal having a foot on the stomach? This may be a quite fanciful although not impossible example of teratology but, anyway, we know from the historical process of evolution that organs have been topographically displaced or shifted (pineal and parietal organs, fish fins, position of nostrils, nerve roots, heart, lengthening of neck). Here again we shall be inclined to call 'normal' what is nearest to the highest statistical frequency. In fact, only a very few of the living structures that we can imagine have really existed.

This takes us to the second class of important differences between the normal and the monstrous. Many forms were indeed produced by evolution but not maintained because their structuration did not satisfy the rules of organismic balance, that is to say, they implied an excessive disturbance of their functions or functioning. So, inevitably, while attempting to define the morphological normal and abnormal, we are taken back to the physiological normal and abnormal.

Thus, although the idea of morphological integration can be dissociated conceptually from the idea of physiological integration, it remains true that the living being is a unified ontological totality in which the overall structure, made up of complex sub-structures, could be produced and maintained only because the functions of each subset were integrated in the functioning of the aggregate, i.e., the organism.

Maybe we should, at this point, ask another question: are the topographical relations prior to the functional ones? It seems that, quite often, it is possible, within a very short ontogenetic period, to dissociate topographical from functional relations and that the former precede the latter in time. In such cases, a topographical relation appears as a necessary condition for making the functional relations possible. It is worth noting here that the contiguity of parts is but one particular case of topographical relations: the important thing is the relation or correlation between parts, whether these are contiguous or not. For example, the hypophysis and the ovaries in vertebrates are in spatio-temporal relation as strictly as the frontal and parietal bones in the mammalian skull, or the testes, the efferent canalicules and the kidneys in the frog. On the other hand, the contiguity of parts does not necessarily determine the functional relation.

To be sure, the spatial grouping (testes-canalicules-kidneys in the frog) is a real factor in thedetermination of the uro-genital function. However, this structural relation seems to be rather contingent, even quite secondary. An example of a deeper and more important determination of functioning by position on structure would be that of the gametic activity being caused by the fact that the cells derived from the embryonic genital ridge undergo a meiosis and so produce sexual elements, whereas the cells of the nearby nephrogenic ridge divide by mitosis and produce kidney tubules. The co-operation seen in the first case appears to be far less significant that the dissociation in the second case.

From such examples we can perceive, in the general activity of the living being, several levels of determination arranged in a kind of hierarchy. This could carry our reflexion upstream so to speak, through the genetic coding up to the first existing cell or even the initial atom. Along this line, the spatial relations in the living are reduced to very little, being no more than contingent stages of a structuration determined by the genetic code. It will be noted here that our insistence on the genetic determination does not imply an underestimation of the epigenetic mechanisms. Both factors, genetic and epigenetic, are necessary. Chronologically, however, the genetic structure comes first and sets the limits for epigenetic intervention. The lesser importance of epigenetic factors is in a way indicated by the fact that these factors enjoy a certain freedom or margin of variability, i.e., if they do not obey rigorously the instructions issued by the genetic code, an approximate conformity to the latter may anyway result in an organ that functions somehow or other. Furthermore, if structure is, after all, determined by genetic instructions, the latter are not a purely theoretical program. They have been tested in the course of evolution. Their emergence itself is a demonstration of their adaptive value with respect to environmental conditions, both past and present. The very existence of a structure in a functioning state proves that it materializes not only a morphological but also a physiological program.

3. CONCLUDING REMARKS

We have thus illustrated with our examples, taken from the correlation of parts, and established with our remarks on the genetic program, that it is really impossible to talk about the morphology of an organism without referring simultaneously to his physiology. One further indication of this relative impossibility to dissociate both aspects is found in the common usage of the word 'system'. In order to describe the morphological structures that collaborate in a vital activity, we currently use the word 'system' coupled with adjectives the meaning of which is clearly physiological: digestive system, nervous system, etc. Every system, being morpho-physiological, is ideally integrating. It will be noted that a narrow spatial connection is again not necessarily implied in the morphological aspect of the system. For example, some invertebrates possess solenocytes dispersed almost everywhere in their body; the total set of such small structures makes an excretory system, although the actual unity between them is probably reduced to a very loose and indistinct nervous mediation. The morphological demarcation of the system becomes also rather vague in the case of the central nervous system where structural territories are not always easy to demarcate [11].

In conclusion, we have two modes of integration, one for the organs and one for the functions. If both can be easily distinguished by the epistemologist, they cannot be separated, i.e., there is a kind of integration of the integrations. In this, we are getting close to the organismic viewpoint, the efforts of which in order to become a general system theory in biology are still in their infancy, although progressing.

We close our paper with two short remarks. Firstly, we have not dealt exhaustively with the problem of causality in connection with the organ-function relation. We have only rejected the introduction of a final cause into that relation, not considering the finality of human action. Whether we should also discuss the applicability of the Aristotelian concepts of formal and efficient causes in this case remains beyond the scope of this paper. We intend, however, to tackle as fully as possible, for the restricted case of the living being and following the example of Bunge on a more general level, the question of causality in our more complete treatment of the subject now in preparation.

Secondly, we are aware of the importance of the contemporary debate regarding the general substitution of a non-teleological for a teleological expression in biology and biophilosophy. Two classic examples are: "The earth happens to be made in such a way that it intercepts millions of small meteorites travelling through space" and "The heart happens to be made so that it produces beating sounds". Such expressions, proposed by mechanistically inclined people, are obviously insufficient for describing the function of the earth or of the heart in spite of being presented as 'functional ascriptions'. Obviously, we need more than that to describe adequately a function. The attempts to change some traditionally teleological descriptions into non-teleological ones remain fairly difficult, as can be concluded from the works of Nagel, Canfield, Beckner and Braithwaite.

Département de Zoologie, Département de Philosophie
Université de Montréal

BIBLIOGRAPHY

[1] Simpson, G. G., *Principles of Animal Taxonomy*, Columbia University Press, New York and London, 1962, pp. 21–22.
[2] Waddington, C. H., *New Patterns in Genetics and Development*, Columbia University Press, New York and London, 1964, pp. 86–87.
[3] Cuénot, L., *Invention et finalité en biologie*, Flammarion, Paris, 1941.
[4] *Ibid.*, pp. 36ff.
[5] *Ibid.*, Part IV: 'les difficultés du mécanisme', pp. 154ff.
[6] *Ibid.*, p. 233.
[7] Simpson, G. G., *This View of Life*, Harcourt, Brace and World, Inc., New York, 1964, p. 202.
[8] *Ibid.*, p. 173.
[9] *Ibid.*, p. 175.
[10] Pittendrigh C. S., 'Adaptation, Natural Selection, and Behavior', in A. Roe and G. G. Simpson (eds.), *Behavior and Evolution*, Yale University Press, New Haven, 1961, p. 394.
[11] Pirlot, Paul, 'Relation organe-fonction et système nerveux central', *Scientia* **106** (1971), 601–612.

MARY B. WILLIAMS

THE LOGICAL STATUS OF THE
THEORY OF NATURAL SELECTION
AND OTHER EVOLUTIONARY CONTROVERSIES*

ABSTRACT. This paper shows that the theory of natural selection is not tautologous and that the belief that it is stems from formulations of the theory which attempt to defy logical impossibility by defining all the words used in the theory. The correct method is to treat some of them as primitives characterized by axioms. The axiomatization used to resolve this controversy also resolves controversies about the units of evolution and the target of selection. The concatenation of the axiomatization, revealing the fundamental structure of the theory, and the controversies arising in the preaxiomatic theory gives insight into the structure underlying controversies about other preaxiomatic theories.

The phrase 'survival of the fittest' is a source of nagging embarrassment to evolutionists. On the one hand it is clearly ambiguous, purportedly tautologous, and (so far) impossible to translate into a statement that is non-tautologous, non-ambiguous, and also captures the essence of natural selection; but on the other hand it is so evocative of the essence of the principle of natural selection that even those who believe that it is tautologous and therefore completely meaningless find themselves using it, albeit with many *caveats*, when teaching novices. The arguments about this phrase and the many suggested replacements are reflected in Lerner's comment ([21], p. 180): "with all of the knowledge now acquired on the process of selection in nature, its logical status in evolution is still uncertain and undoubtedly controversial." This controversy is settled by axiomatization of the theory of natural selection (given in [21]), but it will not disappear until the fallacy underlying the belief that it is tautologous is exposed. The purpose of this paper is to expose that fallacy and to provide a non-ambiguous non-tautologous translation of 'survival of the fittest'.

To give an understanding of the term that is the referent of this phrase it is necessary (and, with the aid of the axiomatization, easy) to resolve the controversies about the units of evolution and the primary target of selection. The paper therefore resolves these controversies and exposes the fallacy which underlies them.

M. Bunge (ed.), The Methodological Unity of Science, 84–102. *All Rights Reserved*
Copyright © 1973 by D. Reidel Publishing Company, Dordrecht-Holland.

1. DESCRIPTION OF THE AXIOMATIZATION

The axiomatization presented in [21] is a naive axiomatization, closer in style to the axiomatizations of Euclid and Newton than to the formal axiomatizations of the Russell-Whitehead school. In this section I will present the main points of the axiomatization even more informally; because definition of the technical terms used in the later axioms would require an inordinate amount of space, the later axioms will be stated in informal 'translations' which do not render their full meaning. These translations should be sufficient, however, to provide the necessary insights into the phrase 'survival of the fittest'.

There are two sets of axioms. The first set delineates properties of the set B of reproducing organisms on which natural selection works. The primitive terms introduced in this first set are *biological entity* and $\succ$. $\succ$ is an asymmetric, irreflexive, and non-transitive relation between biological entities and should be read 'is a parent of'. Some possible interpretations for biological entity are: organism, gene, chromosome, and population.

Axiom B1: For any b_1 in B, $\sim(b_1 \succ b_1)$. (I.e., '$\succ$' is irreflexive.)

The following defines another relation, $\triangleright$, or 'is an ancestor of'.

Definition B1: $b_1 \triangleright b_2$ if and only if $b_1 \succ b_2$ or there exists a finite non-empty set of biological entities, $\{b_3, b_4, \ldots b_k\}$, such that $b_1 \succ b_3 \succ b_4 \succ \ldots \succ b_k \succ b_2$.

Axiom B2: For any b_1 and b_2 in B, if $b_1 \triangleright b_2$ then $\sim(b_2 \triangleright b_1)$. (i.e., $\triangleright$ is asymmetric.)

A set B with a relation $\succ$ satisfying these axioms[1] will be called a *biocosm*. From these axioms it can be proved that $\triangleright$ is irreflexive and transitive and that $\succ$ is asymmetric. $\succ$ is not transitive, although in special cases $b_1 \succ b_2$, $b_2 \succ b_3$ and $b_1 \succ b_3$ may all be true; e.g., let b_1 be Jocasta, b_2 be Oedipus, and b_3 be Antigone.

The primary purpose for stating these axioms is to enable the concepts of *clan* and *subclan* to be rigorously defined. A clan is a temporally extended (over many generations) set of related organisms. (In this description I will, for clarity, usually use the 'organism' interpretation of 'biological entity'.)

Translation of Definition B7: The clan of a set S is the set containing S and all of its descendants.

A crucial biological phenomenon occurs when a part of a clan becomes isolated from the rest of the clan (perhaps by an earthquake) and is subjected for many generations to different selective pressures until ultimately the organisms in one part of the clan are so different from their contemporaries in the other part that they would be described as different species; this is a situation of great interest for evolutionary theory, so it is clearly important to have a word for some particular kinds of parts of a clan. The first one I introduce is a *subclan*, which, roughly speaking, is either a whole clan or a clan with one or several branches removed; a subclan is an organized chunk of a clan, not just a set of isolated descendants.

Translation of Definition B9: C_1 is a subclan of C if and only if C_1 is contained in C and for every organism b_1 in C_1 there exists a lineage (or line of descent) from an organism in the first generation of C to b_1 such that every biological entity in that lineage is in C_1.

Translation of Definition B10: C_1 is the subclan of C derived from $C_1(j)$ if and only if C_1 contains all of the descendants of $C_1(j)$ and all the ancestors of $C_1(j)$ which are in C.

Now I can introduce the second set of axioms. This set uses two new primitive terms, *Darwinian subclan* and *fitness*. The following quotation from [21] gives an intuitive introduction to the meaning of the concept of Darwinian *subclan*:

Using an imperfect but intuitively useful analogy, we may think of selection as a force which is pushing a subclan in a certain direction (e.g. toward longer necks, or toward an optimum proportion of different forms in a polymorphic population). The direction and strength of this force is always an average over the differing forces on different individuals of the subclan, but, as long as cohesive forces (e.g., interbreeding, same environment) hold the subclan together, it is meaningful to speak of selection pushing the subclan as a whole in some direction. If, on the other hand, the subclan consists of two parts which are isolated from each other and subject to different selective forces (e.g. one favoring longer necks and the other favoring shorter necks), it is not very meaningful to speak of selection pushing this subclan in one direction; it is pushing it in two opposite directions and the average of the two directions would be a mathematical abstraction which would only serve to conceal the interesting biological phenomenon. Clearly I need a term to denote a subclan which is held together by cohesive forces so that it acts as a unit with respect to selection; I shall call such a subclan a *Darwinian subclan.*

Darwinian subclan is a primitive term but, unlike the other primitive terms, it does not correspond closely to any familiar intuitive concept. A Darwinian subclan may be an entire clan from which no descendants have been separated; it may be an interbreeding population; it may be an entire species. It cannot be a species which is splitting into two species; such a species will consist of two Darwinian subclans.

Although a Darwinian subclan is a set of biological entities it cannot be defined solely in terms of properties definable within the biocosm; it is determined both by properties of the parent relation among biological entities and by properties of the relationship between a set of biological entities and their environment.

Fitness is introduced as a real valued function on the set of biological entities; $\varphi(b_1)$ is a real number expressing the fitness of the biological entity b_1 in the environment in which it lives. The following quotation from [21] is an intuitive introduction to the concept of fitness:

fitness is a measure of the quality of the relationship between an organism and its environment, where the environment of an organism is the set of all external factors which have influenced it during its life.... This relationship is determined by such factors as fertility, ability to get food, ability to avoid dangers, etc.

Fitter organisms have a better *chance* of surviving long enough to leave descendants, but a fitter organism does not necessarily leave more descendants than its less fit brother.

Translation of Axiom D1: Every Darwinian subclan is a subclan of a clan in some biocosm.

Translation of Axiom D2: There is an upper limit to the number of organisms in any generation of a Darwinian subclan.

(This limit is important in inducing the 'severe struggle for life' which Darwin noted.)

Translation of Axiom D3: For each organism, b_1, there is a positive real number, $\varphi(b_1)$, which describes its fitness in its environment.

Before giving the next axiom we must introduce another term denoting a particular type of subclan. Suppose that at a particular point in time the Darwinian subclan D contains a subset of organisms with a hereditary trait that gives them a selective advantage over their contemporaries, and suppose that this trait continues to give a selective advantage for many generations. Then members of this subset will, on average, have more offspring than their contemporaries, and if we consider the sub-subclan derived from this set of organisms (call it D_1), then in the offspring generation the proportion of the members of D which are in D_1 will be larger than it was in the parent generation. Similarly, since this trait continues to give a selective advantage, the proportion of D_1 will continue to increase in subsequent generations. It is by this increase in the proportion of organisms with particular traits that characteristics of populations (and species) are changed over time. It is the increase of the fitter sub-subclan which causes descent with adaptive modification. This sub-subclan is the referent of 'survival of the fittest'. It will be called a *subcland*.[2]

Translation of Definition D2: Let $D_1(j)$ be a set of biological entities in the jth generation of the Darwinian subclan D. Then D_1 is the subcland derived from $D_1(j)$ if and only if $D_1 = D \cap C_1$, where C_1 is the subclan derived from $D_1(j)$.

Translation of Axiom D4: Consider a subcland D_1 of D. If D_1 is superior in fitness to the rest of D for sufficiently many generation (where how many is 'sufficiently many' is determined by how much superior D_1 is and how large D_1 is), then the proportion of D_1 in D will increase during these generations.

The final axiom asserts the existence of sufficiently hereditary fitness differences.

Translation of Axiom D5: In every generation m of a Darwinian subclan D which is not on the verge of extinction, there is a subcland D_1 such that: D_1 is superior to the rest of D for long enough to ensure that D_1 will increase relative to D; and as long as D contains biological entities that are not in D_1, D_1 retains sufficient superiority to ensure further increases relative to D.

The full formal translation of the law of the survival of the fittest is contained in these axioms, and in particular in Axiom D4. This axiom could be called the 'survival of the fittest' axiom; but an even better informal descriptive phrase would be the 'expansion of the fitter subcland' axiom.

2. FITNESS

Let us first examine the attempts to translate 'fittest'. The fundamental cause of the problems associated with these attempts is the acceptance, by essentially all biologists, of the metaphysical doctrine that all words used in a scientific theory should be defined. It is these problems which have been central in creating the belief that the theory of natural selection is circular and is, therefore, a linguistic epiphenomenon which can be shown by close examination to have no real meaning. (In this controversy the theory is usually accused of being tautological, but 'tautological' is always used in these accusations in the sense of 'circular and therefore vacuous'. Since there are other meanings of 'tautological' which are scientifically respectable, I shall use the term 'circular'.) In this paper I am concerned not so much with proving that the theory is not circular as with exposing the fallacious reasoning which led to the accusations of circularity. [3]

The best introduction to the dilemma is to look at it through the eyes of Ernest Mayr (p. 182 in [15]), one of the most powerful opponents of the idea that Darwin's reasoning is circular:

> Darwin ... has therefore been accused of tautological (circular) reasoning: 'What will survive? The fittest. What are the fittest? Those that survive.' To say that this is the essence of natural selection is nonsense! To be sure, those individuals that have the most offspring are by definition (Lerner, 1959) the fittest ones. However, this fitness is determined (statistically) by their genetic constitution.... A superior genotype has a greater probability of leaving offspring than has an inferior one. Natural selection, simply, is the differential perpetuation of genotypes.

In the last sentence Mayr is simply repeating the usual contemporary description of natural selection. (The virtually complete acceptance by biologists of this description is due to the fact that it does capture the essence of *one* of the Darwinian insights, and possibly also to the compelling, though fallacious, argument: without differential perpetuation natural selection could not occur; therefore natural selection *is* differential perpetuation.) But the context shows that Mayr does not really believe that natural selection is *nothing more than* the differential perpetuation of genotypes; he believes that it is the differential perpetuation of *superior* genotypes. It is essential to his (and Darwin's) conception of natural selection that over the long run the adaptively superior genotypes have more offspring; without some such adjective the important Darwinian insight that the environment has something to do with which genotypes have more offspring is lost. But 'superior', 'adaptively superior', 'adaptively complex' (Maynard Smith [18]), 'greater ability of phenotypes to obtain representation in the next generation' (Bossert and Wilson [2]) 'adaptedness' (Dobzhansky [5]), etc. are all simply disguised ways of saying 'fitter'. How do we know that a superior genotype has a greater probability of leaving offspring? What is superior? In this context 'superior' has the same intuitive meaning as 'fitter' had to Darwin. Therefore, if we accept Lerner's definition of fitness as a true rendition of the meaning of fitness in the Darwinian phrase, we should define 'superior' in the same way; the superior genotypes are the genotypes that have more offspring. Once this is done, of course, 'differential perpetuation of superior genotypes' is just as circular as 'survival of the fittest'.

The real source of the dilemma is that this definition is *not* a true rendition of Darwin's meaning. [4] Lerner's unfortunately all too true comment ([12], p. 176) about this definition is

If there is one thing upon which the most factious partisans of various currents of evolutionary thought agree, it is that fitness of an individual, in the context of the natural selection principle, can mean *only* the extent to which the organism is represented by descendants in succeeding generations. (italics mine)

This definition of fitness makes no reference to the fact that fitness is a property of the relationship between the organism and its environment; it states by omission that the environment is irrelevant to fitness. It is not surprising that the acceptance of this definition has led to statements that the theory is vacuous, for the fact that fitness is related to the environment is absolutely essential for the Darwinian insight. With this definition Darwinian theory is reduced to 'differential perpetuation of genotypes', that is, to a theory which implies that the properties (e.g., morphological characters) of the organisms will change over the generations but gives no indication that this change is systematically related to the environment. (It would be possible for the geneticists to retain the Darwinian insight by stating a new law that differential perpetuation is systematically related to the environment. But the statement of such a law would inevitably require a theoretical term with the same objectionable qualities that 'fitness' has.) Some sternly ascetic geneticists actually do restrict themselves to this reduced version of the theory of natural selection; most evolutionists, however, while using this definition of 'fitness', sneak in a new term (superior, adaptedness, etc.) to take the place of 'fitness' in order to retain as a part of the theory the important Darwinian insight that changes in the properties of species are systematically related to the environment. The controversy, then, is between those who, relying on the deep intuitive knowledge that Darwinian theory is far from being vacuous, save the Darwinian insight by reintroducing a term equivalent to fitness without explicitly defining the new term, and those who, relying on logical reasoning from the accepted definition of fitness, throw away the Darwinian insight. This definition of fitness has put both parties to the controversy into untenable positions; the only way to resolve the controversy is to throw out this definition of fitness.

Both parties to the controversy would probably respond to this statement by stating that they cannot throw out this definition until a suitable replacement is available. And this reveals the deeper source of the controversy: the fallacious doctrine that all words used in a scientific theory can, at least in principle, and should be defined. (In practice this means that definitions are not insisted on for those theoretical terms which (like organism) are close enough to experience that scientists rarely have difficulty deciding what they mean in specific situations, while definitions are demanded for those theoretical terms which (like fitness) are so abstract that scientists frequently must struggle to find an adequate interpretation.) Now it is a simple logical fact that it is impossible to define all words of a theory in terms of other words of the theory without introducing a circularity into the theory. Since the doctrine in question would not allow a definition in terms of words from another theory which themselves ultimately depend on undefined terms, no non-circular theoretical definition of fitness will be acceptable.

The scientist hopes to avoid this problem by using operational definitions for his basic words and defining the rest in terms of them. Theories which contain only terms denoting concepts which are close to experience appear to be stated in simple, operationally defined (or, at least, definable), terms, and it is this appearance which gives rise to the belief that any theory can be so stated. (Also, of course, this belief comes from the reasoning that since the theoretical terms have their ultimate origin in experience, they must be statable in terms of experience. But this is the same as reasoning that since scientific laws have their ultimate origin in observation statements, they must be statable as some conjunction of observation statements. The problem of induction is clearly as much a problem with regard to general concepts as with regard to general laws.) As Hempel has shown ([9], p. 129), there are difficulties which prevent theoretically satisfactory operational definitions of even simple concepts like 'length', but these are not the difficulties that ambush attempts to define 'fitness'. Scientists are generally willing to accept as operational any definition stated in terms of (potentially) directly observable results of manipulations, where what is to count as directly observable is decided not by philosophical analysis but by consensus.[5] The difficulty that ambushes fitness is that abstract terms which are not close to experience (i.e., to direct observation) are not amenable to definition in terms of direct observation. As Einstein pointed out, theories which have been rigorously stated meet this difficulty by "the application of complicated logical processes in order to reach conclusions from the premises that can be confronted with observation", (p. 5 in [6]) though even this philosophically acceptable technique causes "an almost irresistible feeling of aversion [to arise] in people who are inexperienced in epistemological analysis". (*ibid.*) Since evolutionary theory had not been stated sufficiently rigorously to allow the application of complicated logical processes, this way of validating the concept of fitness was not available. Therefore the evolutionists could not, for the full Darwinian meaning of the concept, satisfy the demands of this metaphysical doctrine by using either direct or indirect operational criteria.

Faced with this impasse the evolutionist defined fitness in terms of its most important known property; he defined 'the fittest' as 'those that survive'. This was disastrous for two reasons: (1) Because the law of the survival of the fittest had not itself been explicitly stated, the definition enshrined an extremely impoverished version of this important property. (2) When an axiom is used as a definition of one of its terms it is no longer an axiom; the theory remaining after that axiom has been removed will obviously be less powerful, and, when the axiom that was removed expressed the most important insight of the theory, its removal makes the theory virtually meaningless. (Of course, in a formally stated theory it can be seen that *calling* an axiom a definition does not make it one; it will be a creative definition, and therefore really an axiom. But in an intuitively stated theory once you convert the axiom into a definition you are forced to admit that it is purely circular and gives no power to the theory; no one can save you by proving it is a creative definition.) Thus this definition of fitness weakened the theory both by replacing the intuitive definition, which recognized that fitness is related to the environment, with a definition that ignores this relationship and by removing from the theory its most important law. It is this replacement of an important law by an (apparently) circular definition that is responsible for the belief that Darwinian theory is circular.

The belief that all (non-obvious) terms must be defined is common among scientists. Since the most important explicitly known property of an abstract term is the property stated in the deepest law containing the term, it will always be very tempting to respond to the demand for a definition of the term by using that property as a definition. It is probably because of this that we so frequently see theories accused of being circular on the ground that their most important insights are merely definitions, or of being meaningless on the ground that their most central concepts cannot be defined. Recall, for example, the *reductio ad absurdum*: What is intelligence? Intelligence is what is measured by intelligence tests. Or consider the accusations in the ecological literature that the exclusion principle of Gause, which says that two species cannot coexist in the same niche, is circular because this is the defining property of the niche. Anyone familiar with the 'soft' sciences can give more examples. But an example from a 'hard' science will strengthen our understanding of the theoretical structure which underlies these problematic definitions. Consider the following quotations from Newton's *Principia* (pp. 2, 13 in [17]).

Definition IV: An impressed force is an action exerted upon a body, in order to change its state, either of rest, or of uniform motion in a right line.
Law I: Every body continues in its state of rest, or of uniform motion in a right line, unless it is compelled to change that state by forces impressed upon it.

Let us subject the concept of force to the catechism used in the quotation from Mayr for the concept of fitness. "What will change the state of rest or of uniform motion of a body? An impressed force. What is an impressed force? Something that will change the state of rest or of uniform motion of a body." Clearly Newton's theory of mechanics is just as circular as Darwin's theory of natural selection. (More so, in fact, since Darwin at least didn't give that definition of fitness.)

Fitness is a theoretical term which cannot be explicitly defined. That such terms exist in any axiomatized theory is well known; they are the primitive terms of the theory. That such terms must exist also in the intuitively stated precursor of an axiomatized theory is obvious. In any deep theory some of the terms will be so abstract that the lack of adequate definitions will be painfully obvious. But until the theory is rigorously stated it is impossible to experimentally validate such an abstract concept. If it is a primitive term, only an axiomatization of the theory will allow a full and explicit statement of its meaning in the theory, for its meaning in the theory is completely given by the statements that the theory makes about it. After the theory has been axiomatized, the various successful interpretations of the primitive term give the most comprehensive possible statement about its meaning in the real world. Thus only an axiomatization can provide a final resolution of the problems stemming from the need to specify the meanings of abstract concepts. But during the preaxiomatic stages of a theory it is important simply to recognize that these problems are caused by a fallacious metaphysical doctrine and do not indicate that the theory is worthless; in fact, they indicate that the theory is deep.

3. THE REFERENT

The major source of the controversy surrounding the phrase 'survival of the fittest' is that dealt with in the preceding section. But to understand the referent of this phrase we must first use the axiomatization to resolve controversies arising from the following questions: What is the fundamental unit of selection? What is the primary target of selection? Both spring from the fact that our analytic metaphysics leads us to (incorrectly) assume that there is *one* fundamental entity which is the object of selection and which is such that all results of selection can, and should, be described with reference only to that fundamental entity. (For example, in the argument about whether the target of selection is the gene or the organism, the argument is about which is the fundamental entity with reference to which the basic theory of selection should be stated and all other entities which undergo selection should be described.) This assumption has led to confusion because the world that the evolutionist is trying to describe contains several important independent fundamental entities.

All of these different fundamental entities are physically parts of one another. With respect to the theory of natural selection, they fall into two categories: (1) those that cannot be defined in terms of one another because they correspond to different primitive terms of the theory; and (2) those that are independent of one another because they appear in different models of the theory.

(1) *Different Ontological levels:* My primary plan in this section is to discuss the problem on a relatively intuitive biological level in order to give insight into the way things look at an intuitive (preaxiomatic) stage when the underlying theoretical structure is such that one of the entities being discussed is a collection of entities but cannot be defined as a set of these entities. Since the assertion that the entities under discussion are of this kind is a very strong assertion, I will first point out that the axiomatization makes a rigorous proof of this assertion possible. Because this assertion is equivalent to the assertion that *Darwinian subclan* is inde-

pendent of the remaining primitive terms of the theory, it can be proved by using Padoa's Principle.[6]

First let us try to get some insight into why the theory needs two types of entity. Natural selection changes the characteristics of populations by depriving individuals of offspring (either by ensuring an untimely death for the individual or by interfering with the reproductive process). Thus it acts on individuals to change the characteristics of populations. This is a strange kind of force, since the forces we usually deal with change the characteristics of the objects they act on; for example, an impressed force changes the state of motion of the billiard ball it acts on. Selection is a force which changes hereditary characteristics, but this change does not take place in individuals. Selection cannot change the inherited characteristics of an individual; it may, so to speak, punish the individual for his bad characteristics by preventing him from having offspring; but it is powerless to change his characteristics once he is there. (The insight that selection could change the characteristics of a population without changing the characteristics of any individual was one of Darwin's most valuable contributions.) It is clear that, while the forces of mechanics could be described with reference to a single type of entity which is both acted upon and changed, the forces of selection must be described with reference to two types of entity, one of which is acted on and the other of which is changed. (This is partly an artefact of our human sized viewpoint; we could, theoretically, completely ignore the existence of individuals and consider the killing of an individual as an action on the population of which that individual is a component, just as we consider a knife wound as an action on the organism rather than as an action on the cells that were actually killed. But, because we *do* have a human sized viewpoint and *do* see the individual deaths rather than the wound in the population, it is necessary for the theory to deal with the relationship between the actions on the individual and the results on the population.) This is the reason that in the axiomatization there are two primitive terms referring to types of entities; the biological entity is the thing selection acts on and the Darwinian subclan is the thing whose characteristics are changed.

Let us consider now the effect that this undefinability has had on the definitions used in biology, remembering that biologists have simply assumed that since a species is a collection of organisms it can be defined in terms of the properties of the organisms it contains. Since a species is a

Darwinian subclan and an organism is a biological entity we would
expect that any attempt to define species in terms of organisms would be
doomed to failure. And it is exactly this failure that Beckner has analyzed
so beautifully in [1], where he shows that in the definitions used in
systematics the definiens is typically a set of neither severally necessary
nor jointly sufficient properties of the entities contained in the taxa
being defined. From the point of view of normal logic such definitions
are clearly not legitimate definitions. (Beckner concluded that the concept of definition should be expanded to include these polytypic definitions. Although, as I have argued elsewhere [22], definitions in the
usual logical form are possible once the theory has been sufficiently
rigorously stated to make clear what the defining properties are properties
of, polytypic definitions probably do have a legitimate role in the preaxiomatic stages of theories.)

And finally let us look at how these two types of entities appear in
arguments about the fundamental units of selection. Consider the following statements:

> "The primary focus of evolution by natural selection is the
> individual." ([13], p. 7)
> "Selection is primarily concerned with genotypes." ([12],
> p. 178)
> "Mendelian populations, rather than individuals, are the
> units of natural selection." ([4], p. 79)
> "The species are the real units of evolution." ([15], p. 621)

The first two of these statements are concerned with fundamental
entities corresponding to the biological entity – the entity which is acted
on. The second two statements are concerned with fundamental entities
corresponding to the Darwinian subclan – the entities which are changed.
These statements are not contradictory: the first two are appropriate in
discussions on micro-evolution (i.e., the processes occurring in the short
term which will, after many short terms, result in significant evolutionary
change), while the last two are appropriate in discussions of macro-
evolution (i.e., significant changes in characteristics of populations).
These statements were, in fact, used in the appropriate contexts, but, as
the phrases 'the *real* units' and 'rather than individuals' indicate, the
assumption that there is *one* fundamental entity (and that that one is the

smallest of the entities under consideration) forces biologists to fight for the appropriate recognition of the Darwinian subclan-type entity.

(2) *Different Levels of Selection.* It has long been recognized that natural selection operates on the levels of the gene, the chromosome, the gamete, the organism, and the population, but it is usually assumed that one of these levels is primary and the others subsidiary. Thus:

Asserting the primacy of the organism:

> "To consider genes independent units is ... meaningless from the evolutionary viewpoint because the individual as a whole ..., not individual genes, is the target of selection." ([16], p. 162. See also [8], p. 230; [3], p. 173; [13], p. 7, etc.)

Asserting the primacy of the gene:

> "In its ultimate essence the theory of natural selection deals with a cybernetic abstraction, the gene, and a statistical abstraction, mean phenotypic fitness." ([20], p. 33).

Asserting the primacy of the chromosome over the gene:

> "The selection of the chromosome as a whole is the overriding determiner of allelic frequencies." ([17], p. 725).

Asserting the primacy, in at least some circumstance, of the population:

> "Unless extinction of populations, species, and higher taxa occurs randomly, group selection occurs ... [for the evolution of dispersal] it seems to be important." ([19], p. 596).

Such assertions of primacy are sometimes assertions that selection on a particular level is the primary form determining the evolution of certain types of phenomena, but in other cases (e.g., the first and second assertions given above) they represent a real clash between scientists each of whom thinks that he is speaking of *the* fundamental level of selection in terms of which all other levels of selection should, and ultimately will, be expressed.

The question is: What is the relationship between the different levels of selection? There are two important ways of answering this question. One is to answer it not as a question about the theory of natural selection but as a question about the relationship between genes, chromosomes,

gametes, organisms, and populations; this answer would state that all
phenomena at each level are caused by phenomena at the lowest level.
(At present, of course, this is merely an assertion of a philosophical
commitment to reductionism; we are nowhere near being able to specify
the chain of causal mechanisms.) But when we are trying to decide
whether statements about selection at the gene level *should* be expressed
in terms of selection at the organsim level, or vice versa, it is more important to ask it as a question about the theory of natural selection. Does
the process at each of these different levels actually follow the laws of the
theory, or are the laws of the theory truly applicable only to one level?
Formally, this question is asking whether: (1) the different levels of
selection are different models of the theory; or (2) only one of the levels
is a model of the theory. By substituting gene, chromosome, gamete,
organism, and population for *biological entity* in the axioms, we find
that these different levels of selection are different models of the theory
of natural selection. The levels of selection, being different models of one
theory, are analogs of one another. One level of selection may be more
suitable than the other for studying a particular phenomenon, and the
organism level may seem *primus inter pares* because we are more familiar
with the phenomena for which it is most suitable, but *no* level of selection
has absolute primacy over the others.

It has been difficult to identify the referent of 'survival of the fittest'
because it appears to have different forms in the different levels of selection. To understand this difficulty let us consider what subclands look
like in two different models. With the organism interpretation a subcland
is the set of all organisms which are in the Darwinian subclan and are
descended from (or ancestral to – but we can ignore that part at present)
a particular founder set of organisms; for the present discussion we can
consider the founder set to be a set of contemporaneous organisms with
a particular advantageous hereditary trait; some of the offspring of the
founder organisms will have this trait and some will not; it is natural
when discussing selection on this trait to ignore the ones that do not have
it. But this should not be done: biological traits are affected by many
different genes and even if a particular offspring does not have the trait
it may have many of the genes which positively affect the trait; thus the
fact that it does not have the trait is not an indication that its success in
leaving descendants is irrelevant to the selection for the trait. By including

all descendants we may include some which are irrelevant, but this causes less difficulty than the assumption that the expression of the trait is all that counts. (For some traits, those that are controlled by a single gene, this argument does not hold. But these are traits whose selective fate should be analyzed with the gene interpretation.) Notice that one cannot define the subcland simply in terms of the morphological properties of its members.

With the gene interpretation, the Darwinian subclan frequently used in discussions of selection is the set of all alleles occupying a particular chromosomal locus. (An *allele* is "one of two or more alternate forms of a gene occupying the same locus on a chromosome." E.g., the gene for hemoglobin has several alleles: a normal hemoglobin allele, a sickle cell anemia allele, a thallassemia allele, etc.; each of these alleles has a different molecular structure.) 'The sickle allele' denotes the set of all molecules (or, rather, of all portions of DNA molecules) with a particular molecular structure. In this usage the sickle allele is, barring mutations, exactly the same as the subcland derived from the set of all sickle alleles existing in 1800 A.D. Thus to say that selection is increasing the frequency of the sickle allele is the same as to say that selection is increasing the frequency of this sublcand. Note how much easier it is to visualize the subcland on the gene level than on the organism level; a definition in terms of the molecular structure[7] of the gene includes virtually all members of the subcland while a definition in terms of the morphological structurc of thc organisms includes only scattered portions of the subcland. This is why 'differential perpetuation of genotypes', which expresses the referent in the terminology of the gene level, is used even by organism level biologists.

We saw, in the section on fitness, that the fallacious metaphysical doctrine about definitions led many biologists into the inconsistent position of advocating that all terms be defined while sneaking in undefined terms. Similarly the fallacious metaphysical doctrine that there is *one* fundamental level has led many biologists into the inconsistent position of asserting that the organism level is *the* level while working solely on the gene level. (Although evolutionary geneticists work as if the gene level could be studied independently, it is very difficult to find one who disagrees with the statement that the organism level is the primary focus of selection. But, as Mayr frequently points out (e.g., in [14]), if this

statement is true then most of the work in evolutionary genetics is worthless.) The axiomatization has shown us that in both cases the inconsistency lies not within the theory but between generally accepted metaphysical assumptions and the theory.

4. CONCLUSION

I have shown in this paper that the controversies about the logical status of evolutionary theory and about the fundamental entity of the theory arise from the following two fallacious metaphysical doctrines: (1) All words used in a scientific theory should be defined. (2) When a theory deals with entities which are physically parts of one another, *one* of those entities is the fundamental entity of the theory and all results of the theory can, and should, be expressed in terms of that fundamental entity.

The first of these doctrines is fallacious because it is inconsistent with our logical system; it is logically impossible to define all words used. The attempt to defy this logical impossibility led to definitions which created the impression that the theory of natural selection is tautologous.

The second of these doctrines is fallacious because it denies the possibility that a theory may have two primitive terms denoting entities which are such that one is contained within the other, and because it denies the possibility that a theory may have two distinct, but physically related, models in the real world.

The axiomatization, and in particular Axiom D4, provides a nontautologous, non-ambiguous translation of 'survival of the fittest'. A brief phrase which captures the essence of this translation is 'expansion of the fitter subcland'.

Biomathematics Program,
Department of Statistics,
North Caroline State University

NOTES

† This work was supported by NSF Grant GU 1590.
[1] Axiom B1 is really a theorem, since it can be proved from Definition B1 and Axiom B2.
[2] *Biocosm, biological entity,* $\succ$, $\triangleright$, *subclan, Darwinian subclan,* and *subcland* are all terms that I have coined.

[3] There are two ways of showing that a theory is not circular. The first is by axiomatizing the theory; this I have done in [21]. The second is by exhibiting falsifiable predictions of the theory; this I have done in [22].

[4] The situation is made more confusing by the fact that the concept denoted by this definition is *called* 'Darwinian fitness'! I hope that the users of this term follow Humpty Dumpty's example and pay it extra when it comes round for its wages Saturday night.

[5] Hull's discussion of operationism in [10] provides a useful view of what has been accepted by various groups of biologists as operational.

[6] Padoa's principle states that to prove that a given primitive term, D, is independent of the other primitives it is sufficient to find two different interpretations of the axioms in which D has different interpretations while the other primitives have the same interpretations. I have a sketch of the necessary proof, but because it relies on an understanding of some rather complex biological situations, it would be inappropriate to present it here.

[7] It can be seen from this analysis that those who believe the organism level to be the fundamental one need not be anti-reductionists. They are not denying that laws may some day be found which are expressed in terms of the lowest level and from which all higher level phenomena can be deduced. They are denying that the *Darwinian* laws are applicable on the lower levels.

BIBLIOGRAPHY

[1] Beckner, M., *The Biological Way of Thought*, University of California Press, Berkeley, 1968.

[2] Bossert, W. H. and Wilson, E. O., *A Primer of Population Biology*, Sinauer Associates, Inc., Stanford, Conn., 1971.

[3] Crow, J. F. and Kimura, M., *An Introduction To Population Genetics Theory*, Harper and Row, New York, 1970.

[4] Dobzhansky, T., *Genetics and the Origin of Species*, Columbia University Press, New York, 1937.

[5] Dobzhansky, T., 'On Some Fundamental Concepts of Darwinian Biology', *Evolutionary Biology*, vol. 2 (ed. by T. Dobzhansky, M. K. Hecht, and W. C. Steere), Appleton-Century-Crofts, New York, 1968.

[6] Einstein, A., 'On the Generalized Theory', *Scientific American* (April, 1950), Reprint 209; W. H. Freeman and Company, San Francisco, 1950.

[7] Franklin, I. and Lewontin, R. C., 'Is the Gene the Unit of Selection?', *Genetics* 65 (1970), 707–734.

[8] Grant, V., *The Origin of Adaptations*, Columbia University Press, New York, 1963.

[9] Hempel, C. G., *Aspects of Scientific Explanation*, The Free Press, New York, 1965.

[10] Hull, D. L., 'The Operational Imperative: Sense and Nonsense in Operationism', *Systematic Zoology* 17 (1968), 438–457.

[11] Hull, D. L., *Philosophy of Biological Science*, Prentice Hall, Inc., Englewood Cliffs, N.J., in press.

[12] Lerner, I. M., 'The Concept of Natural Selection: A Centennial View', *Proceedings of the American Philosophical Society* 103 (1959), 173–182.

[13] Lewontin, R. C., 'The Units of Selection', *Annual Review of Ecology and Systematics*, vol. 1 (ed. by R. F. Johnston, P. W. Frank, and C. D. Michener), Annual Reviews Inc., Palo Alto, California, 1970.

[14] Mayr, E., 'Where Are We?', *Cold Spring Harbor Symposia on Quantitative Biology*, vol. 24, The Biological Laboratory, Cold Spring Harbor, New York, 1959.

[15] Mayr, E., *Animal Species and Evolution*, Harvard University Press, Boston, 1963.

[16] Mayr, E., *Populations, Species, and Evolution*, Harvard University Press, Boston, 1970.

[17] Newton, I., *Principia*, 1686 (Quotations from Motte's translation revised by Cajori), University of California Press, Berkeley, 1966.

[18] Smith, J. M., 'The Status of Neo-Darwinism', *Towards a Theoretical Biology* (ed. by C. H. Waddington), Aldine, Chicago, 1969.

[19] Van Valen, Leigh, 'Group Selection and the Evolution of Diversity', *Evolution* **25** (1971), 591–598.

[20] Williams, G. C., *Adaptation and Natural Selection*, Princeton University Press, Princeton, 1966.

[21] Williams, M. B., 'Deducing the Consequences of Evolution: A Mathematical Model', *J. Theoret. Biol.* **29** (1970), 343–385.

[22] Williams, M. B., 'Falsifiable Predictions of Evolutionary Theory', manuscript.

PART V

PSYCHOLOGY

MARIO BUNGE

ON CONFUSING 'MEASURE' WITH 'MEASUREMENT'
IN THE METHODOLOGY OF BEHAVIORAL SCIENCE

ABSTRACT. Several acceptations of 'measure' are distinguished from one another and from 'measurement', which denotes an empirical operation. The concept of quantitative measure, or quantity, or magnitude, is elucidated in mathematical terms. It is argued that a scale is involved in every quantity or magnitude. Also, a unit is involved in the very construction of any magnitude endowed with a dimension. The extensive-intensive distinction, misunderstood in much of the literature, is clarified. It is shown that intensive magnitudes are often theoretically more basic than the corresponding extensive quantities. Finally the notions of index or objectifier, and standard (or materialization of a unit) are analyzed. The departures from the standard theory of "measurement" (introduction and clarification of scientific concepts) are pointed out. It is shown that no *a priori* theory of quantities, independent of natural or social laws, can be adequate, as we should have learned from the non-additivity of mass and entropy for interacting systems.

The methodological discussions in psychology, sociology and politology are often marred by three confusions: those between quantitation (numerical quantification) and measurement, magnitude (quantity) and scale, and objectifier (index) with operational definition. While the third confusion is also common to an obsolete methodology of physics (where it originated), the first two are not and they render much of the behavioral literature unintelligible and even irritating to the physical scientist. This paper attempts to clarify the concepts concerned – mainly that of quantity or magnitude – and some related notions, with the help of the experience gained in the foundations and methodology of physics (see [1], [2], [3]) and in the philosophy of science (see [4]). Our results will prove to be disjoint from the standard theory of "measurement" (formation and analysis of scientific concepts) as represented by Stevens' popular [10], and Suppes and Zinnes' authoritative [11] – a theory that has found its way into a number of psychology textbooks (e.g., [7]).

1. SYMBOLIZATION AND QUANTITATION

The introduction of quantitative concepts is sometimes called *quantifica-*

M. Bunge (ed.), The Methodological Unity of Science, 105–122. All Rights Reserved.
Copyright © 1973 by D. Reidel Publishing Company, Dordrecht-Holland.

tion or, more precisely, *numerical quantification* – to distinguish it from universal generalization, which is a purely logical operation. To forestall confusion we shall call it *quantitation* – a good English word. Quantitation, though not a logical operation, is a purely conceptual one as well: it consists in inventing some concept intended to exactify the corresponding qualitative, hence less precise notion. Quantitating is an armchair occupation scientists engage in when intent on building quantitative theories. It should therefore be kept distinct from measuring, which is a empirical operation – the more so since quantitation precedes measurement. Thus the replacement of "habit" by "habit strength" is a case of quantitation, while the determination of an actual habit strength value for a given organism under certain conditions is a laboratory operation. And the latter cannot be planned, much less executed, unless the quantitative concept of interest is at hand.

Quantitation should not be mistaken for symbolization or even for mathematization although it involves the two. Even class or qualitative concepts, such as "loud" and "restless", can be associated numbers – or at least numerals. The simplest way of doing so is to take the characteristic function of the set S of interest, i.e. the function χ from the set S of individuals of a kind to the set $\{0, 1\}$ such that

$$(1) \qquad \chi(x) = \begin{cases} 1 & \text{iff} \quad x \text{ is in } S \\ 0 & \text{iff} \quad x \text{ is not in } S. \end{cases}$$

This trick can be extended to relational concepts such as that of interaction. If a binary relation holds between two items then we tick the numeral '1', otherwise the numeral '0' (or some other sign). For example, if x and y are things (members of a certain set S), one can introduce a function η from the set $S \times S$ of pairs of things into $\{0, 1\}$ such that, for all x and y in S,

$$(2) \qquad \eta(x, y) = \begin{cases} 1 & \text{iff} \quad x \text{ and } y \text{ interact} \\ 0 & \text{iff} \quad x \text{ and } y \text{ do not interact}. \end{cases}$$

The values $\eta(x, y)$ of the characteristic function of a binary relation can be orderly displayed in a square matrix. If the relation is defined on a set S of cardinality n, then the matrix will be of rank n. For example, if the set S of things has three elements called a, b, and c, then the interactions among them can be represented by the matrix

$$(3) \qquad \|\eta\| = \begin{Vmatrix} \eta(a, a) & \eta(a, b) & \eta(a, c) \\ \eta(b, a) & \eta(b, b) & \eta(b, c) \\ \eta(c, a) & \eta(c, b) & \eta(c, c) \end{Vmatrix}$$

In particular, if the items interact among each other but do not act upon themselves, the aggregate $S = \{a, b, c\}$ together with its mutual actions will be represented by the matrix

$$(4) \qquad \|\eta\| = \begin{Vmatrix} 0 & 1 & 1 \\ 1 & 0 & 1 \\ 1 & 1 & 0 \end{Vmatrix}$$

There need be nothing quantitative about these matrices: the entries might just as well be color names rather than number names. Matrices are valuable because they display information and satisfy definite mathematical laws (among them those of ring theory). Being lawful objects they can be incorporated into mathematical theories, whether pure or applied to physics, psychology, economics, or what have you. Only if every entry of a matrix is a genuine number or a numerical function will the matrix as a whole be a quantitative concept (though with no numerical value). Thus the input-output matrices occurring in mathematical economics are quantitative concepts because their entries are quantities, or rather values of numerical functions (e.g. volume of annual production of a merchandise reckoned in tons or in dollars). On the other hand the matrix of a transformation of a string of letters is not a quantitative concept.

The preceding methods for associating '0' and '1' to qualities and relations look like procedures for "pinning numbers on facts" (Stevens' well-known characterization of "measurement"). They certainly are convenient ways of stating with precision that a certain state of affairs obtains or fails to obtain as well as of roping in the help of mathematics via the notions of function and matrix. However, they hardly qualify as instances of quantitation because the symbols '0' and '1' in the previous lines may not designate the concepts of zero and unity respectively but may be taken as conventional tags subject to the sole conditions: $0 \cdot 0 = = 0 \cdot 1 = 1 \cdot 0 = 0$, and $1 \cdot 1 = 1$.

The same holds for the assignment of numerals to the degrees of some property if such degrees, though ordered, cannot be multiplied and divided to get numbers proper. The numerals in the Richter earthquake scale are in this predicament: they do not represent numbers indicating absolute earthquake intensities. (Hence 'Twice Richter intensity 4' makes no sense and, *a fortiori*, it is not the same as 'Richter intensity 8'.) Many psychophysical "measurements" are based on similar concepts, i.e., ordinal "scales". The fact that the subjects are asked to rate the intensity of their loudness sensation, or of pain, does not entail that genuine quantitation is always involved. What is at stake is order, or partial order, or semiorder – not quantity. In short, the numerals occurring in the treatment of class concepts and comparative (ordinal) concepts need not stand for numbers. Hence classing and ordering do not qualify as quantitative operations – unless, of course, the classing or the comparison are conducted in the light of genuine quantitative concepts, as when "*a* is stronger than *b*" is inferred from "The strength of *a* is *m*, the strength of *b* is *n*, and $m > n$".

To quantitate, in a strict numerical sense, is to introduce a functional correspondence between the degrees of a property and numbers. For example, the concept of an angle quantifies (and *a fortiori* exactifies) the concept of inclination, and the concept of probability quantifies that of disposition or propensity. Quantitation, in other words, consists in the introduction of some function mapping degrees of some property onto *bona fide* numbers. Such a function is called a *quantity* or a *magnitude* in the adult sciences, a "scale" or "measurement scale" ("interval scale" or "ratio scale" as the case may be) in the juvenile sciences. Let us take a closer look at this matter.

2. MAGNITUDE AND SCALE

A quantity, or numerical functor, or magnitude, is a quantitative predicate, such as "response probability", or "brightness", or "surplus value", supposed to mirror some property of a concerete system. A magnitude M is a conceptualization of the corresponding property P: it is a "measure" of the latter – a conceptual measure, not an empirical one or measurement.

Take for example the concept of response probability: this is a behavioral interpretation of the mathematical concept of conditional probability. In fact the propensity for an organism of a certain kind to produce a certain response r to a stimulus s can be construed as: $Pr(r \mid s) = p$, where p is a real number between 0 and 1. The function Pr qualifies as a magnitude because (a) its values are numbers, (b) it is well defined (by the axioms of the probability calculus), and (c) its values are assumed to represent the intensities of a property of a concrete system, namely the latter's disposition to react to an external stimulus of a given kind. (Note that what is interpreted in factual terms is not the function Pr, which is determined mathematically, but its arguments r and s and its values p.)

Other magnitudes (or quantities) are more complex, in that they concern things of several kinds (e.g., organisms and environmental units) or in that they involve some scale or other. Thus the concept of action involves at least two kinds of entity: agents and patients. Indeed, we say, for example,

(5)   Entity a of kind A acts with intensity $F(a, b)$ upon entity b of kind B.

In general terms: F is a certain function, with domain $A \times B$ and range some number set V, where A and B are the kinds of thing involved, and the values $F(a, b)$ are interpreted as "measuring" (representing) the intensity of the action of a upon b.

However, the previous analysis is incomplete, since the same action can conceivably be represented in a number of different ways – in fact as many as action scales are chosen. (A scale is, roughly, a mode of representing the degrees of a property. More on scales in the next section.) Consequently proposition [5] should be replaced by

(6)   Entity a of kind A acts with intensity $F(b, a, s)$ upon entity b of kind B, where s is a particular action scale.

(In the case of probability we did not have to worry about a scale because it is unambiguously fixed by the condition that the probability values lie between 0 and 1 and because probabilities, being dimensionless, are unit free.) If we now take the whole bunch S of possible action scales into account, we build the general concept of action as a certain function F with domain $A \times B \times S$ and range V. Here the ambiguous term 'a certain' suggests that the function F should be fixed by conditions (postulates) that we do not care to state at the moment – perhaps because the grapes are sour.

The concept of a scale is then a constituent of the concept of a magnitude or quantity. We must fix the scale of a magnitude not only if we wish to measure some values of the magnitude but also if we wish to compute its values with the help of theoretical formulas. We say not only 'The value of F, when *measured* on the couple $\langle a, b \rangle$ and on the scale s, equals the number c', but also 'The value of F, when *reckoned* for the couple $\langle a, b \rangle$ and on the scale s, equals the number c'. Therefore it is mistaken to equate "quantity" (or "magnitude") with "scale", even more so to confuse "scale" with "measurement" – as has been done by many psychologists and sociologists following Stevens' influential [10] and its various subsequent versions.

The general concept of a quantity, or magnitude, can be elucidated as follows. A magnitude is a function M from the cartesian product of n kinds of system (e.g. organisms) by a set S of scales, onto a set V included in the real line R or in the collection $\mathscr{P}(R)$ of intervals of real numbers, and satisfying definite law statements (e.g., psychological laws). Furthermore every magnitude represents some property P of the things referred to by the corresponding magnitude M. In symbols:

(7) $M \triangleq P$ and $M: A \times B \times \ldots \times N \times S \to V$,
        with $V \subseteq R$ or $V \subseteq \mathscr{P}(R)$,

where '$\triangleq$' stands for the semantic relation of representation. In short, a magnitude or quantity is a numerical function occurring in a nomological net concerning some aspect of reality.

We see now why it is misleading to call a magnitude a "scale" or a "measurement scale". The scale concept is one ingredient of the magnitude concept whereas the concept of measurement, or empirical determination of (some) values of a magnitude, simply does not occur in either the formation or the analysis of the magnitude concept. Quantitative measurements, i.e. measurements proper, are performed in order to sample magnitude values, not to replace the formation (invention) of the concept of a magnitude. Introducing considerations about measurement in the treatment of magnitudes, or quantities, is a relic of the operationist philosophy.

Let us now proceed to a more precise analysis of the scale concept, one involving the explicit use of the concept of a unit.

3. SCALE AND UNIT

Consider a property P of a thing of some kind, and a conceptual representative M of P. If P is qualitative, such as "able to learn the digits", the concept M will be a dichotomic variable of the kind discussed in Section 1: it will have just two values, 0 (absence) and 1 (presence). But if P comes in different amounts, i.e., if it is quantitied, as is the case with recall capacity, then those amounts can not only be ordered but, in principle, they can be represented numerically. (The thesis that every ordinal "scale" can be replaced by a quantity or magnitude cannot be proved even though it has been taken for granted in physics ever since Galilei: it is an unspoken methodological principle. Whether the principle can be upheld in psychology is not for philosophers with an anti-mathematical bias to decide, but a matter for mathematical psychologists.)

Such a numerical representation of the degrees or amounts of a property, we saw before, may not be unique. Except for dimensionless quantities such as numerosity (e.g. population), propensity (e.g. transition probability), and ratios (e.g. perceived distance over physical distance), every property of a concrete system can be represented in different ways. Every such mode of representation we may call a *scale*. The paradigm is, of course, the set of temperature scales. The concepts of empirical temperature are said to be "interval scales", whereas the concept of absolute temperature, which is the one employed in advanced physical theory, is said to be a "ratio scale". A physicist would say that the concept of absolute temperature has a uniform metric scale attached to it. (For a lucid and brief discussion of the difference between interval and ratio scales of magnitudes see [9].)

A scale is then a conventional component of a concept M representing a property P. Although the P degrees are real, their ordering and spacing can be represented in different ways. If the ordering and spacing is chaotic but fixed (i.e. it does not change from one computation or measurement to the next), we have a scale all right albeit an extremely inconvenient one. (See Figure 1a.) A reasonable scale is one with a lawful ordering and spacing, such as that shown in Figure 1b. Every scale with a lawful ordering and spacing may be called a *metric scale*. (Caution: do not confuse 'metric' with 'decimal'.) If the spacing is uniform and the scale includes a zero, it may be called a *uniform metric scale*. (See Figure 1c.)

The basic interval in such a uniform metric scale is called a *unit* for the magnitude M or for the corresponding property P. Thus the decibel is a unit of sound volume, and the bit a unit of information.

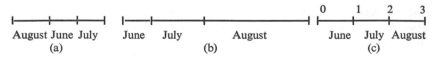

Fig. 1.   Two ways of representing the three most agreeable durations in the Northern hemisphere: (*a*) on an arbitrary scale, (*b*) on a metric scale, (*c*) on a uniform metric scale.

A magnitude $M \triangleq P$ may then be regarded as a way of mapping real (objective or subjective, i.e., felt) P degrees onto M units. Thus amount of information may be construed as representing probabilities of messages onto numbers of bits. This suggests postulating

AXIOM 1. Let $A, B, \ldots, N$ be n kinds of concrete system endowed with a (mutual) quantitative property P. And let R designate the real line and $\mathcal{P}(R)$ the power set of R. Then for every property P of an n-tuple $\langle a, b, \ldots, n \rangle \in A \times B \times \ldots \times N$ there exists a non-empty set U_M, called the set of *M-units*, and there is at least one function

$$M : A \times B \times \ldots \times N \times U_M \to V, \quad \text{where} \quad V \subseteq R \quad \text{or}$$
$$V \subseteq \mathcal{P}(R),$$

called a *magnitude*, such that M represents P.

This assumption involves the ontological (metaphysical) concepts of natural kind and of property, and the semantic concept of representation. We do not apologize for this because we are persuaded that science has ontological and semantical presuppositions (see [5]), but we offer the following explanation. A function, even if characterized unambiguously, is a mathematical concept: it won't represent a property of anything concrete unless we assume so explicitly – and unless we succeed in embedding the function in a nomological net. Note also that the above axiom is optimistic: it asserts that, no matter what the quantitative property, we should be able to conceptualize it as a magnitude. And observe that no explicit mention of a scale is made in Axiom 1: a system of units, together with a zero, is sufficient (not necessary, though) to determine a scale of the uniform metric kind.

So far, we know nothing about the M-units in U_M occurring in our axiom. Units are manipulated by physicists and chemists with the same ease as behavioral scientists neglect them, but nobody seems to care what kind of animal they are. The usual textbook explanation is metaphorical: units, provided they belong to a coherent system such as the CGS system, can be multiplied and divided *as if* they were real numbers. This characterization, though expedient, does not explain why units cannot be added and subtracted as in the ill formed expression 'cm + bit'. We need a theoretical characterization. The precise nature of units is characterized by the mathematical theory of units (see [3]). From this theory we borrow

AXIOM 2. Let $\mathcal{M}$ be a set of magnitudes and $U_{\mathcal{M}}$ a set of units for $\mathcal{M}$. Then there is at least one non-empty finite subset of $U_{\mathcal{M}}$,

$$U^*_{\mathcal{M}} = \{u^*_1, u^*_2, ..., u^*_m, 1_U\} \subseteq U_{\mathcal{M}},$$

called a *system of basic units for $\mathcal{M}$*, such that

(i) the elements u^*_i of U^*_m are mutually independent (not interdefinable);

(ii) the structure $U_{\mathcal{M}} = \langle U_{\mathcal{M}}, \cdot, {}^{-1}, 1_U \rangle$ is an abelian group written multiplicatively, in which the powers are defined as in the field of reals;

(iii) for every $u \in U_{\mathcal{M}}$ there is an n-tuple $\langle \alpha, \beta, ..., \nu \rangle$ of rational numbers such that u is uniquely decomposable in the form

$$u = u^{*\alpha}_1 \cdot u^{*\beta}_2 ... u^{*\nu}_n.$$

(The distinguished element 1_U of $U_{\mathcal{M}}$ is not the number one but the neutral element of the group. It is needed to include dimensionless magnitudes as well as to account for expressions such as 'sec·sec$^{-1} = 1_U$'.)

There is more to be said about units, in particular about their relation to dimensions, but this is not the proper place for doing so. Suffice it to remark that the concept of a unit can be given an exact elucidation together with that of a magnitude (see [3]) and that it should be clarified without any reference to measurement. On the other hand no precision measurement can be designed, let alone performed, unless the magnitudes of interest, if dimensional, are assigned definite units. In general: Think before going to the lab.

Unless units are assigned their place at the very inception of magnitudes endowed with a dimension, mistakes both small and big are apt to creep in. An error of the former kind is, of course, omitting to mention the units, as is frequently the case in the non-physical sciences. Another mistake is to believe that physics is basically unit free (see [12]). Actually the basic formulas of a physical theory are not so much unit *free* as unit *invariant* – just as they are sometimes frame invariant even though they do involve reference to frames of reference. Is it not that units are dispensable at the foundations level but that the need for choosing a particular system of units does not arise until the stage of either numerical computation or empirical measurement is reached.

A far more disturbing consequence of the inadequate analysis of magnitudes performed by the standard theory of "measurement", which ignores the unit component, is the attempt to justify such an omission by resorting to a change of logic. Thus in [12] Suppes has proposed to save freaks such as

(8)   The mass of body b is 5.

by assigning them a value other than truth or falsity and adopting a system of three-valued logic. This tilt at windmills was quite uncalled for: physicists and chemists know how to deal with expressions like [8] – they either discard them as ill formed or non-significant, or they take the trouble of completing them to, say,

(9)   The mass of body b, in CGS units, equals 5.

A final word of caution: Units should not be mistaken for standards – as they must if the operationist philosophy is adopted. Whereas a unit is a concept, a standard is a thing or a process supposed (rightly or wrongly) to materialize that concept. For example, the rotation of the earth around the sun provides a natural time standard – albeit not a perfect one. That is, one may take the duration of that process as a physical correlate of a certain time unit, namely the year. Likewise one may adopt the average daily output of a typical worker in a given industry as the productivity standard or norm in that particular manufacture. This standard will represent or materialize the corresponding unit without being identical with it. Standards satisfy natural laws whereas units obey algebraic laws.

4. EXTENSIVE AND INTENSIVE MAGNITUDES

The magnitudes treated by the so called theories of measurement are *extensive* quantities like volume. These represent systemic properties or properties of a system as a whole. However, the most interesting magnitudes, from a theoretical point of view, are the *intensive* quantities such as the densities. The mathematical difference between these two kinds is that, whereas extensive quantities are measures in the measure-theoretic sense, intensive quantities are not. This difference is clearly exhibited by the following examples. If *a* and *b* are non-overlapping bodies, and we denote their physical addition (juxtaposition or concatenation) by '*a*+*b*', then the volume of this composite body equals the sum of the volumes of its parts:

(10) $V(a + b) = V(a) + V(b)$.

Temperature, *per capita* income, and many other magnitudes fail to satisfy this law: they are not morphisms of addition.

Let us emphasize that, notwithstanding their failure to satisfy an additivity law, densities and other intensive quantities are quantities all right. They can be added, subtracted, multiplied by numbers, often differentiated and integrated, etc. Only, there is no addition theorem for them. Thus the densities of different things can be added but the result does not represent the density of a composite thing. In particular, whereas the expression

(11)   The density of x equals n times the density of y

is unobjectionable, the expression

(12)   The density of x plus the density of y equals n,

though mathematically unobjectionable, tells us nothing about the density of the compound system $x+y$, at least in the non-trivial case $x \neq y$. Likewise the visual acuity of different subjects can be added but it does not yield the visual acuity of some supersubject.

In contrast, if E is an extensive quantity then we may venture to write "$E(x+y)=E(x)+E(y)$", where x and y name different things, provided E is defined at x and y. Still, such a meaningful formula may be false or nearly so. That is, not all extensive magnitudes are strictly additive. For example, the entropy of a system of interacting components is smaller than the sum of the partial entropies. And mass, which is taken to be additive in macrophysics, is seen in microphysics to be subadditive. In symbols: If a and b are material systems, then

(13) $M(a+b)=M(a)+M(b)$ *in macrophysics*
(14) $M(a+b)=M(a)+M(b)-\Delta m$ *in microphysics,*

where $\Delta m \geqslant 0$ is called the mass defect of the compound system. (This departure from additivity, though minute in terms of mass, can be enormous in terms of energy: $\Delta m \cdot c^2$ is the energy that binds the constituents of an atomic nucleus and is released in fission.) The standard theory of "measurement" has ignored subadditive measures just as it has ignored intensive quantities. Worse: that theory *has* to ignore these non-elementary kinds of scientific concept because it wants to be an *a priori* and normative theory concerned with "basic measurement" rather than a mathematical analysis and systematization of the existing scientific concepts.

We have, in sum, the following basic kinds of scientific concept:

$$
\text{Scientific concept}
\begin{cases}
\text{Qualitative}
\begin{cases}
\textit{Unary predicate (e.g., possibility)} \\
\textit{Relation}
\begin{cases}
\textit{Non-comparative (e.g., similarity)} \\
\textit{Comparative (e.g., loudness)}
\end{cases}
\end{cases} \\
\text{Quantitative}
\begin{cases}
\textit{Intensive (e.g., density)} \\
\textit{Extensive}
\begin{cases}
\textit{Subadditive (e.g., mass)} \\
\textit{Additive (e.g., duration)}
\end{cases}
\end{cases}
\end{cases}
$$

The standard theories of "measurement" are not concerned with intensive magnitudes because they assume, more or less explicitly, that the strictly additive ones are basic, the others being either derived or just non-quantitative – e.g., ordinal. (On this point they may have been misled by Campbell's uneven and now dated [6], which misunderstood the distinction drawn in thermodynamics between "extensive" and "intensive" magnitudes. The more's the pity, because [6] was no authority on theoretical physics anyway.) Actually the intensive quantities generate (by integration) extensive magnitudes rather than the other way around. For example, the total mass $M(b)$ of a body b is defined as

$$(15) \qquad M(b) =_{\text{df}} \int_B \delta(x)\,d^3 x,$$

where $\delta(x)$ is the density of b at the point x, and B the point set representing b. Total energy, entropy, charge, and electric flux are parallel. Likewise the basic quantum mechanical bilinear forms $\psi^\dagger A \psi$, where ψ is a state function and A a dynamical variable, are intensive quantities. Their volume integrals, as well the moments of those quantities, are extensive magnitudes. For this reason – which can be spelt out in measure theory – in all continuum and field theories, whether classical or quantal, intensive quantities are often taken as basic (primitive) concepts serving to define others, in particular extensive quantities.

It might be thought that the choice could be inverted, i.e., that extensive magnitudes could have been given the upper hand. This is impossible: densities determine unambiguously (by integration) the corresponding extensive quantities, if any – not conversely. Thus one and the same mass of a given gas can be formed in any number of ways by just varying the gas density – much as different statistical distributions can have the same average. In short, intensive magnitudes are theoretically more basic than the corresponding extensive quantities. What may have mislead the "measurement" theorist in this respect is that, instead of looking at physical theories for inspiration, he looked at physical measurements. In fact in experimental physics extensive quantities (e.g., mass) are more basic than the corresponding intensive quantities (e.g., density) in the sense that the empirical measurement of the latter is reducible (via theoretical formulas) to the empirical measurement of the former. In particular, every objectifier or index of an unobservable trait, whether intensive or extensive, must be extensive. But this is another story.

5. OBJECTIFIER AND MEASUREMENT

Recall is an objectifier of memory and performance an index of learning, much as the height of a barometer column objectifies atmospheric pressure and *pH* is an acidity index. In general, an *objectifier* or *index* or *observable measure* is an observable property such that its computation or measurement yields an indirect measure of an unobservable property. (The latter may be an intervening variable or a hypothetical construct – or both, as is the case with habit strength, which mediates between external variables. Standard indices of habit strength are the probability of correct response, the amplitude of the galvanic skin response, and the number of reactions without reinforcement necessary to produce extinction.) The measure of an unobservable supplied by an observable linked to the former is said to be indirect because some theoretical formula relating the two variables is involved in the process.

An observable O can perform the role of an objectifier for an unobservable U provided there is a law $U = F(O)$ such that F is a one to one correspondence between observable and unobservable values. (Mark: a law, i.e., a hypothesis belonging to some scientific theory, not just a stray conjecture. This condition disqualifies tea leave patterns, dreams, and the like.) When this condition holds one may say that O *measures* U, or that O values constitute *measures* or *indices* of U values. For example, the GNP, unemployment rate, and retail prices are indices of the state of an economy. On the other hand the Dow-Jones index is a joint objectifier of the state of the economy and the psychological mood of share owners and stock market brokers. Even so, it is doubtful whether it constitutes a scientific index, because the Dow-Jones "theory" that houses the index is hardly better than a very coarse black box. In any case the Dow-Jones index does not enjoy the same scientific status as, say, frequency as an index of probability, or coagulation time as an index of physiological age.

The objectifiers or indices of an unobservable item are often interpreted as operational definitions of that property. This is mistaken on several counts. First because an O-U relation is not a matter of definition but of law, hence of theory: O will be a reliable index of U just in case there is a function F mapping U values onto O values and such that every statement of the form '$U = F(O)$' is an instance of a law statement – i.e., if and only if F represents objective relationships to a good approximation. Second because no laboratory operations are involved in conjecturing that O values objectify U values. The operations occur in the actual measurements of O values and in checking the assumed O-U relation by means of alternative objectifiers of the same unobservable. And such measurements, in the strict sense of the word, require measuring instruments. In short,

(16)   *Measurement = Measurable object + Measure (e.g. index)*
         + Measuring instrument + Observer.

There is no measurement without a measure, whether direct or indirect. But there can be measures without any apparatus. For example, the social and economic indicators are established without the help of any measuring instruments. Table I summarizes and exemplifies the instrument-index-unobservable relations.

TABLE I

Apparatus measures index objectifying unobservables

Apparatus »— MEASURES →	*Observable* »— OBJECTIFIES →	*Unobservable*
Anemometer	Angular velocity	Wind speed
Thermometer	Length of thermometric column	Molecular agitation
Electromyograph	EMG waves	Muscle activity
Electroencephalograph	EEG waves	Brain activity
_____	Income	Economic status
_____	GNP *per capita*	Technological level

6. UPSHOT

We have distinguished the following items:

(i) *Quantitation* or *numerical quantification:* the formation of a quantitative concept (quantity or magnitude).

(ii) *Scale* of a magnitude: mode of representation of the corresponding property.

(iii) *Unit* of a magnitude: basic interval of the scale of the magnitude provided the latter has a dimension.

(iv) *Standard* for a magnitude: materialization of a unit of the magnitude.

(v) *Extensive quantity* or *measure:* magnitude E for which "$E(x+y) \leqslant \leqslant E(x) + E(y)$", where x and y denote things.

(vi) *Intensive quantity:* non-extensive quantity – a function that does not obey the additivity law.

(vii) *Objectifier* or *index:* observable measure of an unobservable item to which it is related in a lawful way.

(viii) *Measurement:* effective determination of a value of a magnitude with the help of empirical operations.

Some of these distinctions are often ignored in the methodology of behavioral science, where a number of disparate concepts are lumped together under the "measurement" umbrella. Moreover the so-called theories of basic measurement are exclusively concerned with ordinal "scales" and with quantitation of the extensive kind – and, even so, with neglect of the subadditive measures. They do not care for the intensive magnitudes, which are often more basic, at least theoretically, than the corresponding extensive ones – if any. Nor do those theories elucidate the notions of dimension and unit of a magnitude, which they often ignore altogether or regard as accessory. Finally, they do not care for random errors of measurement either – which is just as well because these are taken care of by the theory of errors of observation, which is a major constituent of the theory of measurement as understood in the natural sciences.

One might suppose that these shortcomings of the "measurement" theories studied by behavioral scientists are unimportant for, given a narrow theory, one should be able to generalize it – e.g., by relaxing some restrictions. This is not the case with the theories at stake because they are *a priori* and prescriptive rather than descriptive. Any attempt to build *a priori* theories of scientific concepts, in particular of quantities, is doomed to failure precisely because it handles such concepts in isolation from their matrix, viz., scientific theory. Indeed only scientific theories, i.e. systems of law statements, can tell us how magnitudes actually behave. For example it was relativity theory, not pure mathematics – nor even a theory free empirical measurement – that taught us that mass is a slightly subadditive function rather than a strictly additive one. Likewise statistical mechanics, not mathematics, shows that entropy is subadditive in the case of interacting components. These features of nature can only be captured by a substantive scientific theory: no amount of mathematical sophistication can make up for the loss of contact with scientific practice.

For these reasons the standard theories of "measurement" are largely irrelevant to advanced science. Worse: they are responsible for a number of muddles, foremost the mixing up of *measure*, in the sense of quantitation, with *measurement* by means of empirical operations. Oddly enough this confusion, like some religious sects, seems to have originated in a translation error. In fact when Hölder's 1901 postulates for *Mass* (measure) – not *Messung* (measurement) – crossed the Atlantic, they were rechristened "axioms for measurement". And so the illusion was born that a purely mathematical, hence *a priori* theory, could account for measurement – of anything and apart from both substantive theories and the praxis of measuring. An illusion, needless to say, in the purest tradition of philosophical idealism.

In this sense the theories of "measurement" discussed in the methodology of behavioral science are as ghostly as the so called quantum theories of measurement spun by some mathematicians following von Neumann's [8]. These other theories, too, claim to concern actual measurements (not just micro-macro interactions) and they attempt to account for them without resorting to the laws satisfied by things in the absence of any measurement, because they ignore the specific design and hardware of the measurement set-ups. Finally these theories, too, have become a pastime of mathematicians and philosophers precisely because they make only modest demands on substantive knowledge. Needless to say, theories of such a high degree of generality can account for no specific measurement process: they can make no particular predictions – whence they go safely untested. (Cf. [1] and [2].) Moreover they do not even serve the purpose of clarifying the ideas involved: rather on the contrary, they have contributed to obscuring them. The parallel with the theories of "basic measurement" in behavioral science is striking.

Moral: Distrust *a priori* theories of nature, society, or science, even if they are clad in beautiful mathematical garb. Another: If you wish to elucidate theoretical concepts, such as that of quantity, look at the way they function in theories. But if you wish to clarify pragmatic concepts, such as that of measurement, look also at practice. This won't prevent you from building theories with a definite mathematical structure: it will merely help you proposing relevant theories.

ACKNOWLEDGMENTS

This paper was written while I was a honorary research professor of philosophy, at Aarhus Universitet, on a Guggenheim fellowship. I am grateful to those two institutions.

Foundations and Philosophy of Science Unit, McGill University

BIBLIOGRAPHY

[1] M. Bunge, *Foundations of Physics*, Springer-Verlag, Berlin-Heidelberg-New York, 1967.

[2] M. Bunge, *Philosophy of Physics*, D. Reidel Publ. Co., Dordrecht, 1973.

[3] M. Bunge, 'A Mathematical Theory of the Dimensions and Units of Physical Quantities', in M. Bunge (ed.), *Problems in the Foundations of Physics*, Springer-Verlag, Berlin-Heidelberg-New York, 1971.

[4] M. Bunge, *Scientific Research*, 2 vols., Springer-Verlag, Berlin-Heidelberg-New York, 1967.

[5] M. Bunge, *Method, Model, and Matter*, D. Reidel Publ. Co., Dordrecht, 1973.

[6] N. R. Campbell, *Physics: The Elements*, Cambridge University Press, Cambridge, 1920.

[7] C. H. Coombs, R. M. Dawes, and A. Tversky, *Mathematical Psychology: Introduction*, Prentice-Hall, Englewood Cliffs, N.J., 1970.

[8] J. v. Neumann, *Mathematische Grundlagen der Quantenmechanik*, J. Springer, Berlin, 1932.

[9] A. Rapoport, *Two-Person Game Theory: The Essential Ideas*, University of Michigan Press, Ann. Arbor, Mich., 1966.

[10] S. S. Stevens, 'Mathematics, Measurement, and Psychophysics', in S. S. Stevens (ed.), *Handbook of Experimental Psychology*, John Wiley and Sons, New York, 1951.

[11] P. Suppes and J. L. Zinnes, 'Basic Measurement Theory', in R. D. Luce, R. R. Bush, and E. Galanter (eds.), *Handbook of Mathematical Psychology*, Vol. I, John Wiley and Sons, New York, 1963.

[12] P. Suppes, 'Measurement, Empirical Meaningfulness, and Three-Valued Logic', in C. W. Churchman and P. Ratoosh (eds.), *Measurement: Definitions and Theories*, John Wiley and Sons, New York, 1959.

RAIMO TUOMELA

THEORETICAL CONCEPTS IN
NEOBEHAVIORISTIC THEORIES*

ABSTRACT. The paper examines in an exact way the role of theoretical concepts within some kinds of neobehavioristic theories, expecially within representational mediation theories (such as Osgood's). Even if Craig's elimination result shows that theoretical concepts are logically dispensable within the *deductive* tasks of neobehavioristic theories, open theoretical concepts are shown to be indispensable within *inductive* systematization and explanation. Furthermore, there are a number of epistemological, ontological, semantical, and methodological features which make theoretical concepts philosophically and heuristically desirable within neobehavioristic theories.

1. THEORETICAL CONCEPTS AND NEOBEHAVIORISM

In this paper we shall make a modest attempt to discuss certain methodological issues arising in neobehavioristic theories, and thereby we shall use tools and results employed in modern philosophy of science. Generally speaking, we are going to examine the role of theoretical constructs in some of the tasks assigned to such theories. Special emphasis will be on questions of definability and interwovenness of theoretical concepts with observational ones.

Neobehaviorism is here simply taken to mean a methodological approach within stimulus-response psychology where theoretical constructs concerning the organism ('organism-variables') play an important role. Hull,Tolman and Spence can be considered important representatives of this approach. Within the investigation of symbolic processes neobehaviorism is represented, for instance, by Osgood and Mowrer. What is essential for our purposes is to distinguish the neobehavioristic approach from extreme behaviorism as represented, for instance, by Watson and Skinner. A discriminating feature is that theoretical constructs are given a more or less important role within neobehavioristic theories, whereas in Skinner's 'single stage' theorizing their presence is excluded (mainly for methodological reasons). What we call a neobehavioristic theory in this paper will incorporate a wider range of theories than what is usually included under the label 'neobehavioristic' or 'neo-

neobehavioristic'. For instance, the TOTE-mechanisms, and theories based on them, which have been investigated e.g. by Miller *et al.* (1960) belong here.

In this paper we are especially interested in so-called *mediation* theories developed, for instance, by Hull, Mowrer, and Osgood. Furthermore, in our illustrations we shall concentrate on psycholinguistic applications of such theories (especially Osgood's representational mediation theory), partly because of the recent lively debate in that field (cf. Fodor, 1965; Osgood, 1966; and Tuomela, 1972). The theoretical concepts, mediators, occurring in mediation theories are usually – at least in the so called representational mediation theories – regarded as non-observable events, states, or processes, which may be of physiological nature. They can thus be thought to represent in some way various endogenous (including innate) dispositions. To these belong also dispositions accounting for symbolic processes.

When the neobehavioristic mediation theories are conceived of like this they are quite close to the neorationalistic approaches which have recently become increasingly popular (cf. Chomsky, 1968). When talking about linguistic behavior it should be emphasized that neobehaviosistic theories are concerned with linguistic performance (*la parole*: how actual people actually use language) rather than with linguistic competence (*la langue*: language as an abstract conceptual system). On the other hand, neorationalistic approaches to linguistic behavior (for instance, Chomsky's approach) have been mainly concerned with linguistic competence. Presently it is far from clear how theories of performance and theories of competence are related. One thing we know for sure is that they cannot be equivalent. Therefore, it seems that one cannot build a theory of performance from a generative grammar representing competence in any straightforward manner. Perhaps the main reason why we know so little about this relation is that, so far, theories of performance have not been formulated explicitly enough (from a conceptual and formal standpoint) so that they could be compared with anything at all. Therefore I think we cannot consider, for example, Chomsky's severe criticism of Skinner's theory of verbal behavior (see Chomsky, 1959) to be decisive for the possibilities of S-R-psychology.

However, there is at least one interesting exception to the claim above. In a paper by Suppes (1969) stimulus-sampling learning theories are compared with generative grammars. Suppes shows that asymptotically a probabilistic stimulus-sampling learning theory becomes (under certain identificatory assumptions) isomorphic to a finite automaton which again is equivalent to a certain generative grammar. On the other hand, Chomsky has argued that generative grammars corresponding to finite automata are not rich enough to represent linguistic competence. Therefore Suppes' S-R approach seems to show that asymptotic and stable verbal behavior (performance) is different from linguistic competence (compare, however, with Suppes' own contrary interpetration of his result). We have mentioned this example mainly because of its great theoretical and heuristic importance, for we think Suppes' approach gives a promising direction for future studies. To repeat, presently there is just an unsolved and conceptually unclear dispute about methodological and philosophical programmes, and this dispute is bound to go on for a long time.

In this paper we shall not really discuss the methodological and philosophical adequacy of neobehavioristic theories of linguistic and other behavior. The main reason for this is just that they are not yet sufficiently developed to be amenable to critical evaluation. What we shall do is to discuss the methodological role of mediators in mediation theories, using Osgood's representational mediation theory as our example. Below we shall briefly outline some of the main features of his theory (see e.g. Osgood, 1953, 1966, and 1968).

Osgood's representational theory is summarized by the following diagram which gives "the basic paradigm for representational mediation theory" (Osgood, 1968, p. 497):

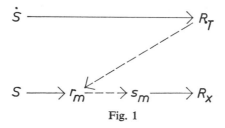

Fig. 1

Let us explain this diagram in Osgood's terminology and phrasing. $\dot{S}$ stands for a non-linguistic stimulus (to become a 'significate' or denotatum), R_T is the total response elicited by $\dot{S}$. S stands for a stimulus capable of becoming a 'sign' (e.g. presentation of a word, like a proper name or a property word). S elicits a mediating response r_m which is an abstract 'stimultaneously occurring bundle of events', presumably of neurophysiological nature. This mediating response is 'a proper part' of R_T, but it bears a part-to-whole relation to R_T only in the sense of being 'derived from' and being 'distinctively representational of' R_T. It is not 'part of' in the literal sense of being a material subset of the overt R's making up the total response R_T. In other words, the dashed arrow between R_T and r_m in our diagram can be considered a kind of semantic abstraction process which abstracts from R_T its semantically distinctive features to the componential event r_m. (It should be evident that this notion of semantic abstraction is loaded with interesting philosophical issues, but we shall not go into them and our own views here.

We interpret from what Osgood has said about the mediating response that it has both response-like and stimulus-like properties. We may denote this mediator by r_m when our emphasis is on the former and by s_m when on the latter. Conceived of in this way, the dashed arrow-relation between r_m and its self-stimulational effects s_m comes to represent a conceptual dependency between the response features and the stimulus features of a meaning response. Hence one can really do with only one symbol for the mediator. The symbol we shall use for it is r_m (even if a more neutral symbol, such as m, might be preferable).

The response R_x elicited by the mediator is usually meant to be an overt response – linguistic or non-linguistic. Naturally e.g. verbal utterances belong here.

The factual relationships incorporated in the diagram above are meant to represent the results of a learning process (though sometimes the eliciting relation between $\dot{S}$ and R_T may be a reflex). Thus, within psycholinguistic applications no account of the learning of language needs to be given here, as only asymptotic and stable behavior is discussed.

2. ANALYSIS OF AN EXAMPLE

Let us consider an example which illustrates the 'non-historic' part of Osgood's neobehavioristic theory outlined above. We shall then proceed to a more general treatment of the role of theoretical constructs on the of this example. In the manner of Osgood we describe this example first by a diagram (Figure 2 below).

It is important to notice that, as it stands, Figure 2 is ambiguous, because we do not know yet the *exact* meanings of the arrows (nor the ontological status and structure of the stimuli S_i ($i = 1, 2, 3$), responses R_j ($j = 1, 2, 3$) and the theoretical concepts P_k ($k = 1, 2$). We shall have to

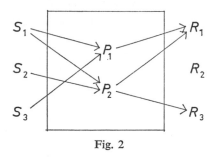

Fig. 2

explicate Figure 2 in various ways. Thus we start our investigation by considering the different ways in which Figure 2 can be formalized, that is, the non-equivalent behavioral assumptions Figure 2 is compatible with.

In this paper no attempt will be made to formalize Osgood's theory or any other neobehavioristic theory in full detail and full generality. We shall rather try to indicate how this could be done, while the actual technical developments only concern some parts or parts of the theory. Furthermore, they are based upon simplifying assumptions. Still, we shall attempt not to distort the theory in a substantial way.

First we shall comment upon the very difficult and important notion of eliciting. What is, strictly speaking, meant by the assertion that a stimulus S_i (which may be a combination of several atomic stimuli) *elicits* (evokes, produces) a response R_j (see below for our notions of stimulus and response)? This relationship is apparently considered to be a causal one, but we shall here avoid using the phrase 'cause' as we believe this phrase to be still more ambiguous than the term 'elicit'. Notice also that some theoreticians would here allow S_i to be a theoretical and unobservable state of the subject.

We shall now consider three simple basic types of explicates for

eliciting, each of which is acceptable under behavioristic standards.[1]
Each basic type consists of an absolute and a (more realistic) conditional
explicate. Let S_i, R_j and C be either statements or sets below:

(a) S_i elicits R_j if and only if the statement '$S_i \rightarrow R_j$' can be
        accepted as true. (We use ' $\rightarrow$ ' for the ordinary material im-
        plication of deductive logic.)

(a') S_i elicits R_j if and only if '$S_i \rightarrow R_j$' can be accepted as true,
        given that certain standard conditions C are satisfied.

(b) S_i elicits R_j if and only if $p(R_j/S_i) \geqslant 1 - \varepsilon$. (We use '$p$' for
        probability here; ε is a relatively small number $<.50$.)

(b') S_i elicits R_j if and only if $p_C(R_j/S_i) \geqslant 1 - \varepsilon$, where C is a
        statement representing standard conditions. Usually we define
        $p_C(R_j/S_i) = p(R_j/S_i \& C)$.

(c) S_i elicits R_j if and only if '$R_j \rightarrow S_i$' can be accepted as true
        and $p(R_j/S_i) \geqslant 1 - \varepsilon(\varepsilon < .50)$. (In the disjunctive cases, e.g.,
        Osgood's divergent hierarchies, where there are competing
        responses for which the same stimulus is a necessary condition,
        the most probable response will occur.) Sometimes still other
        factors, e.g., new contextual ones, are added into this type of
        characterization of eliciting, but they might perhaps also be
        taken into account by the probability clause of the present
        definition.

(c') S_i elicits R_j if and only if '$R_j \rightarrow S_i$' can be accepted as true,
        given C, and $p_C(R_j/S_i) \geqslant 1 - \varepsilon(\varepsilon < .50)$.

Let us comment upon these alternatives. In (a), (a'), (c), and (c') the
phrase 'accepted as true' can be taken to mean simply that the implication
sentence '$S_i \rightarrow R_j$' is well confirmed (perhaps due to its being entailed by
a well confirmed neobehavioristic theory). As we know from standard
logic, '$S_i \rightarrow R_j$' means, among other things, that always when S_i occurs
also R_j occurs. Alternative (a) seems to be too strict an explicate for the
relation of eliciting, even if (a) might be a candidate for an explicate of
causing (in one sense of the notion).

In (a') we require, roughly, that provided certain normal conditions C
obtain the implication '$S_i \rightarrow R_j$' be acceptable as factually true. These
normal *ceteris paribus* conditions (and assumptions concerning them)
can be of quite a diverse nature and their amount is usually vast. They

may include general metaphysical conditions, experimental conditions, 'protopsychological' assumptions, etc. (see e.g. Tuomela, 1968). Some of them can be (and have to be) specified exactly, whereas all of them can never be thus specified (for epistemological reasons). It is conceivable that C incorporates a background theory suitable for uor present theorizing such that implicative sentences of form $S_i \rightarrow R_j$ of our present more specific behavior theory are true within the range of application of this background theory. In such a case alternative (a') might be a perfectly good explicate for the relation of eliciting. However, it seems that in the present stage of theorizing in psychology it is often hard to refute (or corroborate) the views of one who relies on such a background theory in his theorizing.

As to alternative (b), of which (a) is a special case, it seems to be the one favoured by many S-R-psychologists. The justification of this alternative if often based upon assuming that

(i)   An (atomic or combined) stimulus S_i elicits R_j if and only if the associative strength between S_i and R_j is sufficiently great;

(ii)   The associative strenght between S_i and R_j is directly proportional to $p(R_j/S_i)$.

We think that (i) is acceptable but that there are certainly problems with (ii). One problem relevant in this connection is that (ii) does not (and neither (c)) display the deductive and non-probabilistic structure of the theory which accounts for the associative connection between S_i and R_j. For instance, the existence of analytic meaning postulates seems to require such underlying deductive structure to which the upper layer – the probabilities – have to conform. (Such meaning postulates need not be manifest or phenotypic but only implicit as recent investigations indicate (see e.g. Przelecki, 1969).) It is conceivable that in explicate (b') conditions C might capture something of the underlying deductive structure, which makes it preferable to (b).

Next consider proposal (c) which incorporates some non-probabilistic deductive structure into the behavior theory. This alternative requires that the eliciting stimulus has to be a necessary (but not necessarily a sufficient) condition of the response it elicits. Furthermore, the associative strength measured by relative probabilities has to be sufficiently great.

Explicate (c′) still somewhat relaxes explicate (c). Alternative (c) (or perhaps rather (c′)) seems to incorporate the essence of Osgood's notion of eliciting (see e.g. Osgood, 1966).

It should be emphasized that in dealing with eliciting relations where theoretical constructs are involved – as we shall mainly do – it does not make a great *observational* difference which one of the above explicates one adopts. This is, of course, due to the great difficulties in 'operational- izing' (in a broad sense) the theory for purposes of testing, explaining, predicting, etc. This operationalization process needs a 'broad belt' of many kinds of auxiliary hypotheses (e.g., concerning measurement and experimental initial conditions) which prevents the discrimination be- tween our alternatives especially between (a′), (b′), and (c′).

In our subsequent discussion the eliciting arrows can be interpreted either according to (a), (a′), (c), or (c′) (even if (a) and (a') are the ones this author originally had in mind when writing the paper). Alternative (a) does not require any extra comments. If (a′) is adopted, the reader has to think of the conditions C as suppressed implicit background conditions throughout the paper. The alternative (c), which is perhaps the psychologically most realistic alternative, requires the following minor change. In our formulas, which have been obtained from the figures by using interpretation (a) (or (a′)), naturally the roles of the stimuli and responses change. (Or, alternatively, redrawing the figures, all the arrows in them become inverted while the formulas stay as they are.) As our definability formulas for theoreticals are generally symmetric with respect to observable stimuli and responses, there will not be changes in the (deductive) definability relations of theoretical constructs with respect to the observables, which will be our concern later in this paper. As to the degrees of definability of theoreticals due to the probability clause of (c) we shall later indicate how to take care of them. For (c′) conditions C have to be taken as suppressed implicit conditions.

Next we shall comment on the nature of the stimuli. Below we assume in the behaviorist fashion that the *stimuli* S_i are concrete reproducible *physical events* described in the molar language of the experimenter (e.g., showing the subject an inscription of the word 'apple' or the perceptual sign *apple*). The set of our atomic stimuli $S = \{S_1, ..., S_i, ..., S_n\}$ is usually assumed to be (empirically or experimentally) exhaustive.

The set $R = \{R_1, ..., R_j, ..., R_m\}$ of atomic *responses* R_j is here considdered to consist of *behavior-events* described in the molar language of the experimenter. Let us, for the time being, leave open such questions as whether the responses are 'molar' or 'molecular', empirically compatible or incompatible, linguistic or extralinguistic, described extensionally or intensionally, and so on. Furthermore, in the more interesting cases of linguistic behavior some of these R's can be mediating responses as well.

As to members of the set $P = \{P_1, \ldots, P_k \ldots, P_1\}$, the atomic *mediating constructs P_k*, we just assume here in accordance with Osgood and others that they represent 'abstract' and normally unobservable *events* (possibly neuro-physiologically describable, and hence physical), which are clearly something one would have to call theoretical in practically any philosophically interesting sense of a theoretical/observational dichotomy. (Osgood described them as hypothetical constructs in the sense of the famous hypothetical construct/intervening variable-dichotomy of Meehl and MacCorquodale, 1948.) Below we shall require of a theoretical concept P_k occurring in a theory T that, in distinction to an observational one, it is not always directly measurable (assignable to objects) without assuming the truth of T (see Tuomela, 1973 for a detailed characterization).

Below, for simplicity, we mainly deal with cases where our theoretical concepts are not *directly* involved with each other in the kind of neobehavioristic theories we consider, except for some examples discussed in section 4. The indirect involvement or interwovenness between theoretical concepts is due to (1) their separate involvement with the observational concepts and (2) the involvement or relationships found to hold between the observational concepts. It goes without saying that one central characteristic of advanced scientific theories is that theoretical concepts in them are also directly involved with each other. This holds e.g. for psycholinguistic theories, too (see Osgood, 1953, 1968).

Now, what happens in a behavior situation or a 'trial' is, neutrally speaking, a *complex event* consisting of, first, one molar stimulus-event, then at least one mediating response-component P_k (i.e., in Figure 2 P_1 or P_2 or both), and finally at least one behavior-event R_j. In our example we can thus have complex events consisting of exactly one stimulus-event, and one or two mediating responses. In the sequel we shall for simplicity treat all the primitive concepts of our behavior theory as dichotomous or binary (that is, their 'values' are S_i or $\sim S_i$, P_k or $\sim P_k$, R_j or $\sim R_j$, depending on the case). However, it is easy to generalize all of our results to the case where each concept can have any fixed finite number of values (that is, different kinds of stimuli, mediating responses, and behavior-events can then occur with finitely many different intensities. Cf.Tuomela, 1971).

On the assumption that each of our concepts is dichotomous there are 2^m logically possible complex events. Thus, previous to making the above empirical (experimental) assumptions concerning the atomic events corresponding to our concept set $\{S_1, S_2, S_3, P_1, P_2, R_1, R_2, R_3\}$ in our example, we had 2^8 possible complex events (or actually descriptions of complex events). However, if we want to assume the empirical incompatibility and exhaustiveness of the stimulus set $\{S_1, S_2, S_3\}$, we obviously have 2^5 possibilities corresponding to the occurrence of a S_i $(i = 1, 2, 3)$, and thus 3×2^5 possible complex events, of which only 10 are compatible with Figure 2 under the widest interpretation of it.

We can now ask: What kind of behavioral theories are compatible with Figure 2? For simplicity, let us assume that there is nothing more in our behavioral theory (i.e. we ignore the $\dot{S} \rightarrow R_T$ relation and the learning mechanisms obviously needed). We assume that our underlying logic is ordinary (monadic) predicate logic.[2] Then we can describe all this by the following notation:

> '$S_i(x)$' – 'x is an S_i-event' or, more fully, 'x is a complex event including the atomic stimulus event S_i'
> '$R_j(x)$' – 'x is an R_j-event' or 'x is a complex event including the atomic response-event R_j'
> '$P_k(x)$' – 'x is an occurrence of the mediating (theoretical response P_k'.[3]

Thus in our example our observational concepts are given by the set $\lambda = \{S_1, S_2, S_3, R_1, R_2, R_3\}$, and $\mu = \{P_1, P_2\}$ is the set of our theoretical predicates. Of course, $\lambda \cup \mu$ is then the set of all our extralogical predicates.

Everything in our theory will be relativized to one organism (agent, subject). Thus we shall not here complicate our theory by taking into account such individual differences, as this would not give us essentially new aspects.

As an elementary exercise in logic we can now start building theories[4] compatible with Figure 2 to illustrate the possibilities of neobehavioristic theories. We get different theories depending on how we interpret Figure 2.

We assumed above that exactly one of our set of mutually incompatible stimuli $\{S_1, S_2, ..., S_n\}$ occurs on each trial. Formally, we assumed the following conditions to follow from our behavior theory:

(α) $(x)(-(S_i(x) \& S_j(x)))$,   for all $i \neq j$ (incompatibility)
(α') $(x)(S_1(x) \lor ... \lor S_n(x))$ (exhaustiveness)

The analogous incompatibility and exhaustiveness conditions for the responses are called (β) and (β'). We can formulate analogous conditions (call them (γ) and (γ')) for theoretical concepts, too.

What kind of interpretations for Figure 2 do we have? Consider first the stimulus-mediator relationships. We have, in case S_1 occurs, three possibilities initially compatible with Figure 2: we get to P_1 or P_2 or both. Formally speaking: we may accept either

(1) $(x)((S_1(x) \rightarrow P_1(x)) \lor (S_1(x) \rightarrow P_2(x)))$

or

(2) $(x)((S_1(x) \rightarrow P_1(x)) \& (S_1(x) \rightarrow P_2(x)))$.

In case we accept exactly one of the arrows leaving S_1 we still require (γ) in addition to (2).

The cases with S_2 and S_3 are not problematic in our example. It seems natural to assume:

(3) $(x)(S_2(x) \rightarrow P_2(x))$

Furthermore, we assume

(4) $(x)(S_3(x) \rightarrow P_1(x))$.

Of the relations between mediating responses and mediated responses the case with P_1 is the following:

(5) $(x)(P_1(x) \rightarrow R_1(x))$.

In the case of P_2 we again have the possibilities for disjunctive or conjunctive interpretations as in the case of S_1:

(6) $(x)((P_2(x) \rightarrow R_1(x)) \lor (P_2(x) \rightarrow R_3(x)))$
(7) $(x)((P_2(x) \rightarrow R_1(x)) \& (P_2(x) \rightarrow R_3(x)))$.

In Tuomela (1971) the following theories were shown to have some psychological interest:

$T'_1 = (\alpha) \& (1) \& (3) \& (4) \& (5) \& (6)$
$T'_2 = (\alpha) \& (\beta) \& (1) \& (3) \& (4) \& (5) \& (6)$
$T'_3 = (\alpha) \& (\gamma) \& (1) \& (3) \& (4) \& (5) \& (6)$
$T'_4 = (\alpha) \& (\beta) \& (\gamma) \& (1) \& (3) \& (4) \& (5) \& (6)$

Notice especially that of these theories T'_4 could be called a *theory of chains* (for

Figure 2) going through the organism-box; it states that only a certain subset of all the logically possible chains are empirically possible.

In view of this it is now quite easy to see how to formalize within this framework a neobehavioristic theory (or, more correctly, at least the non-probabilistic part of a theory) in this way in terms of stimulus-organism and organism-response relationships. We have not yet discussed probabilistic relationships even if it would have been possible in principle (see Section 4). Hence what we are going to say below about the role of theoretical concepts in our example is immediately generalizable to this kind of situation.

3. DEFINABILITY OF THEORETICAL CONCEPTS

1. We shall below consider different kinds of definability and state some general and well known properties of them.

The definability of a predicate must always be considered with respect to a set of other predicates and a theory where all these concepts occur. We shall below concentrate on four different kinds of definability termed *explicit, piecewise, conditional*, and *partial* definability. The three last mentioned reflect, each in its own sense, *openness* and potential empirical *surplus 'meaning'* of (theoretical) concepts. Notice that within neobehavioristic theories the so-called definitions and partial definitions normally express *contingent* and not analytic (semantic) relationships.

To start, an *explicit* definition of a monadic (theoretical) predicate $P\varepsilon\mu$ on the basis of a set λ of (observational) predicates, given a theory T' in the vocabulary $\lambda \cup \mu$, where for simplicity $\mu = \{P\}$, is of the form

$$(8) \qquad (x)(P(x) \leftrightarrow F(\lambda, x))$$

where $F(\lambda, x)$ is a formula with one free variable in the vocabulary λ.

There are two classical criteria for definitions according to which different types of definability can be evaluated. These are the criteria of *eliminability* (or translatability) and *non-creativity*. In the present context these criteria have to be formulated with respect to observational theories (in the vocabulary λ) and their extensions in the vocabulary $\lambda \cup \mu$. We say that a theory $T'(\lambda \cup \mu)$ is an extension of a theory $T(\lambda)$ if and only if all the statements derivable from (belonging to) $T(\lambda)$ are derivable from (belong to) $T'(\lambda \cup \mu)$. Now assume $T'(\lambda \cup \mu)$ is an extension of $T(\lambda)$. Then we say that $T'(\lambda \cup \mu)$ is a *conservative* (non-creative) extension of $T(\lambda)$ if all the statements in the vocabulary λ derivable from $T'(\lambda \cup \mu)$ are derivable from $T(\lambda)$, i.e., when $T'(\lambda \cup \mu)$ does not give us any new observational statements not previously possessed through $T(\lambda)$. In this case the set of statements defining the members of μ in terms of those of λ can be taken to be the theory $T'(\lambda \cup \mu)$ (or one of its sub-theories in the vocabulary $\lambda \cup \mu$, in general). Now, the members of μ are definable in terms of those of λ by a non-creative definition (set of defining statements) exactly when $T'(\lambda \cup \mu)$ is a non-creative extension of $T(\lambda)$. This is the criterion of non-creativity. Clearly, if $T'(\lambda \cup \mu)$ is obtained from $T(\lambda)$ by adding only statements of form (8), $T'(\lambda \cup \mu)$ will be a non-creative extension of $T(\lambda)$. Hence explicit definitions meet the criterion of non-creativity. As in an explicit definition the definiens $F(\lambda, x)$ fixes uniquely the value of the theoretical concept P, an explicit definition also meets the following much stronger condition of *eliminability*: A statement containing a $P\varepsilon\mu$ must in every context be substitutable *salva veritate* by a statement containing members of λ only.

However, *explicit* definability is perhaps the least interesting kind of definability from a methodological point of view. Other kinds of more interest are: *piecewise* definability, *conditional* definability, and *partial* definability. It goes without saying that all these notions defined for many kinds of languages apply to the neobehavioristic theories formulated here within monadic languages. Let us now briefly define the main notions.

A monadic (for simplicity) theoretical concept P is *piecewise* definable in terms of λ given a theory T' (in the vocabulary $\lambda \cup \{P\}$) if and only if the theory T' implies a finite disjunction of sentences (explicit definitions) of form (8) for P. If there is only one member in this disjunction we of course get explicit definability in this special case. (On the formal properties of our notion of piecewise definability see Hintikka and Tuomela, 1970 and Tuomela, 1973.) Piecewise definability meets the conditions of eliminability and non-creativity.

A concept P is *conditionally* definable in terms of λ, given $T'(\lambda \cup \mu)$, if and only if $T'(\lambda \cup \mu)$ implies a (so-called bilateral reduction) sentence of form

(9) $(x)(L_1(\lambda, x) \rightarrow (P(x) \leftrightarrow L_2(\lambda, x)))$

where $L_1(\lambda, x)$ and $L_2(\lambda, x)$ are formulas of one free variable in the vocabulary λ.

It is easily seen that a conditional definition fulfills the condition of non-creativity but naturally fails to satisfy the requirement of eliminability.[5] In case $L_1(\lambda, x)$ is a tautology (9) reduces to an explicit definition.

A concept P is called *partially* definable in terms of λ, given $T'(\lambda \cup \mu)$, if and only if T' implies the conjunction

$$(10) \qquad (x)\,(L_1(\lambda, x) \rightarrow P(x))\ \&\ (L_2(\lambda, x) \rightarrow \sim P(x))$$

where $L_1(\lambda, x)$ and $L_2(\lambda, x)$ mean the same as above. (In Carnap's terminology, (10) is a conjunction of two unilateral reduction sentences for P.) Partial definition does not meet the condition of non-creativity with respect to the original observational theory T from which we obtained T' by adding the members of μ. For, obviously, (10) implies the sentence

$$(11) \qquad (x) \sim (L_1(\lambda, x)\ \&\ L_2(\lambda, x))$$

which is generally non-tautologous (factual). In the special case when (11) is a logical tautology or if we are willing to assert (11) and to incorporate it into the axiom set T, (11) reduces to the following conditional definition:

$$(12) \qquad (x)\,(((L_1(\lambda, x) \vee L_2(\lambda, x)) \rightarrow (P(x) \leftrightarrow L_1(\lambda, x))))$$

In addition to the above kinds of definability based directly on the (non-probabilistic) deductive structure of a behavior theory one can quite generally define and measure the *degree of definability* or interwovenness of, say, theoretical and observational concepts (See e.g. Tuomela, 1973). The resulting measures of degrees of definability take into account both the non-probabilistic deductive 'understructure' and the probabilistic 'superstructure' (additional probabilistic relationships between concepts). This corresponds directly to our distinction made in connection with our explicates (c) and (c') for the relation of eliciting.

2. Let us now briefly and summarily consider the definability relations obtaining between mediating theoretical concepts and observables (stimuli and responses) in some typical neobehavioristic theories. (The

reader is referred to Tuomela (1971) for proofs and a more extensive and detailed treatment.)

In general, we can divide neobehavioristic theories into 'functional' and 'non-functional'. By functional theories we mean theories which are of form $R=f(S)$ or $R=k(S,P)$, where f and k are appropriate set functions stating which elements of the set R correspond to elements of set S or S and set P, respectively.

Stricter neobehaviorists usually look for a function $R=f(S)$, as we shall see below. It is usually obtained as a composite function from some elementary functions $P=g(S)$, $P=o(P)$, $R=h(P)$ between stimuli and mediators, mediators and mediators, and mediators and responses. The required composite function $f=h\cdot o\cdot g$ exists provided that g is a surjective (onto) function. To what extent are the mediators P_k definable on the basis of stimuli and/or responses in such a theory $R=f(S)=h(o(g(S)))$? It is easily seen that we get the following explicit definition in terms of stimuli:

$$(13) \qquad (x)(P_k(x)\leftrightarrow(S_1(x)\vee ... \vee S_m(x)))$$

for an appropriate numbering and amount of stimuli. However, if we are primarily interested – as we mostly are – in the reducibility or eliminability of the P_k's in terms of *responses* (*and* possibly stimuli) we get the following answer. The mediators can be defined conditionally by means of the following kind of bilateral reduction sentences:

$$(14) \qquad (x)((S_1(x)\vee ... \vee S_m(x)))\rightarrow(P_k(x)\leftrightarrow R_j(x))),$$

for some j and for some amount and numbering of stimuli.[6]

In the case of functional theories of form $R=k(S,P)$ we can again get partial definitions for mediators as follows:

$$(15) \qquad (x)(S_i\rightarrow(P_k(x)\rightarrow R_j(x))).$$

Notice that in theories of form $R=f(S)$ we get non-creative behavioral definitions for our theories, whereas in theories of form $R=k(S,P)$ mediators at most get creative behavioral definitions.

Diagrams like that expressed by Figure 2 clearly cannot be formalized by functional theories of any kind as the responses R_j are not determined by a function on the basis of the stimuli S_i and/or mediators P_k. In these non-functional cases we do not get even partial definitions in terms of stimuli and responses but at best partial definitions in terms of stimuli, responses, *and* other mediators (cf. Tuomela, 1971, p. 16). (For instance, Osgood's convergent and divergent hierarchies represent such non-functional theorizing.) In these nonfunctional theories the methodological usefulness of the mediating theoretical concepts is obviously connected with how much information we can have concerning the internal states of the organism (i.e. how many and how transparent windows the black box-organism has, so to speak). Here obviously the *total* behavior (including all of the previous history) of the organism has to be considered, and not only the part of behavior we happen to be interested in presently.

4. THEORETICAL CONCEPTS WITHIN SCIENTIFIC SYSTEMATIZATION

1. Our main concern in this section will be the role of theoretical concepts within deductive theorizing or systematization. By deductive systematization we mean here, in accordance with Hempel (1965), all the deductive functions of a scientific theory. Among them especially the broad categories of deductive explanation, prediction, and post-diction are central here.

As our focus is on neobehavioristic theories it is of interest to have a look at what some early neobehaviorists say about the aims of behavioral sciences in general and particularly about deductive systematization in them.

It is quite interesting to see that single-stage or 'empty-organism' theoreticians like Skinner and many-stage theorists like Hull agree in their general views about deductive systematization. The minor differences between them concern details and they are only due to their different views on the role of theoretical concepts in scientific theories. For behaviorists and even for some neobehaviorists[7], stimulus-based *control* of observable behavior seems to be the main goal of science (see e.g. Tolman, 1936; Hull, 1943; Skinner, 1953, and the neo-Skinnerians' writings). As we know their background philosophy is (strict) empiricism, and their ideal of scientific theorizing seems to be primarily technological in nature. How is control over behavior to be achieved? If we can predict behavior (dependent variable) on the basis of some (causal) independent variables, and if we can technically manipulate these independent causes of behavior, we can control behavior. Very characteristic of this view is the early Tolman's statement: "The ultimate interest of psychology is solely the prediction and control of behavior." (See Tolman, 1936, p. 101 and also Skinner, 1953, p. 23.)

Tolman's statement indicates that only prediction, rather than, for instance, explanation, and understanding of behavior, are considered to be important. What is then predicted and how? The units of behavior that behaviorists in general have been concerned with are *molar*, not *molecular*. However, this distinction is not too clear (see e.g. Littman and Rosen, 1950; Hamlyn, 1953 and Tuomela, 1971.) But let us here not focus on this problem.

At least extreme behaviorists think that behavior is to be predicted on the basis of some physical stimuli. One has to go outside the organism to look for causal variables *independent* of behavior. It is then assumed that behavior is caused (or elicited) by such stimuli. The task of the behavioral scientist is now to discover and describe (by mathematical equations or otherwise) the causal connections or causal laws existing between stimuli and responses. But behaviorists differ in their accounts of how this can be done. The most extreme behaviorists like Skinner exclude all reference to the subject (organism' for methodological reasons.[8]. Neobehaviorists like Hull, Tolman, Spence, and Osgood think that reference to theoretical organism variables is needed, even if they may and do differ as to the role they give these constructs in behavioral theories.

This point is worth elaborating. Let us first quote an illuminating passage from Skinner's *Science and Human Behavior* (1953) to start the discussion, even if Skinner's view differs somewhat from neobehaviorists' views:

The objection to inner states is not that they do not exist, but that they are not relevant in a functional analysis. We cannot account for the behavior of any system while staying wholly inside it; eventually we must turn to forces operating upon the organism from without. Unless there is a weak spot in our causal chain so that the second link is not lawfully determined by the first, or the third by the second, then the first and third links must be lawfully related. If we must always go back beyond the second link for prediction and control, we may avoid many tiresome and exhausting digressions by examining the third link as a function of the first. Valid information about the second link may throw light upon this relationship but can in no way alter it. (Skinner, 1953, p. 35)

Skinner's view is quite clear, and so is behaviorist Woodrow's: "If you have a secure equational linkage extending from the antecedent observable through to the consequent observable conditions, why, even though to do so might not be positively pernicious, use several equations when one would do?" (Woodrow, 1942, quoted in Hull, 1943, 0. 213)

The message of these arguments by radical behaviorists and neobehaviorists of the more extreme kind is quite clear. They try to show that in psychology at least no organism-constructs – presumably theoretical concepts – are needed. This is actually a special case of the following argument called the *paradox of theorizing* (for deductive systematization) by Hempel. *If the concepts and statements of a scientific theory serve their purpose, i.e., if they establish definite connections between observable empirical events (such as stimuli and responses), then they can be dispensed with since any chain of statements establishing such a connection should hence be eliminable by a statement which links observational antecedent variables (stimuli) directly to observational consequents (responses).*

We saw above that, assuming the responses can be regarded as related by a (mathematical) function $R=f(S)=h(o(g(S)))$ to their stimuli as, for instance, Skinner and Woodrow seem to think, then the eliminability (or reducibility) of theoretical concepts means in that case that they are behaviorally defined by observational reduction sentences in general.[9]

We have claimed above that neobehaviorists do use theoretical constructs in their theories. Does this mean that they do not accept the paradox above? The answer is yes. It is so even if many neobehaviorists (especially the early Hull and Tolman) consider their main task to be to construct an equational linkage ('gross function' $R=f(S)$) leading from stimuli to responses (see Tolman, 1936; Hull, 1943). Naturally their reasons for not accepting this paradox have to be non-logical in nature because of our earlier results concerning the reducibility and eliminability of mediators in functional theories.

Let us now consider what kind of reasons Tolman and Hull give us for not accepting the paradox of theorizing. Both of them state *heuristic* and *methodological* reasons. According to them, intervening concepts and links have to be postulated, because one cannot, at least to begin with, conceive of the gross function $R=f(S)$ because of the complexity of everything taking place between stimuli and responses. In other words, for practical reasons it is easier to start this way. One aspect of this practical convenience is also that theoretical constructs provide suitable quantitative representations or indices of the particular complex of experimental variables for which they stand (cf. Hull, 1943, p. 214).

Another interesting reason for breaking down the gross link between stimuli anz responses into a number of component links and for introducing theoretical constructs is offered by Hull:

> Both for empirical and theoretical purposes behavior must be broken up into relatively coarse causal segments, the interior conditions of which cannot be subjected to observation and measurement. (Hull, 1943, p. 206)
> While it is perfectly possible to put into a single equation the value of events which occur at very different times, it is hard to believe that an event such as stimulation in a remote learning situation can be causally active long after it has ceased to act on the receptors. (Hull, 1943, p. 214)

The third reason for employing theoretical constructs to be found in the writings of some neobehaviorists is simply that one may be interested in theoretical entities in their own right. That is, statements where open theoretical terms appear may have *existential import*. There may be 'something under the skin' that the theoretical construct words refer to and that is worth studying. Especially Hull seems to think this way, though the early Tolman, for instance, does not (cf. Spence, 1948; MacCorquodale and Meehl, 1948).

It is astonishing that (the early) neobehaviorists seemingly have not really found more (philosophical and methodological) reasons for not accepting the paradox of theorizing. (For a comprehensive and detailed discussion of this scc Tuomcla, 1973.) It seems to us that this follows from their strict epistemological and semantical empiricism and hence an unduly restrictive view of deductive systematization and the aims of behavioral science in general. Furthermore, it is at least initially conceivable that in the case of other kinds of neobehavioristic theories even some kind of logical reasons could be found for not accepting the paradox of theorizing. In subsection 4.3 we shall return to the paradox of theorizing again, whereas in 4.2 we shall discuss the need for richer behavioral theories and the role of theoretical concepts in them.

2.   Let us ask to begin with: Why is a behavioral theory corresponding to a gross function $R = f(S)$ too restricted?

The first and the principal reason is that its theoretical concepts do not provide us with new behavioral consequences as they are definable by non-creative observational definitions. The theory thus cannot grow in the proper sense of the notion (i.e., observational growth due to theory). Naturally we may find new stimulus-response connections experimentally but then we have already changed our theory and are dealing with a different gross function f'. Secondly, a functional theory of the above kind is unable to satisfactorily express feedback (effect of reward, reinforcement) which is characteristic of human and animal behavior. One way to argue for this claim is the following. Human beings, considered from a mechanistic point of view, must (for several reasons) be at least as powerful machines as finite automatons. But some kind of finite automaton is the simplest mechanism capable of expressing feedback. Therefore any interesting neobehavioristic theory should be capable of describing such an automaton (or at least its feedback mechanism) if it is to be adequate for describing self-regulating behavior.

But theories of form $R = f(S)$ are not capable of this. This is seen by describing a (finite) automaton in the above vocabulary in terms of its transition function and output function between two succeeding moments of time or trials. Let S thus be the set of automaton inputs, P the set of the internal states of the automaton, and R its output set. Now consider the following functions (from which time indices have been omitted for simplicity):

(16) $g^* : P \times S \to P$
         $h^* : P \times S \to R$

The function g^* is the *transition* function of the automaton, and h^* is its *output* function.

An essential part of what is included in the mechanism of feedback is incorporated directly in the transition function g^*, for g^*, in contradiction to g, describes how the earlier states (or previous history) of the machine combined with new input affect its present state.[10] The output function h^* can actually be compared directly with the gross output function f in the neobehavioristic theories, in which there do not occur any irreducible internal states (intervening variables). Clearly, in empirical research we may succeed in finding a function which makes responses a function of stimuli *and* internal states even if no function is found which relates responses direcly to stimuli. Thus also the composite function $g^* \cdot h^*$ is clearly stronger than the corresponding function $g \cdot h \cdot o$

in the above theories. The difference is roughly that theoretical states play a much more important role in g*·h* in, for instance, that they enable one to express feedback. It should also be obvious that they are not behaviorally reducible by bilateral reduction sentences in the automaton case as they were in the neobehavioristic theory. For a good discussion of the role of internal states in the automaton the reader is referred to Nelson (1969).

In the second argument above against the inadequacy of the theories of form $R=f(S)$ we actually mentioned the following third general kind of reason. It may simply not be empirically possible to find a function $R=f(S)$. The next best thing for a 'predictionist' would then be to look for a function of form $R=k(S, P)$ which is actually a degenerate form form of (16).[11] If he succeeds in finding one he can again get specific predictions as in the previous functional case with $R=f(S)$, provided he is able to measure the values of theoretical concepts. As we saw above, in this kind of theory we get partial definitions of form (15) for our mediators.

Above we have discussed the definability of theoretical concepts and the relationship between definability and a special case of prediction – prediction of responses by means of a function from the stimuli (or stimuli and mediators). In this kind of functional case we get maximally

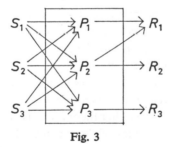

Fig. 3

specific predictions – one single atomic R_j. The condition on which this prediction works is that stimuli (or, respectively, stimuli and mediators) are accessible to knowledge. In the case of unobservable mediators it is not so clear how to measure them. Nevertheless, neobehaviorists use mediators for predictive purposes in the above sense. "We do assume intervening variables and we do try to work forward to them from the independent variables and backward to them from the resulting behavior" (Tolman, 1936, p. 97). The acceptance of strict empiricism by neobehaviorists entails even this: "Symbolic constructs can have nothing more than a rather dubious expository utility unless they are anchored to observable and measurable conditions or events on both the antecedent and consequent sides" (Hull, 1943, p. 201).

Let us still illustrate concretely the predictive gain due to theoretical constructs. Consider the diagram on p. 143.

This diagram cannot be formalized by a functional theory of form $R=f(S)$ or $R=h(S,P)$. But even so, theoretical constructs can be of considerable predictive help, provided one can somehow measure or guess their values.

We may plausibly think that the underlying purely observational stimulus-response theory in Figure 3 is completely tautological as to the predictions of responses, because this observational theory can simply be taken to say that every stimulus elicits every response (disjunctively). Let us assume the conditions (α), (β), and (γ) of Section 2. Then consider the richer theory obtained by inserting the mediators between the stimuli and responses in the same way as in the theory T'_4 in Section 2. (We do not bother to write down the axioms explicitly here.) This richer theory is merely a conservative extension of the observational theory. One can immediately see that the new richer theory combined with suitable initial conditions enables us to infer quite informative response-predictions. For instance, consider an occurrence of a complex event which satisfies S_1, i.e., $S_1(a)$. On the basis of the purely observational theory we can now deductively infer the disjunction $R_1(a) \vee R_2(a) \vee R_3(a)$. However, if we know that $P_1(a)$ we can infer that $R_1(a)$. It thus seems that theoretical constructs really do a great deal of work here. In addition to the mere introduction of the richer theory, this is naturally due to the fact that we can measure the values of the theoretical concepts, and thus add such initial conditions to the theory as are needed for prediction (cf. 4.3).

One important feature about the work performed by theoretical concepts is their role in the explanation of responses. Excepting extreme behavioristic theories, responses are usually explained by reference to theoretical concepts such as the goals (which may be due to drives and needs), plans and past history of the subject. One aspect of such a behavior-explanation is that – in a sense – it redescribes the response to be explained by stating what inner factors (mechanisms) cause the response or what the purpose of the act of behavior is, etc. In general the explaining factors are 'semantically' more general, for a great variety of different responses may be semantically subsumed under the same explaining factor or set of factors. In other words, explanatory factors systematize behavior in a certain way. This can also be seen from our diagrams above. For instance, in Figure 3 the responses R_1 and R_2 are subsumed under the same theoretical concept P_2. The idea of such systematization should be clear. If one succeeds in building a comprehensive theory out of the theoretical concepts, its empirical range, and hence adequacy, will naturally be the greater the more diverse behavior it is capable of explaining.

But it should be noticed that this kind of systematization of responses and the informativeness and accuracy of response-predictions are inversely related. The greater the number of responses a theoretical concept subsumes under it, the less specific response-predictions does it yield. This may seem paradoxical as both goodness of (deductive) systematization and informativeness of (deductive) prediction are usually accepted as desiderata for theoretical systems. But the solution to this apparent dilemma is simple. Goodness of systematization cannot be evaluated as above. Subsuming many different responses under the same theoretical concept must, after all, be understood so that different aspects (values) of the concept are associated with different responses. As shown in Tuomela (1972), Osgood's mediating meaning-responses can be construed within the present frame work as complex concepts have many aspects or components. Thus the seeming paradox between goodness of systematization and specificity of response-predictions dissolves and, indeed, these factors are seen to covary.

3. Our discussion seems to indicate that in sufficiently rich neobehavioristic theories theoretical concepts do a lot of important work, and they are not eliminable or reducible by explicit or conditional observational definitions. However, we have not yet proved that these theoretical concepts are in some sense logically indispensable. That is, even if no term-by-term elimination of theoretical concepts is possible, it may still be the case that the entire theory in which they occur could be replaceable with a purely observational theory which is equivalent with the original

theory with respect to scientific systematization. Let us discuss this possibility.

We say that a (behavior) theory $T'(\lambda \cup \mu)$ *establishes deductive observational systematization* if and only if for some observational statements F and G, (a) T' & $F \vdash G$ but (b) not $F \vdash G$ ('$\vdash$' means 'provability'). The theoretical terms of theory $T'(\lambda \cup \mu)$ are said to be *logically indispensable* for deductive observational systematization if and only if no subtheory $T(\lambda)$ of $T'(\lambda \cup \mu)$ solely in the vocabulary λ establishes (at least) the same deductive observational systematization as $T'(\lambda \cup \mu)$.

We get the corresponding definitions for *inductive* observational systematization and indispensability by simply substituting a relation 'I' of inducibility for '$\vdash$' and by excluding cases of deductive systematization (see Tuomela, 1973). We shall below consider only the interpretation of 'I' as *positive probabilistic relevance*: FIG if and only if $p(G/F) > p(G)$, where p is an inductive probability measure. The above conditions for inductive systematization can still be explicated in various ways; the reader is referred to Niiniluoto and Tuomela, 1973.)

A version of the theoretician's paradox can now be derived for deductive systematization because of a welll-known result by Craig, simply called 'Craig's theorem'. This theorem says that in the case of any richer theory T' in the vocabulary $\lambda \cup \mu$ one can always find a recursively axiomatizable theory T solely in the vocabulary λ such that T consists of exactly the λ-theorems of T'. (Notice especially that no assumptions concerning the definability relationships between theoretical and observational concepts are made.)

However, the Craigian substitute T is in general only infinitely axiomatizable by an unduly complicated and redundant set of axioms. (For a description and a critical evaluation of it see Tuomela, 1973.) Still, as long as the above notion of dispensability of theoretical concepts is used in formulating the theoretician's paradox, the paradox has to be theoretically accepted in the case of *deductive* systematization.[12]

Below we shall not really question the Craigian replacement within deductive systematization as such. One might want, however, to replace the notion of indispensability by a notion of *desirability* of theoretical terms by requiring that the replacing observational Craigian substitute preserve, besides the observational content, also some other desirable features of the original richer theory T'. Among such desirable features of a good theory we have, for instance, *heuristical fruitfulness*, *explanatory power*, *ontological* or *existential import*, *deductive coherence* and *economy*, and *inductive performance*. The Craigian substitute generally seems to lack these. We shall now comment upon some of these features.

We noticed above that *S-R*-theoreticians have tended to concentrate too much on the controlling and predictive aspects of behavioral science and thus de-emphasized the explanatory role of theoretical concepts. (Of course, prediction and explanation are not totally independent notions. Even if one may be able to make good predictions without corresponding good explanations of behavior it should be required, I think, that at least every good deductive explanation should be convertible into a (potential) prediction.) At least on intuitive grounds one may argue that theoretical concepts are introduced into observational scientific theories mainly for their explanatory value (cf. our earlier discussion in 4.2). For instance, theoretical concepts referring to some underlying 'hidden' mechanism have much stronger explanatory value than 'surface' or macro-concepts and concepts which are about the same kind of phenomena they aim at explaining. If this is acceptable, then at least (open) theoretical concepts which refer to hidden but *existing* entities should have greater explanatory value than observational concepts or concepts (somehow) reducible to observational concepts. Actually we have here two separate claims: (1) the explaining entities (to which the theoretical concept refers) should (at least potentially) be of a different kind than those whose behavior is being explained (an *ontological* claim) and (2) the explanatory concepts should be *open* (cf. Section 3.1) and thus have surplus meaning (either a *semantical* or an *epistemological* claim).

Our two desirable features for good explanatory constructs (e.g. Hull's fractional goal response or Osgood's meaning response) are exactly the central features of a hypothetical construct in the sense of MacCorquodale and Meehl (1948) in contrast to their intervening variable. As to the latter, a theoretician who believes that theoretical concepts are merely convenient summaries for observational phenomena must use intervening variables which refer to observable phenomena and are indeed reducible to them by something like reduction chains. Intervening variables are more easily measurable than hypothetical constructs and they have lower explanatory value.

Space does not here allow a further discussion of these features, which are central for at least scientific realists (contra instrumentalists) (see Tuomela, 1973). But we shall briefly discuss the *inductive* performance of theories. Even if an instrumentalist, like Skinner, would not accept claims concerning the explanatory and existential import of theoretical concepts he would have to accept a proof of the inductive indispensability.

We shall assume that in psychology (as well as in other sciences) a property of good theoretical concepts is that they can at least sometimes (but usually not always) be used in *evidence* statements and reports. In other words, on some occasions it should be possible to determine truth values of *atomic* theoretical statements (e.g. '$P_1(a)$').

One cannot really say that these atomic theoretical statements are directly ascertainable evidence-statements comparable to purely observational statements which are about molar behavior. It is just an essential feature about theoretical concepts in psychology that they cannot be directly observed in any interesting sense. Instead, they are more or less indirectly inferred from behavior and from some historical and contextual information concerning the subject (recall e.g. our above quotations from Hull and Tolman). But the important thing is that they are somehow measured, even if there need not be any deductive chain leading from values of observable concepts to values of theoretical concepts; and generally there is no such chain, except in the case $R = f(S)$. The link is not deductive but *inductive* (usually probabilistic).

Or better, the theory may have some nonprobabilistic content (see e.g. Figure 3) but in addition there is information that has not been encoded into the theory proper but which is used when measuring the values of theoretical concepts and when inducing observational consequences of the theory. For instance, in our example there may be some extra-theoretical information available which enables one to infer that $P_1(a)$ rather than, e.g., $P_2(a)$ is the case. This information may, e.g., be due to the 'historical anchorage' of mediating concepts (such as the relationship between Osgood's mediators r_m and the total responses R_T they correspond to). Or it may be contextual information that is regarded as affecting the probabilities of different causal chains (cf. the convergent and divergent hierarchies of Osgood, 1956, 1966). Or it may consist of an inductive leap from the necessary consequences (symptoms) of some theoretical process (cause) to the occurrence of that theoretical process (rather than to some other process). (We cannot here attempt a more exhaustive and detailed account of how one actually measures one's theoretical concepts when no definite deductive criteria are available.)

Let us now comment upon inductive explanations and predictions, supposing that we are sometimes able to measure our theoretical concepts. Consider the following simple probabilistic theory $T(\{S, R\} \cup \{P\})$:

(A1) $(x)(p_0(R(x)/S(x) \& P(x)) > p_0(R(x)))$
(A2) $(x)(p_0(R(x)/S(x)) = p_0(R(x)))$.

Here the probability measure p_0 is assumed to represent an objective (statistical) probability *in re*. Let us now accept Hempel's well known principle for connecting objective probabilities (p_0) with inductive ones (p): If e is the statement '$p_0(G/F) = r \& F(a)$', and h is '$G(a)$', then $p(h, e) = r$. (Hempel, 1965, p. 389)

Consider now some individual a stimulated by S, having property P and eliciting response R. Our theory T in conjunction with Hempel's principle entails the truth of

(17) $p(R(a)/S(a) \& P(a) \& T) > p(R(a))$.

We obviously also get

(18) $p(R(a)/S(a)) = p(R(a))$.

Hence we have (a) '$S(a) \& P(a) \& T$' I '$R(a)$' and (b) not '$S(a)$' I '$R(a)$' when' I' is interpreted as positive relevance. T *cum* P (a) achieves inductive observational systematization. Furthermore, as T has no non-tautological deductive observational consequences (and thus no non-empty observational subtheory), P is *logically indispensable for inductive systematization* within $T \& P(a)$. That is, we have shown the theoretical concept P to be inductively indispensable, not in the theory T *per se* but within T *cum* the initial condition (contextual information) $P(a)$.[13]

Our discussion above is very relevant to Osgood's general behavioral assumptions concerning his associative (convergent and divergent) hierarchies of stimuli and responses. Consider, for instance, a divergent hierarchy – a set of incompatible and competing responses that are (disjunctively) elicited by the same stimulus. Now, according to the behavioral principle for divergent responses, the response with the momentarily highest habit strength will occur (Osgood, 1956). This momentary habit strength depends on the absolute habit strength of the response and the contextual cues and hints present. It seems that at least in the case of relatively stable behavior the information concerning the absolute habit strength can be encoded into the theory non-probabilistically while the additional information concerning momentary contextual cues, etc., is encoded probabilistically. Whether or not this is so, we here a case where our above considerations are directly applicable.

Department of Philosophy,
University of Helsinki

NOTES

* This paper is partly based on an earlier critical evaluation of behaviorism and neo-behaviorism by the author (Tuomela, 1971). That report was addressed to philosophers as well as to theoretically minded behavioral scientists, whence the elementary style of exposition.

1 We are aware that causing and eliciting seem to be best construable as *intensional* and not extensional notions as here. Our extensional explicates for the notion of eliciting seem, however, more in accord with an S-R-theoretician's way of thinking, to which we wish to give a rational reconstruction.

2 Thus we use '$S(x)$' for 'x has the property S'. The quantifier '(x)' reads 'for every x'. As logical connectives we use '&' for conjunction ("and"), 'v' for inclusive disjunction ("or"), '$-$' for negation ("not"), '$\rightarrow$' for material implication ("if-then"), and '$\leftrightarrow$' for material equivalence ("if and only if").

3 Notice that a complex event-description is a redescription of three kinds of atomic events. It is compatible with this to maintain, for instance, that mediating construct are non-observable hypothetical events, while stimulus events and response events are observable events.

4 By a theory we mean, as usually, a set of statements closed under deduction in a certain fixed scientific language. Below, however, we can and will frequently and without harm identify a theory with the conjunction of its axioms (i.e. the statements from which the whole theory is derivable).

5 We shall later be often concerned with theoretical concepts conditionally definable by bilateral reduction sentences. Notice that even if such theoretical concepts are not completely eliminable they are not heuristically fruitful in the sense of helping us in deducing new observational consequences from our behavior theory.

6 These are equivalent to formulas (24) and (25) of Tuomela (1971). The reader is also referred to formulas (17), (20), and (22) of Tuomela (1971) for results concerning slightly different kinds of functional cases.

7 My comments below do not all necessarily apply to the later writings of Tolman and Hull and to neobehaviorists (Mowrer, Osgood, Kendler, etc.) in general. But they are intended to apply to the way of behavioristic theorizing represented, for instance, by the (or some) earlier writings of Tolman and Hull, as well by Skinnerians in general.

8 That Skinner's reasons are methodological rather than ontological, epistemological or semantical is revealed e.g. from this. In describing the drinking of an organism Skinner says:

In each case we have a causal chain consisting of three links: (1) an operation performed upon the organism from without – for example, water deprivation; (2) an inner condition – for example, physiological or psychic thirst; (3) a kind of behavior – for example, drinking. Independent information about the second link would obviously permit us to predict the third without recourse to the first. It would be a preferred type of variable because it would be non-historic; the first link may lie in the past history of the organism, but the second is a current condition. Direct information about the second link is, however, seldom, if ever, available. Sometimes we infer the second link from the third: an animal is judged to be thirsty if it drinks. In that case the explanation is spurious. Sometimes we infer the second link from the first: an animal is said to be thirsty if it has not drunk for a long time. In that case, we obviously cannot dispense with the past history. (Skinner, 1953, p. 34)

[9] Notice especially that it does not mean explicit definability of theoretical constructs in terms of stimuli and responses nor does it presuppose a one-to-one correlation between stimuli and responses (*contra* Fodor, 1965).

[10] We have here just a necessary, but not yet a sufficient condition for feedback. In this case we cannot still explicitly distinguish response-produced stimuli from other kinds of prior stimuli. But how this important aspect can be formalized is easy to see.

[11] It is interesting to notice that even if Skinner does not accept the use of mediators he does accept observational theories of form $R=k(S, P^*)$. In our terminology, 'P^*' is here not a mediator but rather an observational indicator of a mediator. For instance, instead of 'hunger' ('P') Skinner would use e.g. 'hours of deprivation' ('P^*'). (See e.g. Skinner, 1961, p, 320)

[12] Space does not allow us to illustrate this result of Craig's more concretely. However, it is easy to see, for instance, that in Figure 3 it is logically as possible to arrive at the same *deductive* response-predictions (through elimination of superfluous causal chains) without the use of P as with it.

It can be noticed here that a Craigian transcription in terms of observational vocabulary only can always be found for the theory axiomatizing our automation (16) in 4.2. Naturally it will describe only 'relational' behavior, as generally it will not yield a *function* connecting behaviors to stimuli.

[13] For a discussion of other types of inductively indispensable theoretical concepts see Niiniluoto and Tuomela (1973), Tuomela (1971) and (1973).

BIBLIOGRAPHY

Chomsky, N.: 1959, 'A review of B. F. Skinner's *Verbal Behavior*', *Language* **35**, 26–58.

Chomsky, N.: 1968, *Language and Mind*, Harcourt, Brace & World.

Fodor, J.: 1965, 'Could Meaning Be an r_m?', *Journal of Verbal Learning and Verbal Behavior* **4**, 73–81.

Hamlyn, D.: 1953, 'Behavior', *Philosophy* **28**, 132–145.

Hempel, C.: 1965, *Aspects of Scientific Explanation*, The Free Press.

Hintikka, J. and Tuomela, R.: 1970, 'Towards a General Theory of Auxiliary Concepts and Definability in First-Order Theories', in J. Hintikka and P. Suppes (eds.), *Information and Inference*, D. Reidel Publ. Co., Dordrecht-Holland, pp. 298–330.

Hull, C.: 1943, 'The Problem of Intervening Variables in Molar Behavior Theory', *Psychological Review* **50**. Reprinted in Marx, M. (1951), *Psychological Theory*, MacMillan, pp. 203–216; page references are made to the latter.

Littman, R. and Rosen, E.: 1950, 'Molar and Molecular', *Psychological Review* **57**. Reprinted in Marx, M. (1951), *Psychological Theory* **55**, 95–107.

MacCorquodale, K. and Meehl, P.: 1948, 'On a Distinction Between Hypothetical Constructs and Intervening Variables', *Psychological Review* **55**, 97–107.

Miller, G., Galanter, E., and Pribram, K.: 1960, *Plans and the Structure of Behavior*, Holt, Rinehart and Winston.

Nelson, R.: 1969, 'Behaviorism is False', *The Journal of Philosophy* **66**, 417–452.

Niiniluoto, I. and Tuomela, R.: 1973, *Theoretical Concepts and Hypothetico-Inductive Inference*, D. Reidel Publ. Co., Dordrecht-Holland.

Osgood, C.: 1953, *Method and Theory in Experimental Psychology*, Oxford University Press.

Osgood, C.: 1956, 'Behavior Theory and the Social Sciences', *Behavioral Science* **1**, 167–185.

Osgood, C.: 1966, 'Meaning Cannot be an r_m?', *Journal of Verbal Learning and Verbal Behavior* **5**, 402–407.

Osgood, C.: 1968, 'Toward a Wedding of Insufficiencies', in R. Dixon and D. Horton (eds.), *Verbal Behavior and General Behavior Theory*, Prentice Hall, pp. 495–519.

Przelecki, M.: 1969, *The Logic of Empirical Theories*, Routledge and Kegan Paul.

Skinner, B.: 1953, *Science and Human Behavior*, MacMillan.

Skinner, B.: 1961, *Cumulative Record*, enlarged edition, Appleton-Century-Crofts.

Spence, K.: 1948, 'The Methods and Postulates of Behaviorism', *Psychological Review* **55**, 67–78.

Suppes, P.: 1969, 'Stimulus Response Theory and Finite Automata', *Journal of Mathematical Psychology* **6**, 327–338.

Tolman, E.: 1936, 'Operational Behaviorism and Current Trends in Psychology', in *Proc. 25th Anniv. Celebr. Inaug. Grad. Stud.*, Univ. of South Calif. Press. Reprinted in Marx, M. (1951), *Psychological Theory*, MacMillan, pp. 87–102.

Tuomela, R.: 1968, 'The Application Process of a Theory', *Annales Academiae Scientiarum Fennicae, ser. B* **154**, 3.

Tuomela, R.: 1971, *The Role of Theoretical Concepts in Neobehavioristic Theories*, Reports from the Institute of Philosophy, University of Helsinki, No. 1, 66 p.

Tuomela, R.: 1972, 'A Psycholinguistic Paradox and Its Solution', forthcoming in *Ajatus* **35**.

Tuomela, R.: 1973, *Theoretical Concepts*, Springer-Verlag.

Woodrow, H.: 1942, 'The Problem of General Quantitative Laws in Psychology', *Psychological Bulletin* **39**, 1–27.

PART VI

POLITICAL SCIENCE

HARRY BEATTY

VOTING RULES AND COORDINATION
PROBLEMS*

ABSTRACT. Various conditions from social choice theory are discussed as they apply
to *actual* voting procedures. It is found that none of these conditions makes a very
interesting distinction among actual voting rules. Further, many of these conditions
are argued to be not universally acceptable. It is then shown that, especially in cases
in which there are more than two candidates, strategies are an essential part of voting,
and particularly strategies of the type associated with 'coordination problems' as
studied by Thomas C. Schelling. Some tentative acceptability conditions for voting
rules are set forth which attempt to take coordination strategies into account. These
are also found to be not universally acceptable.

1. VOTING RULES

Voting is a device employed by groups of people in order to make
collective decisions. Or, rather, it is a set of devices, for groups of people
adopt different voting procedures or rules. Some voting rules are discussed
briefly in this section.

A. *Unanimity Rule*

A unanimity rule is one which requires agreement by *all* members of a
group to reach a decision. One example of such a rule is the jury procedure
in the Anglo-American legal system, according to which all members
of a jury must vote 'guilty' for there to be a conviction, and all members
must vote 'not guilty' for there to be an acquittal. (Otherwise, in the
absence of unanimous agreement on the verdict, it is said that there is a
'hung jury' and the trial is nullified.)

Unanimity, when adopted by committees as a decision procedure, is
usually interpreted to mean that unanimous consent is required for any
proposed *change*, that and in the absence of complete consensus the
status quo is maintained. Thus this rule is a basically conservative procedure in which each committee member has a veto over any innovation.

B. *Majority Rule.*

If N is the number of people in a society or committee who vote on an

M. Bunge (ed.), *The Methodological Unity of Science*, 155–189. *All Rights Reserved.*
Copyright © 1973 *by D. Reidel Publishing Company, Dordrecht-Holland.*

issue, then for the society to adopt majority rule means that $(N/2)+1$ (if N is even) or $(N+1)/2$ (if N is odd) votes are sufficient to decide the issue. It is easy to see how majority rule functions in a situation in which there are just two alternatives or candidates. In such a situation the alternative or candidate with the most votes wins: if each alternative has the same number of votes, it is a tie. The *status quo* is not favoured in any way over a proposal to change it by this procedure.

It is less clear what majority rule means if there are more than two alternatives. Under one interpretation of majority rule, even if there are more than two candidates, voters just state their first preferences. Then if a, b and c are the three candidates in an election, this interpretation requires that a, to be elected, have one more vote than the other two candidates combined (and similarly for b or c to be elected). If this is the procedure adopted, then often no candidate will be elected. Because of this evident possibility of 'no decision', majority rule in this form is not used too often by committees, and is rarely used in large-scale political elections. When it is used it is usually part of a 'double election' system of some sort, in which another election is held if the majority election fails to give a result.

If a single election is desired, with the majority rule concept retained, what can be done is to obtain from each voter a list of his preferences among all candidates. Then it is possible to take into account second, third and even later preferences of voters in determining which candidate has a majority. An example of this kind of procedure is the alternative candidate ballot system. Under this system, if first preferences fail to produce a majority winner, the low candidate is eliminated and the second preferences on ballots cast for him as first choice are added to the first preference totals for other candidates. This process is repeated until one candidate has a majority.[1]

Majority rule with more than two candidates in a single election is more often interpreted in yet another way. Dahl says:

The principle of majority rule prescribes that in choosing among alternatives, the alternative preferred by the greater number is selected. That is, given two or more alternatives x, y, etc., in order for x to be government policy it is a necessary and sufficient condition that the number who prefer x to any alternative is greater than the number who prefer any single alternative to x.[2]

The basic idea here is that, if we have a list of his preferences among all candidates from each voter, we should see if some candidate has a majority against each opponent. If so, that candidate should be elected: if not, there is no decision. Since this procedure is suggested by the writings of Condorcet, I shall call it the Condorcet rule.

Now we have three procedures, each of which could reasonably be called 'majority rule'. These are:

MAJORITY RULE WITH FIRST PREFERENCES
ALTERNATIVE CANDIDATE BALLOT SYSTEM
CONDORCET RULE

No doubt other interpretations of majority rule are possible. At present, however, let us compare these three procedures by considering some possible situations in a society of 100 voters choosing among a, b, c and d.

It is clear that a winning candidate under majority rule with first preferences will win under the other two systems as well. But often there will be no winner under majority rule with first preferences, and the other systems will still produce a winner. Consider this situation:

Situation I

43	27	18	12
a	b	c	d
b	a	a	c
c	d	b	b
d	c	d	a

If only first preferences are counted, no candidate has a majority. Suppose the alternative candidate ballot system is being used. Then the first candidate to be eliminated will be d, and the second choice will be taken from the ballots on which d is first choice. Now c has 30 votes, and b is the low candidate. So b is eliminated and 27 votes go over to a, who is the winner. If the Condorcet rule is used, a is again the winner, since 61 voters prefer a to b, 70 voters prefer a to c and 88 voters prefer a to d, from a total of 100 voters.

If there is a winner in a given situation using the Condorcet rule, the same candidate must also win using the alternative candidate ballot system. For a can defeat b using the alternative candidate ballot system only if a majority of the voters rank a ahead of b. In the next situation, however, there is no winner using the Condorcet rule, but there is a winner using the alternative candidate ballot system. (*Situation* II is simply an instance of a 'cyclical majority', which gives rise to the 'voting paradox'.)

Situation II

27	26	24	23
a	b	c	d
b	c	d	a
c	d	a	b
d	a	b	c

There is no Condorcet rule winner here. Since 74 voters prefer *a* to *b*, 76 voters prefer *b* to *c*, 77 voters prefer *c* to *d*, but 73 voters prefer *d* to *a*, no candidate has a majority against all other candidates. Under the alternative candidate ballot system, *d* is eliminated first, giving 23 votes to *a* for a total of 50; and *c* is eliminated next, giving 24 more votes to *a* (since *d* has already been eliminated) and making *a* the winner. The alternative candidate ballot system will often declare a winner in situations where the Condorcet rule does not.

C. *Special Majority Rules*

It was mentioned above that unanimity rule makes change from the *status quo* difficult, while majority rule does not favour the *status quo* at all. An intermediate position with respect to the difficulty of instigating changes may be obtained by requiring a 60% or two-thirds majority to pass a new measure.

D. *Plurality Rule.*

Plurality rule is the 'first past the post' system, in which the candidate with the most votes is elected, with no consideration as to whether he has obtained a majority or not. This is the system most used often in general elections in Anglo-American countires.

E. *Borda Count*

Under this system, also called 'the method of marks', if there are *m* candidates each voter assigns *m* points to his first choice, *m*-1 points to his second choice, *m*-2 points to his third choice, and so on. Then the candidate with the highest total of points is the winner.

The voting rules mentioned so far are not meant, of cousre, to constitute any sort of comprehensive list. Many variations on these rules are
possible. Suppose there are three candidates in an election. It would be
possible to allow each voter to vote for *two* of the candidates, and
declare the candidate elected who got the most votes. Or the Condorcet
rule could be applied, followed by the Borda count if the Condorcet rule
failed to provide a winner. Another possibility is to use a system like
the Borda count but with a different distribution of points, for example
a 3-2-0 or3-1-0 rather than a 3-2-1 system.

Because of the variety and complexity of voting systems, actual as well
as possible, it is difficult to develop a formal framework for comparing
them, whether we wish the comparison to be of their respective acceptability, fairness, practicality, or any other characteristic. Consequently, in
this next section I shall discuss problems connected with the acceptability of voting rules informally, leaving the beginning of a formal treatment for Section 3.

2. Informal arguments about acceptability

There are a number of different ways in which voting rules or procedures
may be criticized. Some kinds of criticisms will be outlined and illustrated
in this section. Again, no claim is made that this list of criticisms is in
any way complete – in fact, further kinds of criticisms will be discussed in
later sections.

A. *'Intensities of Preference' Criticisms*

To illustrate this kind of criticism let us start with a simple situation.

Situation III

51	49
a	b
b	c
c	a

In this situation plurality voting or any system of majority voting
requires election of a, even though a is the last choice of 49 people and
b is the last choice of no one. This is true even if the members of the
majority are relatively indifferent among a, b and c while the members

of the minority have an intense preference for *b* over *a*. So the objection can be made that plurality or majority voting allows a diffident majority to have its way against an intense minority.

This kind of criticism of plurality and majority systems can be raised by supporters of the Borda count. For it is clear that the standard 3-2-1 Borda count or any system closely related to it will make *b* the easy winner in *Situation* III. But criticisms based on intensities of preference can be raised against the Borda count and related systems as well. In fact, in *Situation* III it can be pointed out that *b* is chosen by the Borda count even if the majority has an intense preference for *a* over *b* and the minority is relatively indifferent among the alternatives. Thus arguments for the Borda count based simply on intensities of preference are somewhat tenuous.

There are, of course, well-known problems connected with defining and collecting reliable information about intensities of preference. Because of these problems many theorists want to ban arguments based on intensities of preference from discussions of the acceptability of voting procedures. This point will be returned to in Section 7, where we discuss systems which attempt to allow for intensities of preference in a direct way.

B. *Criticisms Based on the Possibility of 'No Outcome'*

It has already been mentioned that systems like unanimity rule, majority rule with statement of first preferences only, and the Condorcet rule carry with them the real possibility that no candidate will be chosen. Systems like plurality voting and the Borda count are less open to criticism on this score, especially if the number of voters is large, even though these systems too leave open the possibility of a tie. For this reason the latter kind of system is often preferable (although a deadlock may in some situations be a desirable outcome).

C. *Criticisms Based on Considerations of Practicality*

Of course, voting rules can be criticized in some instances on the ground that they are too difficult to apply. It should be clear from Section 1 that gadgets of almost limitless complexity could be designed as voting rules. Besides the obvious costs entailed by using a too-complex system, however, there is the more subtle danger that a voter may have difficulty in determining the consequences of his vote. This is not only because he may not understand fully the mechanics of the system, but also because he may have available to him a number of *strategies* which are difficult for him to evaluate. This is a point which will be dealt with extensively later in this paper.

We have given brief statements, then, of a few types of criticism which can be applied to particular voting systems. These statements have been informal and the kinds of criticism have not been linked to explicit criteria for acceptability of voting systems. In the next section I shall begin to discuss some attempts to formulate standards of acceptability more rigorously.

3. FORMAL DEFINITION OF VOTING RULES

Beginning with the publication of Kenneth Arrow's *Social Choice aud Individual Values*[3], a substantial literature has been developed on the formal theory of collective choice. It is this literature which we shall now discuss, but with a somewhat narrower interpretation in mind than that intended by many of the theorists we shall be discussing. Arrow, in *Social Choice and Individual Values*, says explicitly that in developing his theory of social choice "the distinction between voting and the market mechanism will be disregarded." (SC & IV, p. 5) We, on the other hand, want to consider voting exclusively. This restriction in interpretation hopefully will make it easier for us to discuss various conditions which have been dealt with in the literature on social choice.

For discussion of voting procedures a formalism closely related to Arrow's, but slightly different, is desirable. Let us now begin to develop this formalism. The first decision that must be made is the nature of a *ballot*. How are we to represent formally the nature of the information which is obtained from the voters? This presents us with an immediate problem, for different voting rules require different kinds of information from the voters. Although we want a framework to compare different voting systems, the definition of what a 'ballot' is may at once rule out some systems and not allow us to deal with them.

Let us survey briefly how much information different voting rules may require from the electors. A simple statement of first choice is all that is required under unanimity rule or plurality voting. If the Condorcet rule, alternative candidate ballot system or Borda count is used, then voters must present a list or ordering of all alternatives or candidates. Other systems are possible in which voters give their first two or three choices, without necessarily giving a complete list. An example would be the system already mentioned in which each voter casts a ballot for two candidates and the candidate with the most total votes is declared the winner.

Still other systems may require even more information from the electors. Voters can be asked to assign *weights* or *points* to candidates, instead of merely listing them. (Such systems will be discussed in Section 7.) We can also think up systems which would require voters to state their preferences, not just among actual candidates, but also among actual candidates and potential candidates, or among actual candidates and probability mixtures of candidates (e.g., '*a* wins with probability 0.37, *b* wins with probability 0.63'). In such systems ballots could become extremely complex.

In the definition I am about to propose, a 'ballot' will be a list or ordering of all alternatives. Thus the definition corresponds exactly to the notion of a ballot used under the Condorcet rule, alternative candidate ballot system or Borda count. The definition also allows us to deal with systems which require only statements of first preferences, since ballots under such systems may be regarded as orderings in which all candidates except the first choice are ranked together. Similarly, the definition permits us to consider systems in which the first two or three choices are given.

Defining a 'ballot' as an ordering, however, does not let us deal with procedures which require the assigning of weights to candidates, or with systems which require ranking of non-candidates. At least it does not let us deal with such systems in a natural way. Consequently we postpone discussion of such systems until Section 7. In omitting these systems for the present, we allow ourselves to follow closely the formal development of social choice theory in Arrow and later writers; and we restrict our attention to the class of voting procedures in general use, since these seldom require more information from voters than a list. (*SC & IV*, p. 26)

Now for the definition itself. We introduce the symbol 'A' to stand for the set of alternatives or candidates, and say:

(*D1*)   A *ballot* is a transitive and connected relation on A.

By 'ballot' we mean what Arrow means by "individual ordering". (*SC & IV*, p. 23) We also follow Arrow in using 'R_i' to stand for the ballot of individual i, but in accordance with our narrower interpretation, we read 'aR_ib' somewhat differently than Arrow does. For Arrow, this notation means "i prefers a to b or is indifferent between them". (*SC & IV*, p. 12) For us, this notation means "i ranks a at least as high as b on his ballot". Note that this is a report on what i actually *does*: it is not necessarily a report on his subjective preferences with respect to a and b.

Our next two definitions are also taken from Arrow. (*SC & IV*, p. 14)

(*D2*) xP_iy if and only if not yR_ix
(*D3*) xI_iy if and only if xR_iy and yR_ix

We read 'aP_ib' as "i ranks a above b" and 'aI_ib' as "i ranks a and b together".

(*D1*) makes the notion of a list or ordering precise, in requiring that a ballot be a relation which is transitive and connected. Given (*D2*) and (*D3*), we can state the transitivity assumption as follows (for convenience it is broken down into four different sub-assumptions):

A. *Transitivity*

Let V be the set of voters. For every $i \in V$, and for all $x, y, z \in A$

(*T1*)   If xP_iy and yP_iz, then xP_iz.
(*T2*)   If xP_iy and yI_iz, then xP_iz.
(*T3*)   If xI_iy and yP_iz, then xP_iz.
(*T4*)   If xI_iy and yI_iz, then xI_iz.

Some theorists (including Arrow) accept this transitivity assumption as a general constraint on preference rankings. They view transitivity as a necessary condition for 'rationality' or 'consistency'. (*SC & IV*, pp. 12–13) Given our restricted interests, however, it does not seem necessary to defend the dubious connection between transitivity and rationality.[4] It is enough to note that actual voting procedures rarely allow voters to express intransitive preferences, and it is such procedures which we are mainly concerned with here. Further, it would require a considerable complication of theory to allow for procedures which admit intransitive choices by voters. On these pragmatic grounds we accept transitivity.

The situation is similar with respect to connectedness. Using our notation we can put the connectedness assumption as:

B. *Connectedness*

For all $i \epsilon V$ and all $x, y \in A$, either xP_iy or xI_iy or yP_ix.

If we were discussing preferences on an arbitrary set A, this would be a dubious assumption. But as an assumption about ballots connectedness seems uncontroversial. It is true that actual procedures *apparently* allow violations of connectedness. Someone could argue: "Ordinary plurality voting just makes voters name a first choice, not compare other candidates." But this is *only* an apparent violation of connectedness, as may be seen by considering this slightly different description of plurality voting. "Plurality voting allows voters to name a first choice but makes them state all other alternatives to be indifferent." When described in this way, it is clear that plurality voting can be viewed without much distortion as satisfying connectedness, and the same is true of other actual voting procedures.

Having defined 'ballot', we can go on to define 'situation'. We have already used this term to refer to a collection of ballots: our formal definition agrees with this usage. To state the definition we use the expression 'A-ballot' to refer to a transitive and connected ordering on A.

(D4)   Let $R_1, R_2,..., R_n$ be A-ballots. Then $\langle R_1, R_2, ..., R_n \rangle$ is a *situation* (*A-situation*). ($n \geqslant 2$)

Note that we have ruled out the trivial case in which there is only one 'voter', in order to simplify later formal developments.

Next we turn to the main definition of this section.

(D5)   A *voting rule* is a function from a class of situations to sets of alternatives, satisfying the restriction that an A-situation must be mapped into a subset of A. If S is an A-situation, and a voting rule is defined for S, then the value of the voting function at S is denoted by $W(S) \subseteq A$. $W(S)$ is called "the set of winners in S".

There are several comments to be made about (D5). First, note that in each situation a voting rule gives a *set* of winners. It is necessary to allow for a set of winners, rather than a single winner, because of the possibility of ties under voting rules. The possibility of a rule *designed* to give more than one winner (such as might be used in a multi-member electoral district) is also allowed for.

Arrow, in defining a 'social welfare function', requires that it give as values, not just sets of winners, but also a complete ordering of all alternatives. (*SC & IV*, p. 23) Of course, Arrow intends that 'social welfare functions' have interpretations other than as voting rules, and for some of these other interpretations a complete ordering may be desirable. In the voting case, however, the ranking of non-winners is comparatively unimportant, and it is the voting interpretation we are considering here.[5] There is a considerable theoretical advantage to our definition of 'voting rule' as well, in that we do not have to build the controversial assumptions of transitivity and connectedness of *social* preferences for alternatives into our definition. (Sen's definition of 'social decision functions' shares a similar advantage.[6])

A final point. Our intuitive idea of a voting rule, I think, is that it determines the winner or winners in a situation by computing the information on the ballots *in certain specified ways*. If as a voting procedure we were told to invert all prime numbered ballots, interchange the first and fourth choices on the rest and then apply the Borda count, we would object that this was not a voting system at all. Yet by (*D5*) this would count as a 'voting rule', since (*D5*) does not specify how a voting function must be computed.

Amending (*D5*) to specify 'permitted' operations for calculating the outcome of elections, and approximating in this way sufficient conditions for voting rules, seems more or less hopeless. Further, it is not really necessary for the enterprise we have in mind. For in the next sections we are going to consider conditions of acceptability for voting rules. and those conditions we accept should rule out as 'unacceptable' odd procedures for determining winners. Thus it will do no harm to allow odd procedures to be 'voting rules', since we should be able to disqualify them from being 'acceptable voting rules', by formulating necessary conditions for the latter. To this task we now turn.

4. PRELIMINARY CONDITIONS

Various acceptability conditions for social choice procedures have been discussed in the literature. In this and the next two sections I shall reformulate some of these conditions within the present formal development and try to evaluate them. In making these evaluations, emphasis will be placed on the question of which actual voting procedures satisfy the conditions, rather than on questions about how the conditions themselves are formally inter-related.

The conditions discussed in this section are relatively unimportant, although they raise some questions about how our formalism should be interpreted. Consequently my account of these conditions will be brief. More lengthy discussions will be given of other conditions in Sections 5 and 6.

A. *Unrestricted Domain*

The idea behind this condition is that a voting rule must give a result in every possible situation, even though the result may sometimes be a tie.

(*C1*)   A voting rule satisfies the condition of unrestricted domain if and only if for every A-situation S where A is finite there is a non-empty set of winners $W(S)$.

Here we require that a voting rule give a result for every collection of ballots which are listings of a finite number of candidates. We do not worry about the case where there is an infinite number of alternatives because this never happens with actual voting procedures.

Is (*C1*) a reasonable condition? What (*C1*) does is rule out procedures like the Condorcet rule and majority rule with first preferences where 'no outcome' is a likely result. We saw in Section 2 that 'no outcome' may involve serious practical disadvantages, so from this point of view (*C1*) is justified. It is also true, however, that 'no outcome' may in some. circumstances be a better result than election of any particular candidate (It may, for example, give time in which to formulate a compromise.) Practical considerations may be brought in as arguments against (*C1*), then, and from a pragmatic point of view the status of (*C1*) is unclear. Further, even if some kind of 'closure' condition is thought necessary, it arguable that (*C1*) is too strong. For it seems reasonable to admit a voting procedure if it covers all but a few cases, especially if those cases seem unlikely to occur. Thus (*C1*) seems doubtful as a *general* requirement on voting procedures. Whether or not we want to rule out the possibility of 'no outcome' depends heavily on features of the particular situation such as whether the balloting can be repeated and whether there is a real possibility of formulating compromises.

B. *Pareto-Optimality*

Two rules contain the main idea behind Pareto-optimality. The first is that if all voters are indifferent between a and b, neither should win an election while the other loses. The second is that if one voter ranks a ahead of b, and no voter ranks b ahead of a, the outcome of the election should rank a ahead of b. (CC & SW, p. 21)

Let us introduce the notation 'R_i^S' for "the ballot of voter i in situation S", and the analogous notation 'P_i^S' and 'I_i^S'. We formulate Pareto-optimality using this notation.

(C2)   A voting rule satisfies the condition of Pareto-optimality if and only if, for every A-situation S:

(a)   if $xI_i^S y$ for every $i \in V$, then $x \in W(S)$ if and only if $y \in W(S)$

(b)   if $A = \{x, y\}$, $xR_i^S y$ for every $i \in V$, and $xP_j^S y$ for some $j \in V$, then $W(S) = \{x\}$.

(c)   if $xR_i^S y$ for every $i \in V$, and $xP_j^S y$ for some $j \in V$, then $y \notin W(S)$

(d)   if $xR_i^S z$ for every $z \in A$ and every $i \in V$, and if for every $w \neq x \in A$ there is a $j \in V$ such that $xP_j^S w$, then $W(S) = \{x\}$.

By (C2a) we have the condition that if every voter is indifferent between two alternatives, either both are winners or neither is. (C2b) says that if one alternative is ranked first by someone and second by no one in a two-candidate situation, that alternative is the sole winner. (C2c) gives us that a 'dominated' alternative can never be a winner, while (C2d) says that if one alternative is ranked above each other alternative by someone or other, and is never ranked below any other alternative, it is the sole winner. (Clearly (C2d) is a generalization of, and entails, (C2b)).

Do the rules discussed so far satisfy the various parts of the Pareto-optimality rule? All satisfy (C2a), since in any rule we have mentioned no alternative can defeat another without some voter ranking them differently. All satisfy (C2c), since no rule yet discussed allows a 'dominated' alternative to win. Plurality voting and the Borda count also satisfy (*C2b*) and (*C2d*).

Whether the other rules satisfy (*C2b*) and (*C2d*) depends on whether these rules are interpreted as allowing voters to rank alternatives together on their ballots, and, if this is permitted, on how these ties to are be counted under the rule. Consider the unanimity rule. If ranking alternatives together is not permitted, then either there is a unanimous first choice which wins or there is 'no outcome'. In the first case, (*C2b*) and (*C2d*) are clearly satisfied: in the second case, *no* alternative 'dominates' every other so again (*C2b*) and (*C2d*) are satisfied.

Now suppose that ranking alternatives together is permitted. This leads to the question of how to use ballots with ties on them in determining who wins. On one interpretation of unanimity rule, a candidate must be ranked *strictly* above every other on every ballot to win. Thus tied ballots are counted as breaking the consensus. If unanimity rule is interpreted in this way, it violates (*C2b*) and (*C2d*). However, if unanimity rule is interpreted so that tied ballots are disregarded in determining if a consensus exists, then (*C2b*) and (*C2d*) are satisfied.

The same is true of the various kinds of majority rule and of the different special majority rules. If ranking alternatives together is not permitted, (*C2b*) and (*C2d*) are satisfied. If a majority of *all* voters (including those who cast tied ballots) is required, these parts of the Pareto-optimality rule are violated. If a majority of those voters who actually express a preference is all that is required, (*C2b*) and (*C2d*) are satisfied.

How far does (*C2*) take us in distinguishing acceptable voting from unacceptable ones? It rules out all kinds of odd voting procedures that could be devised, of course, but does it provide a useful criterion to be applied to actual voting procedures? I think the answer must be no. First, (*C2*) rules out none of the procedures we have discussed altogether: it just disallows the combination of some of these procedures with extra rules permitting alternatives to be ranked together by voters. Second, it is by no means clear that the special procedures which are ruled out by (*C2*) are *generally* unacceptable. If it is required by a community that a majority be a majority of *all* voters (including those who cast tied ballots) for a new measure to be passed, this gives an interpretation of majority rule which favours the *status quo*. But this may be desirable or not, depending on the circumstances. In some circumstances it is better to favour the *status quo*, especially on issues where many voters are undecided. Thus that this procedure violates (*C2*) may in some circumstances be an argument in its *favour* rather than a criticism.

C. *Anonymity*

This kind of condition was first suggested by K. O. May.[7] The basic idea is that all voters are equal: that a voting rule does not allow for one man's vote counting for more than another's. This condition is easy to state:

> (*C3*)   Let S and S' be situations differing *only* by a permutation of ballots. Then $W(S) = W(S')$.

(*C3*) is met by all rules discussed so far. It is not met by a procedure like that used in the United Nations Security Council, where the permanent members have a veto but the other members do not. Special circumstances may well justify discrimination among voters, so from this point of view (*C3*) does not seem promising as a general requirement on voting systems. However, accepting (*C3*) does simplify matters by restricting our attention to those voting situations in which equality among voters should be assumed, and so I shall accept (*C3*) here. This is just a pragmatic restriction on the scope of our inquiry: (*C3*) does not discriminate among the kind of voting rules we have considered in any interesting way.

D. *Neutrality*

This is another condition due to May.[7] Neutrality is intended to rule out discrimination among alternatives, just as anonymity rules out discrimination among voters.

> (*C4*)   Let S and S' be situations differing *only* by a permutation of alternatives. Then $W(S)$ and $W(S')$ differ only by the same permutation of alternatives.

Like anonymity, neutrality is accepted here as a matter of convenience. What it rules out are those *uses* of unanimity rule, special majority rules or other which favour any special alternative (e.g., the *status quo*). It is useful to limit our inquiry by not considering these special cases, but (*C4*) does not provide any real insight into their acceptability. No *kind* of voting rule which we have discussed is rules out in general by (*C4*).

E. *Non-Dictatorship*

Conditions intended to rule out the possibility of a dictator are common in the literature on social choice, beginning with Arrow's own work. (*SC & IV*, p. 30) However, these conditions are usually much weaker than the equality conditions we have just accepted: that is, it is difficult to formulate a non-dictatorship condition which is not implied by anonymity and neutrality. Hence we shall not discuss such conditions here.

None of the conditions discussed in this section divides up voting rules in any way relevant to their acceptability. These conditions do rule out certain *applications* of voting procedures, but even when they rule out these applications, they do not seem to provide any rationale for doing so. Rather, it seems that in those cases in which applications of voting rules conflict with these conditions, it is more natural to say that the conditions are too narrow than it is to say that reasons have been given against the applications. Neutrality and anonymity have been accepted, but only in a provisional way and for the pragmatic reason that accepting these conditions limits usefully the scope of our inquiry.

5. POSITIVE RESPONSIVENESS

In this and the next section we shall discuss two acceptability conditions which are more important. The condition discussed in this section is based on one of Arrow's original conditions. (*SC & IV*, pp. 25–26)

(*C5*)   Let S be an A-situation and let $a \in W(S)$. Let S' be an A-situation meeting the following conditions:
for all $i \in V$ and all $x \in A$, if $aI_i^S x$ then $aR_i^{S'} x$
for all $i \in V$ and all $x \in A$, if $aP_i^S x$ then $aP_i^{S'} x$
for all $i \in V$ and all $x, y \in A$ such that $x \neq a$ and $y \neq a$, $xR_i^S y$ if and only if $xR_i^{S'} y$.
Then $a \in W(S')$.

What (*C5*) says is that if a is a winner in S, if in S' every voter ranks a at least as high with respect to every other alternative as he did in S, and if no voter ranks any *other* alternatives differently in S' than in S, then *a* should be a winner in *S'* as well. This is intended to guarantee that no alternative should be penalized by voters who *raise* it in their ballots.

Let us see what distinctions (*C5*) is capable of making among the voting rules we have discussed. Unanimity rule, majority rule with first preferences, the Condorcet rule, special majority rules and plurality rule all satisfy (*C5*), since under none of these systems can a voter help defeat a candidate by voting for him or by raising him in his list. Further, the Borda count satisfies (*C5*), since under this system a voter cannot help defeat a candidate by raising his point count. But the alternative candidate ballot system is disqualified by (*C5*).

We show this by comparing *Situation* II (in Section 1) with the following situation:

Situation IV

27	26	22	23	2
a	b	c	d	a
b	c	d	a	c
c	d	a	b	d
d	a	b	c	b

In *Situation* IV, only two voters have changed their ballots from *Situation* II. Since these voters have altered their lists to '*acdb*' from '*cdab*', both have raised *a* in their ballots and neither has raised any other alternative or changed its ranking with respect to an alternative other than *a*. Yet *d* wins under the alternative candidate ballot system in *Situation* IV (note that *c* is eliminated first and *b* second, and both eliminations give votes to *d*). Since *a* won in *Situation* II, this violates (*C5*).

Further, (*C5*) provides a *rationale* for rejecting the alternative candidate ballot system. Consider the two voters who changed their ballots from *Situation* II to *Situation* IV. If these voters really preferred *a* to *d*, then ranking *a* first defeats their purpose of electing *a*. They would have been better off to adopt the *strategy* of ranking the alternatives '*cdab*', misrepresenting their true preferences. Conversely, if they really preferred *d* to *a*, they have successfully adopted a strategy of misrepresenting their true preferences. Thus the alternative candidate ballot system lends itself to strategies of voting contrary to actual preferences, and (*C5*) rules it out on this basis.

Positive responsiveness, then, is basically a 'non-strategy' condition

when applied to voting rules. It rules out one of the voting procedures
we discussed in Section 1, the alternative candidate ballot system. Yet,
as we shall see, this condition is only a small beginning in dealing with
the problems connected with strategies in voting. Strategy will be our
main concern throughout the remainder of this paper.

6. INDEPENDENCE OF IRRELEVANT ALTERNATIVES

In this section we consider one more of Arrow's conditions, the independence or irrelevant alternatives. Arrow gives the idea behind this condition, when applied to voting procedures, as follows:

> Suppose that an election system has been devised whereby each individual lists all
> the candidates in order of his preference and then, by a preassigned procedure, the
> winning candidate is derived from these lists.... Suppose that an election is held, with
> a certain number of candidates in the field, each individual filing his list of preferences,
> and then one of the candidates dies. Surely the social choice should be made by taking
> each of the individual's preference lists, blotting out completely the dead candidate's
> name, and considering only the orderings of the remaining names in going through
> the procedure of determining the winner. That is, the choice to be made among the
> set S of surviving candidates should be independent of the preferences of individuals
> for candidates not in S. (SC & IV, p. 26)

Within our formal development the condition suggested by Arrow in
this passage is best rendered as:

(C6)   Let S be an A-situation, and let $A' \subseteq A \sim W(S)$. If all the
        members of A' are delected from the ballots in S, this gives
        a new situation T such that $W(T) = W(S)$.

(C6) says that if candidates not in the set of winners are dropped from
the ballots in a situation, the set of winners remains unchanged. This
seems to be implied by Arrow's remarks.

Which of the voting rules already discussed are disqualified by (C6)?
We see first that *if* the ballots which voters submit are actually complete
lists of alternatives, *all* of our procedures are disqualified.

Situation V

40	30	30
a	c	d
b	a	a
c	b	b
d	d	c

In *Situation* V there is no majority rule winner, so of course there is no special majority or unanimity rule winner. If the non-winner *c* and *d* are dropped, however, *a* becomes a unanimous first choice and thus a winner under unanimity rule and any kind of majority rule. So unanimity rule, special majority rules and the different varieties of majority rule all violate (*C6*).

Situation VI

40	35	25
a	b	c
b	a	b
c	c	a

In *Situation* VI the plurality winner is *a*, but if the non-winner *c* is deleted, the plurality winner is now *b*. Thus plurality rule aslo violates our version of independence of irrelevant alternatives.

Finally, the Borda count does not satisfy (*C6*), as may be seen by considering *Situation* III (in Section 2). In this situation *b* is the Borda count winner, but if *c* is deleted *a* becomes the Borda count winner.

So independence of irrelevant alternatives, as formulated here, is a powerful condition indeed. It rules out, it seems, all the procedures we have discussed for combining lists of candidates. Why is it so powerful? Intuitively the answer is this. (*C6*) says that if alternatives not in the set of winners are dropped, the set of winners remains unchanged. This implies that if alternatives not in a situation *S* are *added* to it, W(*S*) remains the same so long as the 'new' alternatives do not become members of W(*S*). This precludes any strategy that may be adopted by voters using the new alternatives: it requires that from the point of view of voting strategy the situation without the new alternatives must be just the same as the situation with them. This is truly a strong 'non-strategy' condition.

At this point there are three possible attitudes which we can take towards (*C6*). (i) We can view it as too strong to be an acceptability condition on voting rules and simply reject it. (ii) We can accept it and use it as an argument for demanding *less* information from the voters than a list of all their preferences. (iii) We can accept it and use it as an argument for demanding *more* information from the voters than a list of all their preferences. The remainder of this section will be devoted to (i) and (ii): discussion of (iii) is postponed until Section 7.

If we reject (*C6*), this amounts to accepting a certain number of strategic elements in an 'acceptable' voting procedure. One example is discussed here: there will be a fuller treatment of the acceptability of strategy in Section 8.

Consider a society of 100 voters about to have an election using plurality rule in which a and b are the candidates. Suppose that the supporters of a think that they are in the minority. One strategy they can adopt is to nominate a third candidate, c, as much like b as possible, so that some of the voters may change their votes from b to c. If the majority who favour the viewpoint of b and c split their votes between them, a may well win with a plurality of the vote, despite being a representative of a minority opinion. Such 'vote-splitting' is common in real elections. The strategy adopted by the supporters of a here may be thought unacceptable in a voting system for the reason expressed in (*C6*): c is basically an 'independent alternative', and if it were dropped, b would win. But if we find this kind of strategy to be acceptable in a voting procedure, we may want to reject (*C6*).

Now we turn to possibility (ii). Suppose we accept (*C6*). We can then argue that if voters are limited to stating their first preferences, i.e., handing in 'lists' of one alternative, (*C6*) is satisfied, and thus that the solution to problems of strategy may involve restricting the information required from voters to first choices.

It is easy to see that the 'first preference' procedures we have considered all satisfy independence of irrelevant alternatives as explained by Arrow. In all situations under all such systems, if there is a winner it is the alternative with the most votes. But then deleting the ballots for another alternative cannot give a thrid more votes than the winner, nor can it decrease the winner's percentage share of the total vote. This is what Arrow has in mind when he says that 'every known electoral system' satisfies the condition of the independence of irrelevant alternatives (*SC & IV*, p. 110).

That 'first preference' procedures satisfy independence of irrelevant alternatives is not, however, a strong argument in their favour. For such procedures admit strategies by voters similar to those found in systems requiring lists of preferences. Take the 'vote-splitting' situation discussed above. It is clear that the strategy of introducing c as a candidate is the same whether voters put down their second choices or not, since second choices are not counted under plurality rule. The strategic situation is not affected at all by whether voters submit first choices or lists. Thus that ($C6$) allows 'first preference' procedures while ruling out the corresponding 'complete list' procedures is simply an accidental result of our formal development: it does not tell us anything about the relative merits of the two kinds of procedures.

7. Weighted voting

When we defined a 'ballot' as an ordering in Section 3, we noted that our definition did not allow us to deal with voting procedures in which weights or points are assigned to alternatives. In this section we consider two such systems briefly.

A. *Split Weight Option Scheme.*

Each ballot is assigned a numerical weight. (Since we assumed anonymity, every voter's ballot is assigned the *same* weight.) Each voter distributes the weight of his vote among the alternatives in any way he sees fit. He also has the option of withholding any part of the weight of his vote. The alternative with the highest total weight wins.[8]

B. *Utilitarian Voting System*

Some arbitrary weight range is chosen, say 1 to 10, and each voter assigns every alternative some weight in the range. The alternative with the highest total weight wins.

Variations on these systems are possible, of course. In the interests of simplification we may require that *integral* weights be assigned. Or we can attempt to reduce the effects of extreme judgments by a few voters. This can be done by discarding a few of the very high or very low scores for each candidate, or by adopting a more complicated function than simple addition for combining the scores.

The interest of these systems to us here is that they satisfy the condition of independence of irrelevant alternatives *as we have formulated it*.[9] Suppose we delete the weights assigned to a defeated alternative under the split weight option scheme, i.e., we treat these weights as 'withheld'.

This clearly does not affect who wins. Similarly, deleting the scores for one candidate under the utilitarian voting system leaves unchanged the scores of the other candidates, and does not affect who wins. This illustrates possibility (iii) of the previous section: retain (C6) and demand more information from the voters (in this case information about their *intensities* of preference).

Unfortunately, that these systems satisfy (C6) just point to the limitations of (C6) as a 'non-strategy' condition. For these systems certainly allow for strategic decisions: in fact, they often require such decisions. The split weight option scheme lends itself to 'vote-splitting' in much the same way as plurality rule does. If the opponents have to split the weight of their ballots among similar candidates, so much the better for our candidate.

The utilitarian voting system does not lend itself to 'vote-splitting', or at least not in so straightforward a way. But it shares a second kind of strategic decision with the split weight option scheme. This is the decision of how much weight to assign to one's *second* choice, when there are at least three candidates (and to one's third choice, when there are at least four candidates, and so on). If the second choice is assigned too much weight, this may help it to defeat the first choice. If it is assigned too little weight, this may help a lower choice to win. Further, the more ways one has to fill out one's ballot, the more possible strategies there are. So, while the systems discussed in this section satisfy the independence of irrelevant alternatives, it is arguable that they involve even more strategic possibilities than some systems which do not satisfy this condition.

8. VOTING STRATEGY AND COORDINATION PROBLEMS

Considerations of voting strategy played an increasingly important role in the previous three sections of this paper. In Section 5 we saw that the condition of positive responsiveness rules out voting procedures in some cases where these procedures allow for the strategy of misrepresenting one's true preferences. In particular, the alternative candidate ballot system is ruled out by this condition. In Section 6 it was pointed out that the condition of independence of irrelevant alternatives rules out all procedures allowing for strategies having to do with adding or dropping candidates from the ballot before the election (e.g., trying to induce 'vote-splitting' by nominating an extra candidate). Since none of the procedures we considered met this condition, this raised the possibility that *all* voting rules may inherently contain some element of strategy.[10] This suggestion was strengthened by arguments which showed that even 'weighted voting' systems, which meet the condition of independence of irrelevant alternatives, contain a large element of strategy (Section 7).

The element of strategy in an election is markedly decreased if there are only two alternatives. In a majority rule election with only two candidates, a vector cannot help his candidate to win by misrepresenting his preferences and voting for the other candidate. Nor does a voter have to decide whether he wants to help his first choice to win or his second choice to win. His only reasonable strategy is to vote for his first preference.

This observation gives us some insight into the value of a two-party system, into the usefulness of polarizing opinion into two opposing camps. (c.f. *SC & IV*, p. 48) Strategies multiply as soon as a third candidate is introduced, while the two-party system lends itself to 'honest voting'. Unfortunately, often there are more than two points of view with widespread popular acceptance, and so the number of alternatives increases.

As soon as a third candidate is introduced, however, strategy reappears. This is so even if the candidates are voted on in pairs with losers being eliminated. For under this procedure, if a voter prefers a and b above all other candidates, and there is a vote between a and b, the voter must decide not only which of a and b he likes the best but also which is more likely to defeat all the other candidates.

Since voting rules cannot reasonably be required to be 'strategy-free', then, useful acceptability conditions for voting rules must take the element of strategy into account. Prior to attempting a formulation of such conditions, it will prove useful to look at the nature of voting strategy more closely. We start by considering some examples.

Suppose Jones is a member of a seven-man committee deciding among alternatives a, b and c by plurality rule. Suppose further that Jones has a strong preference for a, and a slight preference for b over c. What strategy should Jones adopt? This depends on several features of the situation.

If Jones has no opportunity to confer with his fellow committee members prior to voting, then he should simply vote *a*, and hope that two or three others agree with him. This is an unusual situation, however. Usually in small committees there is an opportunity for prior discussion.

Now let us assume that Jones does have a chance to talk things over with the others before they vote, and that he is able to find out that three others also have *a* as first choice. Jones should now vote for *a*, but he should also take steps to ensure that the others who have *a* as first choice actually vote for *a* as well. For if one of these others adopts the strategy of voting for his second choice, *a* may not be elected, even though a clear majority prefers *a*.

Jones and the other committee members who favour *a* are faced with what is known in game theory as a 'coordination problem'. (Such problems are studied in great detail in Thomas C. Schelling's *The Strategy of Conflict*.[11]) Each prefers *a*, and they can elect *a* if they all vote for it. The only problem they face is that one of them may not believe that *a* can win and may vote for his second choice. To overcome this problem Jones may announce that he is going to vote for *a*: if he is permitted to do so, he can even mark his ballot publicly for *a*. This is a *strategy of commitment* (such strategies are discussed at length by Schelling). By committing himself to vote for *a*, Jones encourages the other supporters of *a* to do the same. If all four committee members who favour *a* announce their intention to vote for *a*, this will constitute a strong coalition to elect *a*. No one is likely to have a good reason for entering such a coalition and then *not* voting for *a*, since the whole purpose of the strategy of commitment is to induce others to vote for *a*, and one would ordinarily not want to induce others to vote for *a* unless he himself supported *a*.

We can bring out the nature of other possible strategies by assuming the same circumstances with only one change: Jones is able to find only *two* friends, say Brown and Smith, who also support *a*. What Jones, Brown and Smith decide to do depends on the *information* they have about the preferences and probable behaviour of the other four members of the committee. If they find out that the other members of the committee all support *b* and have a firm commitment to vote for *b*, no strategy will help them elect *a*. (More precisely, *no voting strategy on the present balloting* will help them elect *a*. They can, of course, try to induce supporters of *b* to vote for *a* by means *external* to the present election. They can offer side payments or bribes to the other committee members: alternatively, they can threaten them. Such external inducements can be in the form of money or promises to vote in a certain way on later matters or any currency that the other committee members will accept. Such 'external strategies' will be disregarded in the present section: we return to them briefly in Section 10.)

What if Jones, Brown and Smith find out that two other members of the committee are irrevocably committed to vote for *b*, while the remaining two members are committed to *c*? In this case Jones, Brown and Smith can vote for *a* confidently, knowing that they are a plurality although not a majority.

Another possibility is that Jones, Brown and Smith may learn that there is a three-man coalition backing *b*, while the seventh member of committee, Russell, is undecided. Clearly in this case what they need is for Russell to vote for *a*. If they know that *a* is Russell's first choice, they can adopt a straightforward strategy of commitment, trying to convince Russell that all of them are going to vote for *a*. Then if Russell likes *c* almost as well as *a*, he will have a good reason for deciding in favour of *a* when it comes time for him to vote.

Suppose that Russell prefers *c* to *a*, however, while preferring both of these to *b*. Here Jones, Brown and Smith can commit themselves to *a*, but they must allow for the possibility that Russell may vote for *c* in the hope that the other three committee members will support him. Now it is in Jones', Brown's and Smith's interest to adopt a *strategy of information*. They should inform Russell that all the other committee members have joined in a coalition backing *b*, as well as informing him that they themselves are committed to *a*. This hopefully will convince him that *c* has no chance of winning, and that he should vote for *a* which is his second choice. By showing Russell what the true situation is, Jones, Smith and Brown may very well be able to induce him to vote for *a*.

If Jones, Brown and Smith can get Russell to vote with them by telling him that no one else supports *c*, as in the previous example, might it be in their interest to do so if it is *not* true? The answer is yes. Consider Russell's position. He prefers *c*, but he will vote for *a* if *c* has no chance of winning. If Jones, Brown and Smith can convince him not only that they will not vote for *c* but also that no one else will either, he will vote for *a*.

Thus it is in the interest of Jones, Brown and Smith to convince Russell that the unnamed committee members are all committed to *b*, even if this is not true. This is not a strategy of information on their part but a *strategy of misinformation*. They hope to convince Russell falsely that a vote for *c* is pointless, and thus complete their majority for *a*.

The possibilities for strategies of misinformation are endless. Russell may lie about *his* preferences: he may say that he prefers *c* to *b* but also prefers *b* to *a*. If he informs Jones, Brown and Smith that these are his preferences, he can also threaten to vote for *b* unless they all vote for *c*. The success of this strategy depends on Russell's convincing Jones, Brown and Smith that he really holds the 'balance of power' and that he really will use his position to elect *b* if necessary.

Yet another possibility is that two members of a seven-man committee may represent themselves as a three-man coalition. If they can convince another member that they speak for three voters rather than just two, their bargaining position with respect to that member is greatly strengthened. It is easy to see that the possibilities for forming coalitions and adopting strategies of commitment, information and misinformation are extensive even for a small committee. It is also clear that such opportunities exist under voting rules other than plurality rule, although this is the rule that was discussed in our examples.

It will be useful at this point to list the kinds of voting strategies we have encountered thus far. It should be emphasized again that this list is highly selective: it does not include many of the 'strategies' that would be encountered in a real election. Rahter the strategies listed here are those which I think meet two rather vague criteria: (a) they are strategies connected with the balloting itself rather than with the wider social context in which an election is held; (b) they are strategies connected with a *single* balloting rather than with a series of votes. (Mention will be made of some strategies *not* meeting these criteria in Section 10.)

A. *Misrepresentation of Preferences*

This refers to 'dishonest voting': putting a less preferred alternative over a more preferred one on a ballot.

B. *Strategies of Altering the Set of Candidates*

These include all strategies aimed at preventing or inducing the phenomenon of 'vote-splitting', by controlling the nomination of candidates.

C. *Strategies of Commitment*

D. *Strategies of Information*

E. *Strategies of Misinformation*

In concluding this section I shall indicate briefly how these strategies work in a large society as opposed to a small committee. Communication is typically much more uncertain if it is among a large number of people. This uncertainty of communication can be expected to have an effect on voting strategy.

Under plurality voting in a large society, it is often in one's interest not to vote for one's first choice. Just as in a committee, one must take into account which alternative is likely to win. Strategies of altering the set of candidates to *avoid* 'vote-splitting' are also common. In particular, candidates often eliminate themselves from an election in an effort to help another candidate with similar views. Strategies of altering the set of candidates to *produce* 'vote-splitting' are less usual. In a plurality election, one faction may be tempted to nominate a candidate with *opposing* views to theirs in order to increase the number of opposition candidates, but they are usually prevented from doing this by nomination procedures, and by the fact that a candidate will almost certainly not accept a nomination if it comes from the opposing camp.[12]

We saw earlier that *information* plays a crucial role in committee voting. It is important in the same way in a larger society, but as the size of the society increases, the information becomes increasingly unreliable. It is instructive to look at communication, and its relation to strategies of commitment, information, and misinformation, in an actual electoral situation.

In Great Britain, general elections in recent times have involved two major parties, Labour and the Conservatives, one smaller party, the Liberals (who get typically between 5% and 10% of the popular vote), and some tiny parties which can be disregarded for our purposes. Pulzer describes some of the strategies adopted in British election campaigns as follows (remember that plurality rule is used in Britain):

In 1964 and 1966 Liberal posters bore the slogan 'If you think like a Liberal, vote like a Liberal'; in 1950 a Conservative poster (showing a torn ballot paper) read, 'A vote for a Liberal is a vote wasted'. In both 1950 and 1952 the Gallup Poll asked electors whether they would vote Liberal if they thought the Liberals could win. In 1950 34% said 'yes', compared with 9% who actually did: in 1962, just after the Orpington success, 46% said 'yes'.[13]

Clearly the Liberal supporters, especially in 1962, were faced with a coordination problem they did not solve. If they had actually been able to muster 46% of the vote in the next general election in 1964, and Labour and the Conservatives had divided the rest of the vote at all evenly, they would have stood an excellent chance of forming the government under the single-member plurality rule system. Yet when the election actually took place they received just over 11% of the vote and remained a small third party with 9 out of 630 seats.[14]

After the results of the 1962 Gallup Poll became known it was clearly in the interest of the Liberal Party to publicize these results. By doing so they would try to convince voters that a vote for a Liberal was not 'a vote wasted'. This is a straightforward example of a strategy of information.

But this strategy by itself would not be very effective. To convince voters that they were a real alternative, the Liberals would not only have to inform them that other voters were *in principle* ready to vote Liberal. They would have to convince the voters that other voters were actually *going* to vote Liberal, and in large numbers. What would be required in addition would be a strategy of *commitment*. A better slogan than 'If you think like a Liberal, vote like a Liberal' would have been 'People are thinking Liberal and are going to vote Liberal'.

Strategies of commitment are much trickier in large societies than in committees, however. It doesn't help much in this situation to have a few undistinguished voters announce that they are going to vote Liberal, even if others believe them. What is needed is a way of committing large numbers of voters to the Liberals. This can be done by a prominent individual announcing that he is going to vote Liberal and that he urges others to do the same. If this individual is the leader of some interest group (e.g., a union) and if it is generally believed that he can 'deliver' most of the votes of his followers, then his announcement serves to commit a sizeable number of votes. Commitment can also be achieved by having large crowds of supporters at Liberal rallies, large numbers of Liberals canvassing door-to-door, and so on. (Schelling mentions that "mutually perceived" signals are an essential part of this kind of 'bandwagon behaviour".[15])

Finally, strategies of misinformation are also open here both to the Liberals and to the other parties. A biased poll showing the Liberals with huge popular support would be of great strategic use to them if it were accepted as genuine. This is especially true if the report of the poll is that the Liberals have large *committed* support (i.e., if the poll reported that a large number of people would *actually* vote Liberal regardless of what others did). Conversely, a poll showing the Liberals with small support hurts the Liberals and helps the other parties. Newspaper reports about size of rallies and probable support for a political party are of similar strategic importance to polls: these too can easily be manipulated by one party or another to gain a strategic advantage.

In this section an attempt has been made to give persuasive evidence that voting rules contain necessarily a large number of strategic possibilities, expecially in situations in which there are more than two alternatives to be voted on. (The examples have mostly been given with respect to plurality voting, but the reader should be able to convince himself easily that similar examples can be constructed for the other kinds of voting procedures we have discussed.) If strategy is an intrinsic part of voting, however, it is useless to develop 'acceptability' conditions for voting procedures which require that they be entirely 'non-strategic'. It may be more promising to try to formulate acceptability conditions which *allow* for strategic considerations and which even are *based* on such considerations. Some remarks on this approach will be made in Section 9 and 10.

9. COMPARISON OF VOTING RULES WITH RESPECT TO STRATEGY

In this section we try to compare voting rules from a strategic prespective. That is, we discuss voting rules by considering what kinds of coordination games they lead to. The goal of this discussion is to find some basis for *comparing* voting procedures as to acceptability. We have thus retreated somewhat from our original goal of formulating 'absolute' standards of acceptability for voting procedures. Still we are limited to making tentative and informal remarks: no precise criteria of acceptability are forthcoming.[16]

A. *Complexity of Ballots*

The voting rules we have discussed require varying amounts of information from the voter, as was pointed out in Section 3. Some, like plurality rule, have very simple ballots, Others, like the utilitarian voting system, have quite complex ballots, which can be filled out in many different ways. Can the acceptability of a voting procedure be tied to the complexity of the ballot it requires?

Well-known pragmatic reasons favour simpler systems, especially in large societies. Complicated systems cost more to operate; there is more possibility of mechanical error on the part of the voter and in the computation of the result under complex systems; there is more possibility of a voter simply misunderstanding a complicated system. These considerations are not so decisive in committees, where it is more feasible to allow sophisticated procedures.[17]

How do simple and complex systems compare from the strategic point of view? Many contrasts can be drawn, of course, but the sharpest contrast occurs in large societies and with respect to information. Briefly, if ballots are simple, the voter in a large society can obtain some information about how others voters will mark their ballots: he can then at--tempt to coordinate his behaviour with that of others who have preferences like his. This information may be biased for strategic reasons, and it is always to some extent incomplete, but the voter can get *some* information. If ballots are complex, however, this leaves the other voters with many more possible ways of voting, and so the individual voter has much more information to obtain before deciding on a coordination strategy. He is left much more in the dark about what other voters may do: consequently, he has much less idea of how to coordinate his behaviour with that of other voters of similar preferences.

Take the example of the British situation already discussed. Under plurality rule, what a voter has to determine is roughly what the proportion of the vote among the three parties will be.[18] He can get information about this from a poll he believes to be reliable, and then choose his coordination strategy in the light of this information. If Britain used the utilitarian voting system, however, he would have much less chance of getting reliable information from a poll. For in this situation the poll-taker would have to ask voters what their *distribution* of points among the parties was going to be. And on *a priori* grounds it seems much less likely that voters could answer this kind of question reliably before an election than that they could answer the simpler question of which party they were going to vote for under plurality voting. Our individual voter would have a much more incomplete picture of what other voters would do under the utilitarian voting system: consequently he would have much less idea of how best to employ his vote strategically.

It seems plausible, then, that more complex ballots have the effect of reducing the reliable information available to voters. Thus voting procedures involving complex ballots should tend to increase the likelihood of voters 'wasting' their ballots on a minority party or otherwise misunderstanding the strategic effects of their votes. An argument could be constructed on this basis for the greater acceptability of simpler procedures.

But this kind of consideration could be turned into an argument for the greater acceptability of more complicated procedures as well. First, if we accept that complex procedures lead to unreliable information, then if such procedures are used we may expect that voters will come to *view* information about the voting intentions of others with suspicion. Thus they will be less likely to be misled by a strategy of *mis*information as discussed earlier.

Second, while complicated voting procedures may inhibit the forming of coalitions in a large society, it could be argued that this is an argument in their favour rather than a criticism. For if the strategic situation is uncertain, voters may return to 'honest' (i.e., 'non-strategic') voting. Not knowing how to coordinate their voting behaviour with that of others with similar beliefs, voters may vote simply in accordance with their own preferences. Those who view democracy as based on individual free choice rather than on the formation of interest groups or coalitions would presumably be sympathetic to such an outcome.

B. *Difficulty of Forming Coalitions to Obtain a Certain Goal*

Now we shall consider the problem of voters trying to coordinate their behaviour from a slightly different point of view. We begin by comparing two voting procedures strategically. We assume a large society and an election among three candidates, a, b and c. We shall compare plurality voting in this situation with the procedure in which voters must vote for each of *two* candidates and the candidate with the highest total wins. (This is equivalent to the procedure in which votes are cast *against* one candidate and the candidate with the *lowest* total wins.)

Consider a group of people in this society who can muster a large number of votes and who want to elect *a*. Which of these two procedures should they prefer? If this group is relatively indifferent between *b* and *c*, they should prefer ordinary plurality voting. For under plurality voting, it is clear what each member of the group should do: he should vote for *a*. Under the 'two votes' procedure, on the other hand, the members of the group cannot vote for *a* alone. Each must also vote for one of *b* or *c*. Which should they choose to vote for? If they regard *b* and *c* as candidates of similar strength, then some of the memebrs of the group should vote for *a* and *b* while the rest vote for *a* and *c*. This requires that they solve a further coordination problem in deciding who votes for *b* and who votes for *c*, and this may be an extremely difficult coordination problem if the group is large. If *b* is seen as a much stronger opponent than *c*, they have a still more difficult coordination problem. They would lika to vote for *a* and *c* so that their votes would count against *b*, but if e large number of supporters of *b* vote for *b* and *c* on similar grounds, there is the danger that *c* may win. Here they must coordinate their behaviour not only with each other but with the supporters of *b*, in order to defeat *c*. Thus, if a group has as its main goal the election of a particular candidate, plurality voting is better for them than the 'two votes' system, since it does not present them with extra coordination problems of the kind discussed above.

Now suppose we change the goal of this group. We assume that their main purpose is to defeat *b*, and that they are relatively indifferent between *a* and *c*. Now the 'two votes' system is better for them, since they can just vote for *a* and *c*. Under plurality voting, they have to coordinate their behaviour to support one of *a* or *c*, and they have to do this in the light of their information about how other voters are likely to vote. This is not as severe a coordination problem as that which arose in the other case, but it is a coordination problem nevertheless.

Thus voting rules can be compared as to the difficulty of forming coalitions to obtain a certain goal, where a goal may be the election of one candidate, the defeat of one candidate, the defeat of both of two candidates, and so on. Translating such comparisons into judgments about the relative acceptability of voting rules would require specifying certain of these goals as *in general* more important. (Thus the 'more acceptable' rules would be those which facilitated reaching the 'more important, goals.) It is by no means clear, however, that this kind of goal can be evaluated in a general way as to importance. And, to complicate the situation further, we can note again that those who value 'individual choice' may regard *difficulty* of forming coalitions as a virtue and *ease* of forming coalitions as a vice.

10. Conclusion

In this paper we set out to investigate *general* standards for acceptability of voting rules. Many of our efforts to give or defend such general standards met with only partial success. In particular, this was true of the four conditions treated in Section 4: Unrestricted Domain, Pareto-Optimality, Neutrality, Anonymity. While we found that these conditions do capture some important intuitions that we have about acceptable voting procedures, we also found that in some particular circumstances it seemed reasonable to violate them, so that we should not regard them as completely general. Further, these conditions did little to distinguish among actual voting procedures as to acceptability.

Positive Responsiveness (Section 5) and Independence of Irrelevant Alternatives (Section 6) were found to be essentially 'non-strategy' conditions, when applied to voting procedures. There is no strong argument against accepting Positive Responsiveness as a general condition of acceptability on voting rules. Further, it does rule out a voting system, the alternative candidate ballot system, which has had actual use in electoral systems, and it provides a sensible rationale for doing so.

Independence of Irrelevant Alternatives, on the other hand, was found to be unacceptable simply because it is too strong. As long as there are more than two alternatives, actual voting rules simply fail to meet this condition. Since Independence of Irrelevant Alternatives is essentially a 'non-strategy' condition, and since actual voting rules fail to meet it, this raised the possibility that voting *necessarily* involves strategic elements. In Sections 7 and 8 this suggestion was considerably elaborated and defended: further, it was shown that voting procedures are rich in 'coordination problems' as studied by Schelling.

In Section 9 a few remarks were made suggesting how relative or comparative standards of acceptability for voting rules might be set up if voting is seen from the strategic point of view. Even our tentative standards, however, were seen to depend on particular circumstances, such as reliability of the information available, the goals of particular interest groups and the desirability of permitting coalitions (explicit or tacit) to form easily.

All this indicates that general standards for acceptability of voting rules, standards which apply independently of particular circumstances, may be hard to come by. Perhaps we can accept Positive Responsiveness, and we may be able to add a general condition to the effect that all information should be as accurate as possible, in an attempt to rule out strategies of misinformation in general. Apart from this, however, it seems necessary to accept that different voting rules may be acceptable in different circumstances, and to study the relations between rules and circumstances in more detail. Further, the latter part of this paper should be sufficient to indicate that in any such study of voting rules considerations of strategy, particularly as it applies to coordination problems, must play a crucial role.

Finally, it may be useful to note certain problems which were *not* dealt with in this paper. There are many strategies connected with the electoral process which are not too closely related to the voting rule in use. Such strategies include: misrepresenting a candidate (e.g., lying about his qualifications); overt coercion; side-payments; 'log-rolling'. These were not discussed. Nor was there any consideration of many other issues clearly related to the 'fairness' of an election. Two such issues are the question of who should be allowed to vote on a given issue and the question of what matters can properly be voted on publicly. These are all topics for further research.

Department of Philosophy,
McGill University

NOTES

* I read a primitive version of this paper under the title 'What is a Fair Voting Procedure?' at the Colloquium in Exact Philosophy, McGill University, 1969–70.
[1] The 'alternative candidate ballot system', as described here, is a simplified version of the Australian voting system. See Douglas W. Rea, *The Political Consequences of*

Electoral Laws, revised edition, Yale University Press, New Haven and London, 1971, p. 24.

[2] Robert A. Dahl, *A Preface to Democratic Theory*, The University of Chicago Press, Chicago and London, 1956, pp. 37–38.

[3] Kenneth J. Arrow, *Social Choice and Individual Values*, second edition, John Wiley & Sons, New York, 1963. This book will be referred to in this paper as '*SC & IV*'.

[4] For arguments against the identification of transitivity with rationality, see Duncan Black, 'On Arrow's Impossibility Theorem', *The Journal of law and Economics* **12** (1969), 227–48.

[5] I say "*comparatively* unimportant" because who comes second in an election, for example, may affect the outcome of future elections or the actions taken by the winner (if he is a representative).

[6] Amartya K. Sen, *Collective Choice and Social Welfare*, Holden-Day, San Fransisco, 1970, pp. 48–52. This is the most complete review to date of the literature on social choice. It will be referred to as '*CC & SW*'.

[7] K. O. May, 'A Set of Independent Necessary and Sufficient Conditions for Simple Majority Decision', *Econometrica* **20** (1952), 680–84.

[8] This system is discussed in Alex C. Michalos, 'Decision-Making in Committees', *American Philosophical Quarterly* **7** (1970), 91–106.

[9] As Sen points out, the condition Arrow calls "independence of irrelevant alternatives" *includes* the requirement of *non-cardinality*. (*CC & SW*, pp. 89-90) So these voting procedures would not meet Arrow's condition, as they involve assigning weights to alternatives.

[10] This is one way of interpreting Arrow's famous 'impossibility' theorem *with respect to voting procedures*.

[11] Thomas C. Schelling, *The Strategy of Conflict*, Oxford University Press, Oxford, 1960.

[12] If nomination procedures are lax, however, a disreputable variant of this strategy is available. A faction may nominate a candidate with a similar *name* to the opposition candidate, rather than one with similar views, in an attempt to split the opposition vote by confusing opposition voters.

[13] Peter G. J. Pulzer, *Political Representation and Elections: Parties and Voting in Great Britain*, Frederick A. Praeger, New York, 1967, p. 57.

[14] *Ibid.*, p. 96.

[15] Schelling, *The Strategy of Conflict*, p. 90.

[16] It may be wondered why no attempt is made to use standard results of n-person game theory in this section. Briefly, the reason is that most of these results are about games in 'normal' form in which only the *payoffs* of complete sets of moves are shown. The strategic problems we are concerned with, however, require consideration of 'voting games' in *extensive* form, in which individual moves are considered. See Schelling, *The Strategy of Conflict*, p. 99.

[17] Examples are the complicated points systems used in determining winners of athletic contests (e.g., gymnastics) in which there are groups of judges.

[18] More precisely, he has to determine what the proportion of the vote will be *in his riding*.

PART VII

HISTORIOGRAPHY

WERNER LEINFELLNER

HISTORICAL TIME AND A NEW CONCEPTION
OF THE HISTORICAL SCIENCES

ABSTRACT. Historiography and systematic history deal with the same problem: why have the events of history occurred? In the first part of the article the answer given by the deductive-nomological model is discussed. The Hempel-Oppenheim model is characterized as a krypto-reduction of historical sciences to natural ones, since the covering law has to be taken from the natural sciences. The trend to replacement of the deductive-nomological explanation by statistical forms finally leads to Gardiner's, Greeno's, Danto's and Dray's weakened forms using no general law-like statements in historical sciences at all. Thus the hiatus between natural sciences and humanities (*Geisteswissenschaften*) opens up again. In the second part, the approach of Hegel, Rickert and Dilthey and the modern hermeneutic approach to history of Gehlen, Gadamer and Schelsky is reduced to its bare essentials: history and historical science conceived of as an evaluation of man's past. Consequently, the third part offers a scheme of interpretation (evaluation) as a two-dimensional manifold of evaluation and calendar time under uncertainty and risk. The axiomatic definition of this form of historical time plus an empirical interpretation serves as an explicatum for history. The concept of a common history of a group is defined; re-evaluation and re-interpretation are regarded as a repetition of the comparison of evaluated events of the past, leading to different rankings, even if the underlying quasi-order (political, ideological or cultural) remains the same. That means that the individual's or nation's momentary experience or estimations are decisive for the evaluation of its history. Evaluation of the past may even depend on the future (prospects). A definition of traditionalism and activism is given. This result does not need psychological, ideological motives for re-interpretation of history. It is based solely on uncertainty facing the future or past, uses no absolute values and needs no teleological interpretation of the course of history.

1. THE RISE AND FALL OF EXPLANATION IN
HISTORICAL SCIENCES

The purpose of this Section is not to reject the concept of explanation for the natural sciences; rather, our purpose is to demonstrate the futility of attempts to introduce the methods of the natural sciences into the social sciences, especially into the study of history. We are attacking the dogma that perfect empirical sciences have to be (i) cognitive sciences and (ii) have to use laws solely to make predictions and retrodictions, as well as explanations, possible. This dogma has led to the widespread attempt of a hidden (krypto)-reduction of historical sciences to natural sciences. The phrase 'krypto-reductionism' is used because the original

M. Bunge (ed.), The Methodological Unity of Science, 193–215. All Rights Reserved.
Copyright © 1973 by D. Reidel Publishing Company, Dordrecht-Holland

intention of the propounders of this dogma was certainly not to reduce
the historical and social sciences to the natural sciences, but rather to
make these sciences more precise in the manner of the natural sciences.
One can easily show that this attempted reduction is a repetition of a
mistake committed by philosophers of science for several decades. These
philosophers fail to realize that most of the social sciences, including the
historical sciences, are not solely concerned with making predictions,
retrodictions or explanations, but are creative sciences more in the manner of technical engineering. Historical sciences can be considered as a
reconstruction of man's most important decision procedure. When man
makes his decisions concerning future actions on the evaluation of the
past, such an evaluation of the future event can easily become history.
For example, there is no law covering Napoleon's mis-estimation of
Grouchy's efforts to stop Blücher's army on June 18, 1815. The whole
defeat at Waterloo can be seen as a decision procedure in which Napoleon's
decision to attack Wellington's army too swiftly and too eagerly was
critical for Napoleon's famous defeat. The consequences of Napoleon's
evaluation and decision making became history. For this evaluation
and decision making coupled with random events, e.g., Blücher's early
arrival allowing him to save Wellington, accounted for the complete
defeat of Napoleon's army. But still the dogma is tempting. One can
only hope that today's krypto-reductionism of historical sciences to
natural sciences was the last one.

Historiography, systematic history of groups and nations and autobio-
graphies of individuals deal with the same fundamental problem: "Why
have the events of the past occurred?" C. G. Hempel, P. Oppenheim,
R. Braithwaite and E. Nagel, to mention a few, regard the solution of the
problem as a merely methodological one, namely a concern with the
application of the explanation scheme to historical sciences. These philosophers were certainly fascinated by the splendid success of explanation
within the natural sciences; where, according to Hempel's remarks, it
works best.[1] The precise scientific answer to the question: "Why is it the
case that p?" (where 'p' symbolizes an empirical statement, S^e, describing in a true manner the facts to be explained) is given, according to
Hempel, by using the metatheoretical, prefabricated scheme of explanation. The first and most powerful model, the 'deductive-nomological'
as suggested by Hempel,[2] or the 'covering-law' model according to Dray's

label, offers an answer to the question 'why' simply by a detailed tactic of subsumption; viz., subsume the phenomenon to be explained (the explanandum) under, or cover it by, a law. This maneuver shifts the thrust of the problem to the question: Are there at all enough sound laws in the historical sciences to furnish scientific explanations? The krypto-reduction of the historical sciences to the natural sciences lies in the answer to this question. Hempel, for example, never uses specific historical laws within his explanation scheme, but instead, he supplies historical explanations with the laws of natural science, thus making historical laws superfluous. The deductive-nomological scheme of explanation, as sketched in Table I, demands that the explanans has to consist of empirically true statements, S_i^e, describing the relevant initial conditions to be explained, together with the corresponding explanatory laws, (L_j), from which, by means of subsumation of the former under the latter, the explanandum is derived. It demands categorically that every scientific explanation must invoke some existing general laws and that there is some logical relation between the explanans and the explanandum, such that the explanandum must be obtained logically from both, but never from S_i^e alone.[3] It seems that most of the explanationists were seduced by the multiplicity of the application of such a scheme. For with such a scheme one does not need genuine historical laws at all because one can produce so-called historical explanations merely by using economic, psychological, physical laws. Hempel expresses this krypto-reductionism explicitly: "Many of the universal hypotheses underlying historical explanation, for instance, would commonly be classified as psychological, economical, sociological." But the hidden reduction goes on: "In addition historical research has frequently to resort to general laws established in physics, chemistry and biology. Thus, e.g., the defeat of an army by reference to lack of food."[4] Therefore he concludes that history is not methodologically autonomous and independent[5] and, consequently, so-called historical laws are functionally replaceable by means of this explanation scheme. The importance of historical laws is thus denied. The real result of this krypto-reductionism was in fact the opposite of what one has expected. Physical, chemical and biological laws lose their nomothetical universal character very quickly if they are used in historical explanations, for they degenerate to mere statistical law-like statements which permit exception; e.g., in the case mentioned above, precisely the lack of food may incite soldiers to a desperate victory. Nevertheless, the astonishing rise of deductive-nomological explanations in historiography and the following corresponding decline in the increasingly weaker statistical models of explanation have borne out the opposite of Hempel's view. In contrast to Hempel's account, the social sciences, including the historical sciences, are methodologically autonomous in the sense that they use their own specific methods, as will be shown in Sections 2 and 3. It enforces the conjecture (1.1) to the criticism of using an explanation scheme at all. For what reason should we use an explanation scheme, when any well-formed theory delivers the same results by covering empirical instances automatically under a law? The whole question of explanation seems to be a luxury of a methodologically enriched science possessing powerful and well-formed theories. But do we possess such sort of theories within historical sciences?

Before entering into a discussion of history disburdened of the distorted view of the natural sciences, some objections to the deductive-nomological model of historical explanation must be dealt with. These objections will provide indirect support for conjecture (1.1): To each model of explanation there must exist some kind of theory or hypothetical framework supporting the explanation. (This conjecture is made explicit in Tables I and II.) With reference to this conjecture one can easily see that the covering law model of explanation is not a viable concept without the hidden presupposition of a universal law with application to a particular reference class within the framework of a well-formulated theory. Alternatively, in the case of the narrative model of explanation, the hidden presupposition is that there exists a hypothesis with a belief statement, U, based on the evidences $\{S^e\}$.

It would be easy to repeat the criticisms of the covering-law model of explanation for the historical sciences as offered by Dray, Gardiner and others. However, the approach used here will be more general in application, but perhaps less direct. The intention then is to show that the demand of the covering-law model of explanation for history is much too extravagant and completely displaced, simply because we now possess no theories within historical science. The covering-law model of explanation for history, if accepted, would require firstly the abandonment of strictly historical sciences for theoretical sciences of the natural scientific sort; it would really reduce historical sciences to natural ones. Consequently, there would be no intrinsic difference between the methods of explanation applied to natural or social, including historical, sciences. The main objection to this reductionism is therefore embodied in conjecture (1.1). The explanation-scheme never achieves more than what can be done by well-formed theories possessing laws or law-like statements which are defined for a specifically described empirical field of reference (D^i); e.g., observational statements (S^i_o), where the superscript i denotes the specific theory, i, to which laws and observational statements belong. Therefore, any explanation scheme for theoretical sciences may be substituted by subsuming the empirical statements, (S^i_o), belonging to the empirical language of the theory, Th^i, under laws or law-like statements; e.g., statistical rules, (L^i), of the same theory, Th^i. Only if theories are similar,[6] i.e., their field of reference is the same or partially overlaps, may we connect the obtained consequences by 'and' as C_1 & C_2. In Table I the scheme of explanation is compared with subsumptions within the theories

TABLE I

Scheme of explanation	equivalent to:	Scheme of subsumption	
explanans $\begin{cases} S^e \\ L \end{cases}$		For Th^1: S^1	For Th^2: S^2
		L^1	L^2
explanandum E		C^1	C^2

Th^1 and Th^2. This proposal may be helpful in solving most of the general objections against the explanation scheme, such as deducibility-vagueness, law-dependency and statistical weakness.[7]

1.2. *Deducibility Vagueness*

The precise characterization of the nature of the relation between the explanans and the explanandum is still an unsolved problem. Is the relationship a deductive-nomological one or is the relationship to be characterized as an inductive statistical inference? Or, perhaps, the relationship is that of a physical-material principle of inference. The final answer to this question demands an examination of the theory which is the context for any specific explanation. Only after this examination is completed will the nature of the relationship which holds between empirical statements and law-like statements be known. Thus we must in any specific case, especially in history, rely on already existing wellformed theories.

1.3. *Law Dependency*

The critical question of explanation is: How good are the laws which are used in a particular explanation? Generally, we may assume that the better the laws, the less exceptions, the better the explanation. In the following table on the left hand side a distinction among classical-deterministic, inductive-statistical, indeterministic-statistical and belief-formu-

TABLE II

Thesis: Each viable explanation model on the right hand side would require a corresponding equivalent theoretical framework which is exhibited on the left hand side.

Law-like statements and their corresponding theoretical context:

1. General, exhaustive and verifiably true statements of the form $L = (x)\,(Fx \supset Gx)$, $S = (Fx \supset Gx)$ in classical deterministic theories of natural sciences, classical economics.	Deductive-nomological explanation (covering-law model) e.g., causal explanations used in natural sciences.
2. General, restrictive statements, testably true with respect to a class of statements, (S^o), such that the degree of statistical confirmation, r, is high or almost 1. $p(L, S) = r$; used in probabilistic-statistical theories, social sciences, historical sciences of discrete states.	Statistical explanation in a narrower sense (Hempel-Oppenheim, Gardiner, Dray).
3. General, restrictive statements about mixtures of evaluated strategies $(S)\ d(S_i), d(S_j)$; v_{ij} of S_{ij}, partially true, and about transition (conditional) probabilities $p_{jk}(d(S_{ij})) = p(L, S) = t$; Used in game-theory, statistical-decision theories, action theory, historical sciences, here only for two persons (ij).	Statistical explanation in a wider sense (J. G. Greeno, Leinfellner).
4. General, restrictive universal statement, U, where the degree of belief in U, given evidence, (S^e), should be as high as possible. The degree of $b(U, S^e)$ can be found on the basis of subjective-quantitative or subjective-qualitative estimates.	Danto's and Dray's narrative model of explanation which belongs to statistical explanation in a wider sense of Louch, Winch, Nettler, Scriven's empathic model of explanation.

lations of law-like statements is made. In respect to strength these statements are listed in descending order, permitting more and more exceptions. On the right hand side of the table, the corresponding possible theoretical models of explanations are listed, in spite of the fact that we do not possess such statistical historical theories. Since each of the explanation-models requires a specific form of law-like statements, we have to refer to possibly corresponding theories in which these law-like statements are used to find the corresponding empirical statements, (S^i), and vice versa. The real question is: Do we possess today historical theories which would fulfill the demands 1–4? Theories of the first kind (1) would reduce historical sciences to natural ones, i.e., would replace all explanations within historical sciences by explanations of natural sciences.[8] But theories of the kind 2–4 can exist within historical sciences, if the consequences of the last chapter are drawn, and if historical sciences are considered as a theoretical reconstruction of history seen from a value and decision theoretical point of view.

1.4. *The Weakening of the Explanation Scheme within the Historical and the Social Sciences*

From the above table we can see immediately that the deductive-nomological explanation requires a theory of the classical deterministic type which is hardly to be found in any social science and *a fortiori* hardly to be found in any historical science. If we give up the krypto-reductionism we have to choose a statistical form of explanation as Gardiner and Dray, among others, have suggested. But an inevitable consequence of this choice is that history could only be described by more or less vague statistical correlations of events, even assuming that we possess a suitable statistical theory. But this may be detrimental to historical investigations because statistical historical knowledge carries the odium of a 'weak science', consisting only of *ad hoc* hypotheses seen from a classical point of view. History, as statistics, would reduce to a mere estimation; this estimation or evaluation of events being subjectively incomplete because of the lack of information concerning past events. Thus, historical science conceived in this manner would seem to be a deficient and underdeveloped science which would share the same disrepute with which Einstein held for quantum theory with its statistical character. With all this there remains the final problem concerning the exact application of even statistical explanation in historical sciences; viz., the requirement of unrestricted evidence. The requirement of unrestricted evidence is easily fulfilled by the deductive-nomological type of explanation, but it is much more difficult to meet this demand in the social and historical sciences in which the gathering of the totality of all evidence may be nearly impossible. Thus, it is little wonder that the continual weakening of the explanation concept in historical science led, consequently, to Danto's and Dray's narrative model[9] and finally cumulated with Louch's, Winch's and Scriven's empathetic model. Scriven's model can only be regarded as a heuristic device or an intuitive tool for producing proto-stages or mere sketches of scientific explanations without any reference to 'empathy'.[10] Consequently, the bold attempt to introduce strict classical scientific methods into the historical sciences foundered. This withdrawal to the traditional dualism of the natural sciences on one side and the humanities, the *Geisteswissenschaften*, viz., the social sciences and especially the historical sciences, on the other side seemed inevitable. But still we are pressed to answer the critical question, "Why?" Is causal explanation to be restricted exclusively to chemical or physical histories, since even biological 'histories', e.g., the evolution of the species, are not amenable to strict deterministic theories?[11] Thus, the attempted application of explanation to history has led to a methodological dilemma: either to weaken explanation to statistical models, and by doing so, to give up the deductive, strict character of the explanation and forego the possibility of making general statements about history or about the future, based on historical experience, or to maintain a rigorous scientific demand for explanation which would entail explaining history by physical or chemical laws and essentially reducing history to the physical sciences. The way to solve this dilemma consists in demonstrating that historical sciences can be regarded in a positive sense as statistical sciences, if and only if history itself is regarded as a prototypical 'hermeneutic', i.e., evaluating view of the past for finding possible decisions with respect to the future. The theoretical reconstruction of such a 'hermeneutics' has to concentrate on the evaluative character of historical sciences *(Interpretation)* and has to show clearly how such an evaluation can be used for making decisions for the future. Therefore, in the next Section the evaluative 'hermeneutic' view of history and historical sciences will be discussed, and in the Section 3 historical time will be regarded as an evaluation manifold of specific kind.

2. EXPLANATION VERSUS INTERPRETATION

According to the non-analytic, even non-methodologically oriented, approach to solving the problem of history as proposed by Ortega y Gasset, Gehlen, Schelsky, the hermeneutic and existentialist philosophies, man has no intrinsic nature at all, he has only his history. But what is meant by this slogan? Most of the non-analytic philosophers assume that the analytic approach has overlooked one fundamental fact, namely that history must take account of evaluation and values. Carr and Gardiner have recently pointed this out.[12] Perhaps it was the dogma of a value-free science which prevented the analytic philosophers from clearly seeing the role of interpretation in history. Whatever the cause of this blind spot, non-analytic interpreters of history, as well as practitioners of modern hermeneutics, following the lead of Rickert, Windelband and Dilthey, have sought to solve the problem of history more by an evaluation of past events than by the famous 'empathy'. Evaluation of single unique events of the past is the hard core of the ideographic method. This interpretation holds that events of the past do not become the history of an individual or of a group simply by virtue of their belonging to the same causal lines, nor in virtue of their calendarian ordering, nor in virtue of a mere historiographic presentation of past material. History, or the concept of it, historicity, has been regarded since the contributions of Dilthey and Rickert as an evaluative undertaking which only gives meaning to an individual's life. This human evaluation serves in modern hermeneutics, as fashioned by Gadamer and Heidegger, as a foundation of philosophy in general. It does not matter whether this interpretation of past events is based on external goals (e.g., the teleological and eschatological goals of St. Paul and St. Augustine) or on the ideals of the Enlightenment (Herder and Kant), or on philosophical immanent goals (Hegel) or on ideological strivings (Marx and other dialectical materialists or the utilitarians), evaluation is the cornerstone of this approach. Of course, problems are readily apparent with this concept of history. Generally speaking, evaluations based on immanent, past goals, past standards, or past norms which are abstracted from history, tend to degenerate into vicious circles. Prime examples are the systems of

Hegel, Marx and Croce. Rickert as the original promulgator of the ideographic method in history never did regard history as the realization of an ideal goal or system. Rickert believed this method would only allow for the evaluation of single unique events of the past. It is obvious that the ideographic method which deals with the single concrete phenomenon is in sharp contrast to the nomothetic, generalizing method of science which deals with the single case by subsuming it under a nomological law. Dilthey, in a similar ideographic vein, used the word 'empathy' to convey the specific uniqueness of this evaluation. Given this antagonism, four challenging problems arise: (i) to formalize and define axiomatically the intuitively given notion of interpretation for historical sciences; (ii) to discuss all the possibilities and consequences of using the scheme of interpretation in history and historical sciences; (iii) to show that the concept of explanation is redundant in historical science and history because people do not look at everything for laws when demanding an answer to the question, "Why did I make this or that decision?" (iv) The redundancy of explanation does not mean to give up the search for a characteristic theoretical framework as the methodological basis of historical sciences. Such a framework will be proposed here and will be called the decision-oriented framework.

3. THE SCHEME OF INTERPRETATION

To avoid the Scylla of explanation and the Charybdis of the vicious hermeneutic circle, one first must reformulate the crucial initial question. We should not ask why events have occurred; but rather why do people evaluate events of the past in a particular, perhaps peculiar way. It very simply is a category mistake to confuse deductive-nomological explanation with evaluative interpretation of acts, decisions; each belongs to completely different categories. The problem of the evaluative interpretation scheme more closely resembles the problem of time rather than the problem of a deductive nomological explanation. Kant proposed to define classical Newtonian time by imposing a strict serial order on temporal events by means of the relations of simultaneity and succession. Such a temporal order or structure has been axiomatized earlier by the author.[13] An axiomatization of the structure of evaluation taken jointly with a calendar time order will be based on preference and indifference relations of an individual as he evaluates past, or, in a reverse sense even the future possible events and thus creates his own history.[14] In this axiomatization it is imperative that we include the factor of uncertainty with respect to evaluations, as well as the factor of personal risk involved in the evaluations. The problem is therefore to analyze the preconditions of 'creating history' by means of evaluations and decisions, and of theorizing the historical sciences by defining the formal structure of historical time in the same way as we define our clock-time or Euclidean space as preconditions for classical sciences. According to a proposal of Bunge, such an analysis of presuppositions can be regarded as 'scientific metaphysics' if it is concerned with the most general feature of reality and real objects; (1) if it is a systematic theory rather than an array of views; (2) if it makes explicit use of logic or mathematics; (3) if it is compatible and even continuous with the science of the day; (4) if it elucidates key concepts in philosophy or in the foundations of sciences; and (5) if it may be made to occur among the presuppositions of a scientific theory; or (6) if it may develop into a scientific theory by specialization or addition of specific hypotheses.[15]

As an aid for the understanding of the following axiomatization, the interpretational scheme will be called historical time, or historicity, and will be regarded as the basic theoretical 'representational system' for historical sciences just in the same sense as we regard space and time as the basic framework for natural sciences.

3.1.   This section deals with the concept of historical time; the time of an individual's or a nation's history. Throughout the history of philosophy, many attempts have been made to explicate or define the peculiarities of historical time or historicity. There are some common features in the traditional view of historicity, primarily the distinction between calendar time and the interpretation of calendar time. Augustine's teleological characterization of historicity was a theological, 'eschatological' evaluation of calendar time. Rousseau and Kant regarded historical time as composed of calendar time plus an evaluation of its events by means of the ideas of the Enlightenment. Only an interpretation or evaluation of the calendric ordered facts and events of the past transforms this mere listing of past facts and events into historical time; i.e., into one's personal or national history. Hegel, Marx, Windelband, Rickert, Husserl and

Dilthey, as well as the existentialistic and hermeneutic approaches, differ only in respect to the norms or standards by which events of calendar time are evaluated. There has been a shift in philosophy away from religious and metaphysical norms and evaluations to secularized material norms and standards such as the economic ones proposed by Marx, or the pragmatic ones set forth by Dewey. Without going into more historical details we may delineate the traditional concept of historical time or historicity (*Geschichtlichkeit*) as a two-fold one: first, calendric ordered facts, viz., events which are regarded as the content of history and hence get a calendric index; and secondly, a certain evaluation of these events. To be explicit, this means that these events have to be given a hermeneutic evaluation or interpretation before a particular conception of historical time is complete.

3.2. *Axiomatization of the Scheme of Interpretation*

In spite of the enormous literature about historicity and historical time, and in spite of the recent 'explanatory' approach which attempts to use natural laws to save historical law covering explanations, there is as yet no formal definition of the properties of a two-dimensional 'evaluative manifold' composed of calendar time, as one axis, and of at least one evaluation-vector, as the other axis. We now propose the following definition:

3.21.   The form (structure) of historical time is at least a two-dimensional manifold, composed of the calendar time dimension ($\mathscr{K}$) and the evaluation dimension (vector-space $\mathscr{H}$).

   Calendar time based upon mathematical time will be regarded as the usual one-dimensional continuum which provides the calendar indices for all events, acts, goods $\mathfrak{A}$, $\mathfrak{B}$ of the past. Calendartime, ($\mathscr{K}$), and the evaluation-vector, ($\mathscr{H}$), will be combined to produce the ordered pair $\langle \mathscr{K}, \mathscr{H} \rangle$, defining historical time by means of the axioms:

3.221–3.237.   Historical evaluation is, therefore, from a formal point of view, a value theoretical vector-space depending on the set of values, X, and on objectively or subjectively given probabilities (propensities), P. Some important symbols and basic concepts of historical time are the following ones: simple values: $x_i \in X$; probable values or propensity-values: $p_i x_i$; these latter may be put together to form prospects or retrospects: $(p_1 x_1, p_2 x_2, \cdots, p_n x_n)$, consisting of at least two propensity-values. Empirically given preferences or behavioristic preferences are denoted by the preference relation, $\mathscr{P}$, and the indifference relation, $\mathscr{I}$. The evaluated goods, facts, events of calendar time, $\mathfrak{a} \in \mathfrak{A}$, or $\mathfrak{b} \in \mathfrak{B}$ are ordered according to the calendar time and have the calendar time index, $\mathfrak{a}^t$ or, e.g., x^t. These basic concepts permit a general axiomatization; i.e., a definition of the form of historical time, which will even include our uncertainty about the historical information of the past as well as our uncertainty about the future.

3.23. $\langle \mathscr{K}, X; P \rangle$ defines the form of historical time (historicity) if and only if the following conditions are fulfilled:[16]

3.231. The set, $x_i \in X$, of simple values is quasi-ordered and has a minimal and a maximal simple value called norms or standard-values. Quasi-order means the greater-relationship holding between values, '$\succ$', is transitive; the equivalence relationship holding between values, '$\sim$', is transitive, symmetric and reflexive; and that both relationships are strictly exclusive; i.e., either $x_i \succ x_j$ or $x_j \succ x_i$ or $x_i \sim x_j$. The interpretation of the form (or the formal structure), outlined by the axioms, defines the historical time in the usual empirical sense. Thus the basic order of values of a certain society or a certain individual should be quasi-ordered and should possess minimal and maximal (standard) values. This characterizes a formal condition, underlying all basic philosophical, cultural, religious or economic ordering of simple values. Since, according to theorem 4.1 the empirical preference-order is preserved by the order of values, we may use, instead of the quasi-ordered values, the quasi-ranked empirical preferences of a certain society or a certain individual. Any fixed, stable, empirically describable order of a group or society, called their basic underlying value-order, either inherited or upheld by constant education, tradition, culture, religion, etc., is important to make such an evaluative collective system Arrow-immune, simply by fulfilling Black's condition. Stable, means of course, over a certain period of time, where the axioms are ideally fulfilled.

3.232. Prospects and retrospects are at least introspectively equivalent to a chosen value, x_j^t, at the present time point, t:

If $x_i \succ x_j \succ x_k$, then $(p_i x_i, p_k x_k) \sim x_j^t$ at the present time, t.

Interpretation of 3.232: In contrast to all other traditional conceptions of historical time, we do not believe that future or past values remain unchangeable or absolute. Rather we believe that values are matched with propensities, p_i, and put together as prospects, if they belong to the future, or synthesized as retrospects, if they belong to an individual's past or a nation's calendar time. In this manner, a personal-subjective or an objectively given uncertainty about historical information may be expressed by propensity-values. Moreover – and this is the most decisive point – any values may be compared for the establishment of historical time at a present time epoch, t, regardless of whether they belong to the future (prospects) or to the past (retrospects). Thus, evaluations of the past or of the future are dependent upon the evaluations in the present time interval (point), t. The axiom 3.232 is an open condition in the sense that, in principle, the determination of values is possible at least by ordinal scales and at most by interval scales. Therefore, it is clear that an economic interval evaluation of an individual's recent past can permit a better and finer scale of values than a cultural, ideological or metaphysical evaluation, being a more ordinal scale of evaluation.

3.233. Propensities are used as finitely additive probability-measures and should satisfy the Kolmogoroff axioms for the finite case.[17]

ADDITIONAL AXIOMS (3.234–3.237):
3.234. The set of propensity-values such as $(p_1 x_1, p_2 x_2, \cdots, p_n x_n)$ is quasi-ordered (see definition of quasi-order in 3.231) and has minimum and maximum elements.

3.235. Prospects and retrospects are indifferent with respect to augmentation by constant finite values:

$$(p_i(x_i + x_c), p_j(x_j + x_c)) = (p_i x_i, p_j x_j) + x_c$$

3.236. $\quad a_i \sim a_j \rightarrow (p_i x_i, p_j x_j) = (p_j x_j, p_i x_i)$
3.237. $\quad a_i \underset{\sim}{\succ} a_j \rightarrow (p_i x_i, p_j x_j) \geqslant (p_i' x_i, p_j' x_j) \leftrightarrow p_i \geqslant p_i'$

Interpretation of the axioms 3.234–3.237. 3.234 demands comparability of propensity-values; 3.235 excludes incoherent relativity of values used in historical evaluation; 3.236 defines by means of commutativity the admissible present interval, t, of historical evaluation; 3.237 introduces a strict monotonicity for quantitative values (utilities).

4. Consequences of the above axiomatization

4.1. In a qualitative sense, for the representation of preferences by values, we get the theorem defining a quantitative monotonic scale for values:

$$(\mathscr{P}(a_i, a_j) \vee \mathscr{P}(a_j, a_i) \vee \mathscr{I}(a_i, a_j)) \rightarrow$$
$$(x_i > x_j) \vee (x_j > x_i) \vee (x_i \sim x_j)$$

4.2. In a quantitative sense, we get, for interval scaling: $x' = \alpha x + \beta$, $\alpha > 0$ either in the sense of Morgenstern or Allais (α and β are constants).[18] The interpretation of both theorems may be regarded as an explication of a common history if based upon common minimal and maximal norms (standards) x_i, x_k, given Black's condition. In sum, all individuals of a group, nation, etc., which have a common understanding (evaluation scale) of their calendar time can be defined by either possessing a monotonic transformation of their individual evaluation of the past, or at best they may use a linear transformation of their historical values attached to the events, acts, goods of their history.

4.3. *Time Dependency of Historical Time or Evaluation of Calendar Time*
From the axioms 3.231–3.237 we get:

$$p_j^t = x_k - x_j^t / x_k - x_i, \text{ if } p_i = 1 - p_k.$$

This interpretation uses the time indices over p_j and x_j indicating that the comparison of values for the purpose of evaluation of calendar time takes place at the present time interval, t. Given the case 3.232 and a fixed order (3.231), the only variable is p_j^t, i.e., the objectively or subjectively given propensity, p_j^t. Therefore, we may conclude that any evaluation of calendar time, of historically given facts, etc. a_i, b_j is dependent solely on the underlying basic order (3.231) and from the uncertainty expressed by the propensity, p_j^t, at the present time interval, t. From the point of

view of historical information about events of the past, we may state that
the more distant an event, the greater the uncertainty and the more
smeared the attached propensities.

Since our axiomatization by no means prescribes only prospects or
retrospects in the interpreted axiom 3.232, we may define a traditionalist,
or someone who uses a conservative historical evaluation, as one using
only retrospects in 3.232. On the contrary, an activist or revolutionary
evaluation of calendar time is based solely on prospects. This means
that even if the standards and the underlying order of values were shared
by a conservative and a progressive activist we still might obtain a completely different evaluation of their common past.

4.4. *Re-Evaluation of History*

A reinterpretation of history or a rewriting of the history of a group or
nation can be regarded as a repetition of the comparison (3.232) at different present time points $t_1, t_2, \cdots, t_n$. This may lead to different evaluations of the same calendar past even if the underlying order (3.231)
remains the same. From this point of view, we have to regard historicity
and historical time as a dynamic fluctuating frame of evaluations. We
must cease to regard historicity as concerned solely with the 'frozen
aspect' of the past since both future and past may interact in this dynamism of evaluation and re-evaluation. An example, taken from an individual
history, may illustrate this paradoxical situation. This example emphasizes the point that the evaluation of the past is dependent on the prospects, the future. A person may learn a language (a_e) in anticipation
of the prospect of immigrating in the near future to the country where
this language is spoken. In such a case he will evaluate 'learning this
language' very highly, according to an activist's attitude. But if this same
individual, after arriving in this new country, becomes involved in an
accident, he may devalue this same act of the past, (a_e), after he has experienced all the troubles which were consequences of the accident.
Now this individual will change (according to axiom 3.237) his evaluation
of his past at least in respect to this particular act. Thus, neither
the 'frozen aspect' of the past, i.e., a strict causal or deterministic ordering of events from past to future, nor the 'final aspect' of the future, i.e.,
a teleological ordering of events from past to future, is sufficient to explain historical time. Therefore – if we understand historical time in

the sense defined above – we should avoid any misconstrual of 'historical laws' as concealed natural laws and should not use a law covering scheme of explanation. Rather, our axiomatic treatment of historical time exhibits the dynamical personal aspect of historicity. In this axiomatic system the future as well as the past is included in one unit of evaluation which is dependent solely upon the present actual evaluation at the time, t. The most astonishing result of this brief investigation is that we did not require psychological, ideological or cultural motives, nor causal reasons to explain the fluctuating evaluations (interpretations) and re-evaluations (re-interpretations) of the past. We have obtained our results solely by analyzing the *form* of historicity. This form is certainly a *conditio sine qua non*, or a formal *a priori*, for any understanding of historical time as a manifold evaluation.

5. Consequences

There are two kinds of consequences, one negative, the other positive, which will be discussed in the summation of this whole chapter.

5.1. *Negative Results*

One may regard the explanatory power of a science as a criterion or a measure of its effectiveness according to the proposals of Section One. Historical sciences, like most of the social sciences, are statistical sciences, which can at best provide us with a statistical explanation, either in a wide or narrow sense. An exception to this characterization of the historical sciences might be made in the case in which the mere physical or chemical aspects of human history are recounted. Yet Monod has recently pointed out that even in this particular case we should have doubts. Historical sciences resemble social sciences. They can deliver us only statistical regularities, or perhaps only even vague correlations between events. In either case, these explanations will always admit of exceptions. How can we be sure that a statistical explanation, using a 96% confirmed statistical law, will cover exactly the confirmed cases in exactly the time period under consideration? Or, how can we be sure that our information about the death of Marcus Aurelius on March 17, 180 A.D. in Vienna is really so complete that we can make a clear decision as to whether he was murdered, poisoned, died of senility or by accident? But more importantly, why do we really need explanations of any kind of past events? Perhaps the whole business of historical laws is misguided, born out of imitation of the natural sciences. If we do not believe that pure curiosity, as Aristotle suggested, is the motive for using historical knowledge, we may give a different and final formulation of the answer to the question, "Why?" It seems we are not so much interested in the law subsuming answer to the question, why did events occur, but rather, how should we make future decisions on the basis of our historical information and evaluations of this information. Similarly, we are interested in answering the question, why did our ancestor, or even our own past historical self, act in a specific manner, given a specific evaluation of the past? It rather seems that we have reached a point where we are making laws, not obeying blindly already existing ones. This fits very well into decision theory, where we have no laws at all, but only rules or guidelines for future optimal decisions. Briefly, can we learn from history anything that will help us in the future? Hegel's pessimistic position on this question is well known. He said, "We learn from history that we have learned nothing from history." One may deepen this pessimism and ask, "Has history any sense at all?" Sedillot's answer was: History has no sense, the immense past was only the rehearsal of the mistakes that the future is destined to make on a larger stage and scale.[19] Camus' answer was even more damning: History, and even the future, is in itself absurd.

These indictments point out the enormous difficulties and even paradoxes, which arise if we regard history as a study which ca be covered by classical laws. But, of course, this kind of prediction or retrodiction by means of laws, was precisely the hidden goal of explanation-theorists, and also of all those who believe in historical laws. Unfortunately, this kind of prediction of future actions can never be achieved by using classical or even statistical laws. It is clear that from statistical information, which is partial and incomplete, we cannot draw binding and exact deterministic consequences. In terms of learning theory and problem solving – if we allow a fluctuating evaluation of experiences of our past – learning from historical information would never result in automatic learning and automatical problem solving, i.e., learning in the sense of not repeating mistakes when we have to make future decisions. Thus, the result of the first section, along with the consequences of the interpretation scheme, amounts to an impossibility theorem of precise and exact learning from history; or to the impossibility of making automatic (mechanisable) decisions on the basis of past events (with the exception of dictatoric societal systems).

5.2. *The Positive Results*

The whole axiomatization of the third chapter delineates the consequences of these negative results. This axiomatization is to be regarded as a means to overcome the difficulties discussed above by regarding historical sciences in a completely new way, as a generalized creative decision procedure under uncertainty and risk, permitting partial (optimal) learning from past experience by evaluation at the present time-point, whenever we have to make decisions for the future. This generalized decision procedure will consist of two parts: (1) gathering of information and (2) proposing optimal future decisions on the basis of the available information. A throughgoing axiomatization and discussion of the scheme of such a statistical decision theory has been published elsewhere [20] and will be presented in a forthcoming book by this author, *Philosophy of the Social Sciences*. It is shown that sciences can be founded in a new way based on information and on an evaluation of this information. Further suggestions are provided for possible future decisions on the basis of this available information by means of a theoretical decision-formalism under uncertainty and risk. For such an approach classical or statistical laws are not required at all. All that is required is to establish specific decision rules, based on the oikological-social obligation (see [20] Chapter 1). With this approach, all kinds of historical laws become superfluous. Of course, such a systematic decision-making discipline as is being proposed has the same liabilities as any other statistical theory, namely, that for most cases the solutions for problems will not be uniquely determined in a classical deterministic sense, but rather a set of possible outcomes will be provided. From this set, the individual decision maker, e.g., a politician, is relatively free to select one possible solution. Naturally, in this situation, the members of a society as decision makers have a free choice unless they are in a dictatorship. On the other hand, the individual decision maker bears the full responsibility for his final decisions, since he is free in this situation to choose as he wishes. This relativized freedom and responsibility guarantees that an individual decision maker makes future and history his own. Accordingly, we are led to our last conclusion. Our theoretical reconstruction of historical time by a scheme of evaluation, together with a theory of decision-making under uncertainty and risk, indicates the fundamental limitations of any historical science. Under this conception of historical sciences, we understand these sciences (i) as decision-finding disciplines which will aid us in selecting certain future actions on the basis of evaluation of our past, but will scarcely provide us with absolute solutions. (ii) We may apply these schemes to explain why we, or any historical person decided in a unique way; (iii) why we would decide in a different way, if put into the same historical situation again, simply because our information – in this highly utopian case – is changing constantly. Therefore, no decisions practically can be repeated in one and the same way. We are confronted with a general indeterminacy as regards the future. But this indeterminacy should not be cause for pessimism. If there were no indeterminacy with respect to historical decision making, the whole procedure would become automatic and would best be performed mechanically by a machine or computer. Fortunately, this is impossible. Thus, we need the free decisions of men, restricted by and based on a reasonable evaluation of the past or future, for another important purpose. Self-realization and the realization of new states and situations within our society would be impossible without this relativistic or 'reasoning' freedom of decision making. While historians may be the ultimate advisers of future governments and politicians, they will never be able to take away the burden of making the last responsible decision unless they become politicians themselves.

Generally speaking, the limited set of best possible actions or decisions furnished by such a decision-theoretically oriented historical science guarantees only the opportunity to select a reasonable or plausible future. The ultimate decision is the task of everyone. But only this very act of ultimate decision making gives personal meaning to an individual's life (= history) and establishes finally meaning for the life (= history) of his nation. Our proposal frees the historical sciences from the danger of automatization and mechanical decidability by covering laws, which is yet so useful for classical physics. For we see that history is not frozen and unchangeable. The real philosophical problem of history is now what decisions with respect to tomorrow can be made today on the basis of our evaluative knowledge of the past. Since our evaluation of past events influences our evaluation of our future acts, it consequently follows that the past and future belong to one decision procedure, whether an individual, a group or a nation is involved. Each decision procedure is for purposes of reducing the uncertainty of the past as well as the uncertainty and risk of the future. Such a conception of historical sciences as has been offered frees these sciences from the cognitive aspect of the natural sciences. This conception makes of the historical sciences realizing, creative sciences in which we find the possibility of realizing something completely new, our future life and, by so doing, our history. If the decision-making is done in accordance with the oikological-social obligation, then even the moral problem with respect to decisions of politicians, statesmen and other responsible individuals in a society can be reformulated. Given the best available information of the past, any moral decision would be not to know exactly which single actions should be done – this is quite impossible – but to choose from an optimal set of actions one which fulfills the oikological-social obligation best, with respect to the society and decision maker involved. The finding or even computing of the optimal set of actions, which will determine the future, can be achieved by using the decision-theoretical formalism. The final selection can only be done by free decisions of man. Thus, history can be 'theorized' or reconstructed theoretically within historical sciences, which serve as a decision-finding procedure, where the final decision has to be made in a unique, human way.

Department of Philosophy,
University of Nebraska

NOTES

[1] Hempel, 1965, p. 351.
[2] Hempel, 1965, p. 345.
[3] Hempel, 1965, p. 345.
[4] Hempel, 1965, p. 242.
[5] Hempel, 1965, p. 243.
[6] Leinfellner, 1967, p. 107.
[7] Edwards, 1967, p. 162.
[8] Hempel, 1965, p. 243.
[9] Dray, 1954, pp. 15–27.
[10] Evra, 1970, p. 378.
[11] Monod, 1971, p. 112.
[12] Gardiner, 1959.
[13] Leinfellner, 1966, p. 218.
[14] Leinfellner, 1972, p. 340.

15 Bunge, 1971, pp. 507–508.
16 Leinfellner, 1969, pp. 196–210.
17 Leinfellner, 1969, p. 76.
18 Leinfellner, 1969, p. 201.
19 Durant, 1968, p. 11.
20 Leinfellner, 1973 (*Forschungslogik*).

BIBLIOGRAPHY

Bunge, M., 'Is Scientific Metaphysics Possible?', *Journal of Philosophy* **17** (1971) 507–520.

Carr, Edward H., *What is History?*, Knopf, New York, 1961.

Croce, Benedetto, *History – Its Theory and Practice*, New York 1921 (transl. from: *Teoria e storia della storiografia*, Bari 1917).

Danto, A. and Morgenbesser, S. (eds), *Readings in the Philosophy of Science*, New York 1960.

Dewey, John, *Philosophy and Civilization*.

Dilthey, Wilhelm, *Gesammelte Schriften*, Leipzig and Berlin 1957 – 1960 (2nd. ed.). About one hundred pages of selected passages representing the central thought of Vol. VII have been translated and edited by H. P. Rickmann, *Meaning in History: Dilthey's Thought on History and Society*, New York 1962.

Dray, W., 'Explanatory Narrative in History', *Philosophical Quarterly* **4** (1954) 15–27.

Dray, W., *Laws and Explanation in History*, Oxford 1957.

Dray, W., ' 'Explaining What' in History', in P. Gardiner, (ed.), *Theories of History*, New York 1959, pp. 403–408.

Dray, W., 'The Historical Explanation of Actions Reconsidered', in S. Hook, (ed.), *Philosophy and History*, New York 1963, pp. 105–135.

Durant, Will and Ariel, *The Lessons of History*, New York 1968.

Edwards, P., *Encyclopedia of Philosophy*, New York 1967, Vol. 3, p. 162.

Evra, J. W. V., 'On Scriven on 'Verstehen' ', and Scriven, M., 'Verstehen again', *Theory and Decision* **1**, 377–386.

Gadamer, Hans-Georg, *Wahrheit und Methode*, 1961.

Gardiner, P., 'Historical Explanation', *The Nature of Historical Explanation*, London 1952, 1962 (2nd ed.).

Gardiner, P. (ed.), *Theories of History*, New York 1959.

Gehlen, Arnold, *Der Mensch, Seine Natur und seine Stellung in der Welt*, 1962 (7th ed.).

Gehlen, Arnold, *Urmensch und Spätkultur*, 1964 (2nd edition).

Gehlen, Arnold and Schelsky, H., *Düsseldorf Soziologie*, 1964 (5. edition).

Greeno, James G., *Theoretical Entities in Statistical Explanation*, in *Boston Studies in the Philosophy of Science*, Vol. III, D. Reidel Publ. Co., Dordrecht-Holland, 1971, pp. 3–27.

Herder, Johann Gottfried, *Outlines of a Philosophy of the History of Man*, London 1803, 2 Vol. 2nd edition.

Hempel, C. G., *Deductive-Nomological vs. Statistical Explanation*, in *Minnesota Studies in the Philosophy of Science*, Vol. III, University of Minnesota Press, Minneapolis 1962, pp. 98–169.

Hempel, C. G., *Aspects of Scientific Explanation*, The Free Press, New York, 1965.

Hempel, C. G. and Oppenheim, P., 'Studies in the Logic of Explanation', *Philosophy of Science* 15 (1948) 135–175.

Hilgard, Ernest R., *Theories of Learning*, Appleton, New York 1956 (2nd ed.).

Kaplan, David, 'Explanation Revisited', *Philosophy of Science* 28 (1961) 429–463.

Leinfellner, W., 'Werttheorien und ihre formale Behandlung', *Wissenschaft und Weltbild* 17 (1964) 195–214 and 268–278.

Leinfellner, W., *Struktur und Aufbau wissenschaftlicher Theorien*, Physica Verlag, Würzburg, 1965.

Leinfellner, W., 'Logik und Psychologie', *Studium Generale* 19 (1966) 218.

Leinfellner, W., *Einführung in die Erkenntnis- und Wissenschaftstheorie*, B. I. Hochschultaschenbücher 41, 41a (1967). 2 ed.

Leinfellner, W., 'Generalization of Classical Decision Theory', in K. Borch and J. Mossin (eds.), *Risk and Uncertainty*, London 1969, pp. 196–210.

Leinfellner, W., 'An Axiomatization of Historical Time', *Abstracts of the IVth International Congress for Logic, Methodology and Philosophy of Science*, Bucharest 1972.

Leinfellner, W., 'Wissenschaftstheorie und Begründung der Wissenschaften' and 'Epilinguistische Aspekte sozialwissenschaftlicher Theorien' in G. Eberlein, W. Kroeber-Riel and W. Leinfellner (eds.), *Forschungslogik der Sozialwissenschaften*, Bertelsmann Verlag, Düsseldorf (forthcoming 1973).

Leinfellner, W., 'The Normative Incompleteness of Social Sciences', in *Transactions of the Nebraskan Academy of Science*, Lincoln (forthcoming 1973).

Louch, A. R., *Explanation and Human Action*, Basil Blackwell, Oxford:, 1966.

Monod, J., *Chance and Necessity*, New York 1971.

Nettler, Gwynn, *Explanation*, McGraw-Hill, New York, 1970.

Ortega y Gasset, José, *Geschichte als System*, 1943.

Rickert, Heinrich, *Kulturwissenschaft und Naturwissenschaft*, Freiburg 1910 (2nd edition).

Rickert, Heinrich, *Die Grenzen der naturwissenschaftlichen Begriffsbildung*, Freiburg 1913, 2nd edition.

Rickert, Heinrich, 'Vom System der Werte', *Kantstudien* 19 (1914).

Rousseau, Jean-Jacques, *Contrat Social*, 1762.

Schelsky, H., *Wandlungen der deutschen Familie in der Gegenwart*, Stuttgart 1955 (3rd edition).

Sedillot, René. *L'Histoire n'a pas de sens*, Paris 1965 (History has No Sense).

Suppes, P. and Zinnes, J. L., 'Basic Measurement Theory', in R. D. Luce, R. R. Bush and E. Galanter (eds.), *Handbook of Mathematical Psychology*, Vol. I. John Wiley and Sons, Inc, New York, 1967.

Winch, Peter, *The Idea of a Social Science and its Relation to Philosophy*, Routledge and Kegan, London 1958.

Windelband, Wilhelm, *Geschichte und Naturwissenschaft*, *Rede*, Strassburg 1904 (3rd edition).

Windelband, Wilhelm, *Lehrbuch der Geschichte der Philosophie*, Tübingen 1948 (revised by Heimsoeth).

PART VIII

ETHICS

PETER KIRSCHENMANN

SOME PROBLEMS OF OUGHT-UTILITARIANISM, VALUATION, AND DEONTIC LOGIC

ABSTRACT. The paper contains a discussion of H.-N. Castañeda's claim that merely maximizing value is in general neither a necessary nor a sufficient condition even for the *prima facie* obligatoriness of an action. I show that his arguments against the compatibility of act ought-utilitarianism and deontic logic do not conclusively establish this claim. I urge that one should rather blame deontic logic than utilitarianism for the alleged incompatibility. I supply a modified notion of openness of actions, elaborate on how valuing disjunctive actions and implication relationships between obligations depend on the openness of actions, and specify a method of merely comparing disjunctive actions as to their values. Because of the problems raised by disjunctive actions I question whether prescriptions univocally refer to actions and combine logically like propositions.

1. INTRODUCTION

In his examination of various formulations of act-utilitarianism, Héctor-Neri Castañeda comes to the conclusion that "merely maximizing value is in general neither a necessary nor a sufficient condition even for the *prima facie* rightness, or the *prima facie* obligatoriness, of an action" ([3], 257). He arrives at this verdict by examining, in particular, the compatibility of act-utilitarianism with deontic logic. One of the main purposes of this paper is to check whether his arguments against act *ought*-utilitarianism conclusively justify this verdict. For it seems to me that the principle that in given circumstances the agent in question ought to do the action with the best consequences is sound enough to escape decisive criticism from the side of deontic logic. One may, of course, have strong objections of another nature against such a principle. Some of the difficulties involved in connecting ought-utilitarianism to deontic logic can be delineated as follows.

A principle of deontic logic, of which Castañeda makes ample use, can roughly be stated in the following way. If an action ought to be done, then any action entailed by it ought to be done as well. In order to avoid difficulties it is advisable to formulate this principle not in terms of actions, but rather in terms of actions prescriptively considered, or prescriptions for short (cf. [2]). I shall use capital letters '*A*', '*B*', etc.

M. Bunge (ed.), The Methodological Unity of Science, 219–241. All Rights Reserved.

to designate prescriptions, and '$O(A)$' for the obligation 'the agent ought to do A', etc. Following Castañeda, we may assume that prescriptions combine logically like propositions, and that obligations are propositions (cf. [5]). According to the former assumption, if A and B are prescriptions, then $\sim A$, $A \& B$, $A \vee B$, etc. are prescriptions, too. The principle mentioned can then be stated as the following rule of inference (where '$\rightarrow$' stands for 'entails', and quotations marks to indicate names of prescriptions are omitted):

(DR$_1$) If $A \rightarrow B$ then $O(A) \rightarrow O(B)$.

Since $A \rightarrow A \vee C$, we have, in virtue of (DR$_1$), the following theorem:

(D$_1$) $O(A) \rightarrow O(A \vee C)$.

A rough formulation of a typical kind of act ought-utilitarianism is the following: In given circumstances, the agent ought to do a certain action if and only if its consequences are better than those of any other action open to him. Castañeda assumes that the balance of good consequences of an action over its bad consequences can be represented by a valuation function assigning a numerical value, a real number, to the action. It is clear that actions, and not the corresponding prescriptions, have good or bad consequences. It is only on the assumption of a one-to-one correspondence between actions and prescriptions that the value function may be designated by '$V(A)$', as Castañeda does. With this convention, the utilitarian principle above can be stated as follows (where '$\leftrightarrow\!\!\!\!/$' is used for 'is not equivalent to', and '$\leftrightarrow$' will be used for 'is equivalent to'):

(U) $O(A)$ if and only if (Z) (if $Z \leftrightarrow\!\!\!\!/ A$ then $V(A) > V(Z)$).

Principle (U) can be broken up into two parts according as the value relation provides a necessary or a sufficient condition for obligatoriness.

(UN) If $O(A)$ then (Z) (if $Z \leftrightarrow\!\!\!\!/ A$ then $V(A) > V(Z)$),
(US) If (Z) (if $Z \leftrightarrow\!\!\!\!/ A$ then $V(A) > V(Z)$) then $O(A)$.

Since principle (U) provides a necessary and sufficient condition for the obligatoriness of an action one would expect it to validate principles of deontic logic, as it were, automatically (cf. [1], 299). However, unless further restrictions are imposed on the actions considered, principles

(U) and (DR$_1$) are incompatible. This can be shwon by simple arguments like the following.

Argument I. Let A be obligatory, and $A \lor C$ a prescription not equivalent to A. Then, by (DR$_1$) or by immediately using theorem (D$_1$), we find that $A \lor C$ is obligatory. On the other hand, we find, by (U) or (UN), that $V(A) > V(A \lor C)$. This implies that $V(A \lor C)$ is not greater than the value of any other open action. Thus we have to conclude, by the contrapositive of (U) or by that of (UN), that $A \lor C$ is not obligatory, which contradicts our previous result. Since (UN) can be blamed for this contradiction, utilitarian reasons seem to be incapable of providing necessary conditions for the obligatoriness of actions.

Castañeda's main arguments are not as simple as argument I, because they concern more sophisticated versions of act-utilitarianism which involve precisely specified notions of alternative action, a clarified notion of open action, and specific assumptions about valuing disjunctive actions. I shall deal with such specifications before examining his arguments. However, I shall begin with a discussion of argument I and, in particular, theorem (D$_1$): for it is, of course, not necessarily the utilitarian principle that is to blame for the resulting contradiction. One can just as well find fault with deontic logic.

2. DISCUSSION OF THEOREM (D$_1$)

Argument I may be taken to show that theorem (D$_1$) and, consequently, rule (DR$_1$) are open to objection, rather than principle (U) or (UN). Indeed, this theorem, which is known as Ross' paradox (cf. [6], 383 f.), has been considered as highly implausible, if not unacceptable. Ross takes it to be outright false ([9]; [10], 159f.). The reason given for his rejection is that the obligation $O(A \lor C)$ expresses a freedom of choice which is incompatible with the choiceless duty $O(A)$, whence "the obligation to post a letter does not imply an obligation to either post it or burn it" ([10], 161).

However, theorem (D$_1$) is a consequence of the rather plausible principle

(D$_2$) $O(G \ \& \ H) \leftrightarrow O(G) \ \& \ O(H)$,

which is adopted by Ross [10], 163f.), provided one accepts the following more restrictive rule of inference:

(DR$_2$) If $G \leftrightarrow H$ then $O(G) \leftrightarrow O(H)$.

Clearly, $A \rightarrow A \vee C$ implies $A \& (A \vee C) \leftrightarrow A$. Hence, by (DR$_2$), $O(A \& \& (A \vee C)) \leftrightarrow O(A)$. This equivalence, together with (D$_2$), yields $O(A) \leftrightarrow \leftrightarrow O(A) \& O(A \vee C)$, which in turn implies theorem (D$_1$).

Insofar as (D$_2$) or (DR$_2$) is not rejected or regarded as paradoxical, theorem (D$_1$) should not be so either. The feeling of paradox in regard of this theorem seems to arise from mistakenly considering obligation $O(A \vee C)$ not only as deducible, but also as separable from the antecedent obligation $O(A)$; as if one first were faced with a choiceless obligation, but then only with an obligation involving a freedom of choice. However, there is no reason to regard $O(A \vee C)$ as offering a choice as long as the obligation $O(A)$ is not forgotten. In other words, we still have the conjunctive obligation $O(A \vee C) \& O(A)$, and not $O(A \vee C)$ alone. According to (D$_2$), this conjunctive obligation is equivalent to $O(A \vee A \& C)$. Because $A \vee A \& C \leftrightarrow A$, we find ,by (DR$_2$), that the conjunctive obligation is equivalent precisely to the original obligation $O(A)$.

In cases of mutually exclusive alternatives it is even more evident that theorem (D$_1$) need not be rejected, and that no paradox is involved. Consider Ross' example; let 'A' stand for the prescription 'to mail the letter', and 'C' for 'to burn it'; and assume again that the agent ought to do A. Then, by (D$_1$), he also ought to do $A \vee C$. In the present case, A and C can be regarded as incompatible, whence $A \rightarrow \sim C$. Thus the agent has, amongst others, the conjunctive obligation $O(A \vee C) \& O(\sim C)$, which, in virtue of (D$_2$), is equvalent to $O(A \& \sim C \vee C \& \sim C)$. The latter is, by (DR$_2$), equivalent to $O(A \& \sim C)$, which is precisely the intended obligation. In general, it seems correct to say that the apparently paradoxical character of theorem (D$_1$) vanishes as soon as one takes the entire context of the obligation $O(A \vee C)$ into account (cf. [6], 384).

3. DISJUNCTIVE PRESCRIPTIONS AND OPENNESS OF ACTIONS

Whereas theorem (D$_1$) has turned out to be logically unimpeachable, there still remains something obscure about the meaning of obligations of the kind $O(G \vee H)$. According to the few stipulations made so far, G and H are prescriptions which combine like propositions to form other prescriptions, whence $G \vee H$ is another prescription. Consequently, '$O(G \vee H)$' says that one ought to do what is prescribed by '$G \vee H$'. Any further interpretation of '$O(G \vee H)$' will have to draw upon additional data and assumptions. The usual approach is to inquire into how the obligatory disjunction can be fulfilled. On the basis of the assumed one-to-one correspondence between prescriptions and actions we can merely say that $O(G \vee H)$ is fulfilled once the action corresponding to prescription $G \vee H$ has been performed. But what does it mean to do $G \vee H$?

Suppose that G and H are incompatible alternatives which are not themselves disjunctions of other alternatives, for this case will be of particular relevance to the subsequent discussion. Such actions will be called 'basic alternatives' (Castañeda's "basic utilitarian actions"; [3], 261). Doing $G \vee H$, then, is usually taken to mean that one does either G or H. More precisely, since $G \vee H$ is equivalent to $G \& \sim H \vee$ $\vee \sim G \& H$, the obligation $O(G \vee H)$ is considered fulfilled when one has done what either one of these disjuncts prescribes. For this reason, the obligation $O(G \vee H)$, when taken by itself, does seem to offer a choice. But as we have seen, this need not actually be so, depending on other obligations, or rather the total context relative to which $O(G \vee H)$ holds. In particular, it depends on the set of actions which in given circumstances are open to the agent.

The open actions are those which the agent not only can perform, but also can actually choose to perform. To fix ideas, Castañeda considers the agent to be in such circumstances that the only way for him to act is through a particular kind of push-button machine, an 'action machine' ([3], 262f.; and also [4]). In terms of this machine, the open actions are taken to be those for which there are operating buttons. The machine itself is assumed to be a physical realization of the logical connections between prescriptions. Thus it is assumed that, if prescription A entails prescription B, depressing the button for A depresses the button for B. This implies the following principle of openness:

(OP) If $A \to B$ then open $(A) \to$ open (B).

Reconsider the ways in which a disjunctive action $G \vee H$ can be performed, assuming that circumstances are such as can be represented by a push-button machine of this kind. In general, it can be performed either indirectly, by depressing the button for G or that for H, or directly, by depressing the button for $G \vee H$. Concerning the latter way Castañeda assumes that the machine will then realize either G or H. Thus, in performing $G \vee H$ directly, i.e., in depressing the button for $G \vee H$, the agent takes a risk as to the eventual course and outcome of his action. The circumstances can be of the following two essentially different kinds:

> (0.1) At least one of the actions G and H is open, and consequently, by principle (OP), $G \vee H$ is open.
>
> (0.2) $G \vee H$ is open, but none of the actions G and H are open.

Clearly, in case (0.2), the agent has only one way to perform $G \vee H$. Furthermore, we can see now how the set of open actions may determine whether the obligation $O(G \vee H)$ involves a choice or not. In case (0.2), this obligation does not leave any choice to the agent. In case (0.1), the agent has a choice of how to fulfill $O(G \vee H)$ unless, of course, he has the obligation $O(G)$ or $O(H)$ at the same time.

Some comments on Castañeda's action machine are in order. Its most appealing feature lies in that it seems to assign a definite act, if only a releasing push, to disjunctive prescriptions, insofar as the machine has a button for the corresponding disjunctive action. Yet it is only in case (0.2) that 'doing $G \vee H$' can be given this definite sense. Obviously, this sense goes beyond the purely logical meaning of '$G \vee H$', because performing $G \vee H$ by depressing the button for $G \vee H$ has been assumed to involve a risk as to the eventual course of the action. This interpretation of '$G \vee H$' would be analogous to regarding the proposition $p \vee q$ as involving some uncertainty or indeterminacy. In cases other than (0.2), however, 'doing $G \vee H$' remains ambivalent in that the disjunctive action can be performed either directly and with a risk, or indirectly and without risk, i.e., by pushing one of the buttons for the disjuncts. In a sense, allowing this ambivalence amounts to a breach with the assumed one-to-one correspondence between prescriptions and actions. It is at least in part because of this ambivalence that, as we shall see later, there can be several ways of valuing disjunctive actions.

Moreover, because of the ambivalence of disjunctive prescriptions, Castañeda's assumption that depressing the button for A will depress the button for B, if A entails B, may lead to inconsistencies. According to this assumption, depressing the button for G will depress the button for $G \vee H$. Now depressing the button for G does not involve any risk, whereas depressing the button for $G \vee H$ does, since it has been assumed that the machine itself will then realize either G or H. This is an inconsistency on the level of interpretation. It does not mean that the logic of prescriptions adopted harbors an inconsistency. The interpretational device, i.e., the push-button machine, can therefore be modified so as to rid it of the blemish. One can assume that the wiring in the machine is such that depressing the buttons for G and $G \vee H$ together will have the same effect as depressing that for G alone, in accordance with the fact that $G \,\&$ $\& \,(G \vee H)$ is equivalent to G (cf. also [4]). Although the push-button machine will, through this and similar assumptions, become a physical realization of the logic of prescription, such assumptions, including that of Castañeda above, seem to go too far. It is enough to say that prescription G logically entails prescription $G \vee H$ and possibly numerous other disjunctive prescriptions with G as one of their disjuncts. One may even assume that the *internal* wiring of the machine is such that depressing the button for G will realize $G \vee H$ and all other disjunctive actions which correspond to the disjunctive prescriptions mentioned. But one need not presuppose that there must be operating buttons for all these disjunctive actions. This pressupposition would indeed restrict the kinds of circumstances considered. In general then, one should assume only that depressing the button for A will realize B, if A entails B. Making this assumption does not mean rejecting principle (OP), although a less restrictive principle can then be formulated. To this end, the conception of open actions as those for which there are operating buttons has to be expanded. The open actions are to be described as those for which there are such buttons or which are entailed by open actions. Calling the former 'directly open actions', the latter 'indirectly open actions', and using 'open'' to abbreviate 'directly or indirectly open', we have the following less restrictive principle of openness:

(OP') If $A \rightarrow B$ then open' $(A) \rightarrow$ indirectly open (B).

(When 'open'' is replaced with 'open', principle (OP') implies principle (OP) in the form stated above.)

In view of this modification, the circumstances in which a disjunctive action $G \vee H$ is performable can be divided into the following cases:

(0'.1a) G is open', H is not, and $G \vee H$ is not directly open.

(0′.1b) H is open′, G is not, and $G \vee H$ is not directly open.
(0′.1c) G and H are open′, and $G \vee H$ is not directly open.
(0′.2) $G \vee H$ is directly open, but neither G nor H is open′.
(0′.3a) G is open′, H is not, and $G \vee H$ is directly open.
(0′.3b) H is open′, G is not, and $G \vee H$ is directly open.
(0′.3c) G and H are open′, and $G \vee H$ is directly open.

It goes without saying that, according to principle (OP′), $G \vee H$ is indirectly open in all cases, in case (0′.2) trivially so. Evidently, it is only in case (0′.2) that doing $G \vee H$ necessarily involves a risk as to the final outcome of the action. In case (0′.1c), no risk can be involved.

4. Obligatoriness and openness of actions

Concerning the connection between openness and obligatoriness of actions, Castañeda adopts the following principle (e.g. [3], 268, where it is used, but not stated);

(O-OP) If $O(A)$ then open (A).

The question is whether, in the light of the preceding considerations, this principle – by itself or when combined with other principles governing obligatoriness or openness adopted by him – is adequate. Consider the following situation and the subsequent arguments.

Argument IIa. Let circumstances be such that action E is obligatory and action F not open, and that E entails F. Since E is obligatory, it follows, in virtue of (O-OP), that E is open. However, since F is not open and E entails F, we must, by (OP), conclude that E is not open, in contradiction to our previous finding.

Inasmuch as 'open' is ambiguous the contradiction can be avoided. Once we distinguish between directly open and indirectly open we have to use principle (OP′) instead of (OP). Analogously, we have to replace (O-OP) with the following principle:

(O-OP′) If $O(A)$ then open′ (A).

If, then, what is assumed in argument IIa is that F is *not directly* open, no contradiction arises. We simply find that F is indirectly open and E directly or indirectly open.

If, however, what is assumed in argument IIa is that F is *not* even *indirectly* open, we are still faced with a contradiction even though we are employing (OP') and (O-OP') instead of (OP) and (O-OP). Yet does this assumption make sense? Since by doing what E prescribes the agent is doing all the logical consequences of E, amongst them F, it is inconsistent to assume that action E is open and F not even indirectly open. In other words, rather than rejecting principle (OP'), or (O-OP') which quite reasonably says that E cannot be obligatory unless it is directly or indirectly open, we should reject as impossible the assumed situation.

The same situation leads to still another contradiction when principles adopted by Castañeda are employed. This comes about as follows.

Argument IIb. Again, let E be obligatory and F not open, and E entail F. In virtue of (O-OP), since F is not open, it is not obligatory. However, since E entails F and E is obligatory, we must, by principle (DR$_1$), conclude that F is obligatory. We are faced with another contradiction.

As before, no contradiction arises if what is meant is that F is *not directly* open and, (O-OP') is used instead of (O-OP). We simply find that F is obligatory and indirectly open.

If, however, the assumption about F means that F is *not* even *indirectly* open, then, as we have found, the assumed situation is itself inconsistent. In order to stave off such situations I suggest making explicit the requirement that the obligatoriness of an action not be *inferrable* unless it is open. As to the present example, this can be done as follows:

(DR$_1'$) If $A \rightarrow B$ and open' (B) then $O(A) \rightarrow O(B)$.

Clearly, using (DR$_1'$) instead of (DR$_1$), we are not led to a contradiction even when F is not indirectly open. We simply find, by (O-OP'), that F is not obligatory.

The situation assumed in arguments II is so clear-out, especially when the meaning of 'open" is specified as directly or indirectly open, that it hardly seems worth while discussing it. Yet less conspicuous situations such as the following in which the same lines of argument may reappear are conceivable.

Argument III. Let actions A, B, C be incompatible alternatives; let the two disjunctive actions $A \vee B$ and $B \vee C$ be obligatory; and assume that B is not open. Then, from $O(A \vee B)$ and $O(B \vee C)$, it follows, by (D$_2$), that action $(A \vee B)$ & $(B \vee C)$ is also obligatory. As A, B, C are incompatible, prescription $(A \lor B)$ & $(B \lor C)$ is logically equivalent to B. Thus, by (DR_1) or (DR_2), we find that B is obligatory. However, since B is not open, it is, according to (O-OP), not obligatory. This contradicts what we just found.

An examination of this argument shows, that except for the first step, which involves principle (D_2), it is exactly parallel to argument IIb (with $(A \lor B)$ & $(B \lor C)$ taking the place of E, and B that of F). For this reason, another contradiction can be obtained along the lines of argument IIa; and our discussion of arguments II applies as well to argument III.

The first step deserves some further comments with regard to the more serious case of the two discussed above, viz., when it is assumed that B is not even indirectly open. We shall discuss this step in terms of the action machine introduced in the preceding section. In the present case, the machine could have operating buttons for $A \lor B$ and $B \lor C$, since both are assumed to be obligatory; hence, by (O-OP'), they are open', which can mean that they are directly open. Now, the wiring of the machine can be such that depressing the buttons for $A \lor B$ and $B \lor C$ together will make the machine perform their logical conjunction $(A \lor B)$ & $(B \lor C)$ and also any action logically implied by it. In this case, the conjunctive action would be indirectly open (which would also follow from the assumptions in virtue of (D_2) and (O-OP')), and so would be all the actions it entails, amongst them action B. Therefore, if the situation is such as can be represented by this particular machine, then assuming that B is not indirectly open means assuming a contradiction at the very outset. This suggests again, as in the case of arguments II when the assumption concerning F was taken to mean that it was not indirectly open, that the situation specified in argument III should be rejected as inconsistent. And again, we can protect ourselves against such situations by adopting the following principle instead of (D_2):

(D_2') If $O(G)$ and $O(H)$, and open' $(G \& H)$ then $O(G \& H)$.

Indeed, (D_2') precludes the very first step of argument III; the conjunction $(A \lor B)$ & $(B \lor C)$ is neither directly nor indirectly open if B is not even indirectly open (principle (OP')).

Other rules of inference of deontic logic are to be modified correspondingly. Instead of (DR_2), which could have been used in argument III in the place of (DR_1), I suggest adopting the following principle:

(DR'_2) If $G \leftrightarrow H$ and open' (G) and open' (H) then $O(G) \leftrightarrow O(H)$.

5. ALTERNATIVENESS, AND VALUES OF DISJUNCTIVE ACTIONS

There is a straightforward way of evading the contradiction derived in argument I or other similarly simple arguments. This is achieved by replacing principle (U) with a utilitarian principle that refers to alternative actions alone (cf. [3], 258). More precisely, this means that two actions A and Z shall not be compared as to their values unless they are incompatible. Obviously, if we adopt the following principle

(U^+) $O(A)$ if and only if (Z) (if $Z \rightarrow \sim A$ then $V(A) > V(Z)$)

instead of (U), we can no longer argue along the lines of argument I, since A and $A \vee C$ are not incompatible.

Principle (U^+) is still in need of further precision. It does not specify the relevant set of alternative actions. There are two ways of specifying such a set. Both make use of a set of basic alternatives (Castañeda's "basic utilitarian actions"; cf. [3], 260ff.) which are pairwise incompatible and exhaust the possibilities regarding the eventual course and outcome of the agent's actions; they are not themselves disjunctions of other alternatives. In other words, eventually, the agent will necessarily have performed one of the basic alternatives. Any action is then either a basic alternative or a disjunction of basic alternatives. As the set of alternative actions relevant in given circumstances one can take the set of all (directly) open actions Z_A which are incompatible with the action A (Castañeda's "μ-alternativeness"); or one can take a set of (directly) open actions which are pairwise incompatible and jointly exhaustive of all performable basic alternatives (Castañeda's "α-alternativeness"; cf. [3], 260ff.). Qualifying principle (U^+) accordingly we obtain the following two distinct principles:

(U_μ) $O(A)$ if and only if (Z_A) (if Z_A is μ-alternative to A then $V(A) > V(Z_A)$),

(U_α) $O(A)$ if and only if there is a set α_h of α-alternatives such that $A \in \alpha_h$ and (Z) (if $Z \in \alpha_h$ and $Z \neq A$ then $V(A) > V(Z)$).

As was done with principle (U), principles (U_μ) and (U_α) can be split up into parts (U_μN) and (U_μS), and (U_αN) and (U_αS) respectively, according as the value relations provide a necessary or a sufficient condition for obligatoriness. These four partial principles are related in the following way ([3], 266):

(RN) If (U_μN) holds, then (U_αN) holds.
(RS) If (U_αS) holds, then (U_μS) holds.

Consequently, if (U_αN), or (U_μS), can be shown to be invalid, then (U_μN), or (U_αS), will also be invalidated.

Later on I shall examine arguments that can be brought forward against principles (U_αN) and (U_μS). In these arguments, disjunctive actions will play a crucial role and will have to be compared with other actions as to their value. It is therefore expedient to adopt some method of assigning values to disjunctive actions. In view of the complications we have so far encountered in treating disjunctive prescriptions, we should not expect that there will be only one possible method of valuing disjunctive actions.

It seems plausible to assume that the value of a disjunctive action is a function of the values of its disjuncts which cannot exceed the value of its highest-valued disjunct, and cannot be exceeded by the value of its lowest-valued disjunct ([3], 264). In the case of two basic alternatives G and H with values $V(G)=g$ and $V(H)=h$, we can assume, then, that $V(G \vee H)$ is a function $F(g, h)$ subject to the condition

(V) $\max(g, h) \geqslant F(g, h) \geqslant \min(g, h)$.

This condition leaves a great choice of functions. Amongst them are the following two extreme cases:

(V.a) $F(g, h) = \max(g, h)$,
(V.c) $F(g, h) = \min(g, h)$.

All intermediate cases fulfill the condition

(V.b) $\max(g, h) > F(g, h) > \min(g, h)$ if $g \neq h$,
          $F(g, h) = g = h$ if $g = h$.

Castañeda combines these three possibilities of valuing disjunctive actions with principles (U_α) and (U_μ). This yields six distinct varieties of what he calls "simple ought-utilitarianism" ([3], 265). It is these forms of simple utilitarianism that he examines and finds wanting with respect to their capability of generally providing necessary and sufficient conditions for the obligatoriness of actions. The above approach to valuing disjunctive actions is, however, open to various objections. For one thing, one may insist that the value assigned to an action be a measure of its *actual* consequences. The actual consequences of a disjunction of two basic alternatives G and H will be either the consequences of G or those of H. Hence the value assigned to the disjunctive action $G \vee H$ should be exactly the value of just one of its disjuncts (cf. [3], 264). To be sure, this fact might be taken to support condition (V). But it may quite as well be taken to imply that a disjunctive action cannot be assigned a definite value at all. It would seem that it has to remain undecided whether $G \vee H$ should be given the value of G or that of H.

One might think of overcoming this difficulty by regarding the value of an action not as a measure of its actual consequences, but rather of its *possible* consequences. It may be doubted whether a utilitarian would be willing to make such a concession (cf. also [8], 80ff.). At any rate, the possible consequences of basic alternatives can be taken to be the same as their actual consequences. Yet the possible consequences of a disjunctive action $G \vee H$ are either the consequences of G or those of H. Thus, this disjunctive action should be given two values, according to the following principle:

(V') $V(G \vee H)$ equals either $V(G)$ or $V(H)$.

This means that $V(G \vee H)$ is not a single-valued function of the values of G and H. Consequently, none of the assumptions (V) would be justifiable.

It is clear, however, that function F in assumptions (V) is not at all supposed to be a measure of the possible consequences of disjunctive actions. In general, F is rather a measure mediating between the values of the disjuncts of a disjunctive action. Because of some parallels to the concept of expected utility in classical utility theory, this measure can be called the '*expected value*' of a disjunctive action. The particular methods (V.a) and (V.c) equate, as it were, this expected value of a disjunctive action with one of its possible values. mThis akes some sense in cases where the action having the value which is equated with the value of the disjunction is itself open to the agent (which is possible in cases (0'.1) and (0'.3), listed in section 3). But when disjunctive actions involve a risk (which they necessarily do in case (0'.2)), it seems highly unreasonable to use method (V.a) or (V.c) to determine their expected value.

According to assumption (V.b), the expected value of a disjunctive action lies somewhere between its possible values, which can be considered an expression of the fact that risk is involved. Undoubtedly, any method complying with (V.b) will fulfill the task of providing a means for comparing disjunctive actions with other actions. In general, however, when employing such a method we shall in fact compare the expected value of disjunctive actions, which in some way depends on the risk as to their final outcome, with the actual values of riskless alternatives. This kind of comparison is certainly an interesting subject matter for decision theorists, but hardly a solid basis for utilitarianism, which intends to provide firm grounds for obligations (cf. [4]).

One may therefore conclude that, for the sake of a utilitarian theory, disjunctive actions and basic alternatives are not generally comparable. However, in particular cases, disjunctive actions and basic alternatives can still be considered comparable, for instance, as to their possible values. Let G, H, and K be basic alternatives with values $V(G)=g$, $V(H)=h$, and $V(K)=k$. In view of principle (V'), one can make the following assumptions:

(V'.1) If $k \geqslant \max(g, h)$ and $k > \min(g, h)$ then $V(K) > V(G \vee H)$,
(V'.2) If $\max(g, h) > k$ and $\min(g, h) \geqslant k$ then $V(G \vee H) > V(K)$.

Clearly, these assumptions do not cover any 'risky comparisons'. More precisely, the assumptions do not legislate anything about the relationship between $V(G \vee H)$ and $V(K)$ when $\max(g, h) > k > \min(g, h)$. Note that except for these cases any method of type (V.b) yields the statements (V'.1) and V'.2). However, in contrast to such methods, assumptions (V'.1) and (V'.2) do not presuppose that a disjunctive action be assigned just one value. Mere comparison, which is all that is required in order to apply principles (U_α) and (U_μ), is possible without such a presupposition.

Assumptions (V'.1) and (V'.2) are easily generalized for comparing disjunctive actions with one another. In the case of two-membered disjunctions we can make the following assumption, where L is another basic alternative with value $V(L)=l$:

(V'.3) If $\max(g, h) > \min(k, l)$ and $\min(g, h) \geqslant \max(k, l)$ then $V(G \vee H) > V(K \vee L)$.

(Somewhat different assumptions could be made by replacing the partial condition $\max(g, h) > \min(k, l)$ with stronger ones, $\max(g, h) > \max(k, l)$ or $\min(g, h) > \min(k, l)$. Assumption (V'.3) has been chosen, because it yields (V'.1) for $G=H$, and (V'.2) for $K=L$.)

6. ARGUMENTS AGAINST $(U_\alpha N)$

As we saw in the preceding section, one of the utilitarian principles to be examined is $(U_\alpha N)$, which reads explicitly:

$(U_\alpha N)$ If $O(A)$ then there is a set α_h of α-alternatives such that $A \in \alpha_h$ and (Z) (if $Z \in \alpha_h$ and $Z \neq A$ then $V(A) > V(Z)$).

By means of a number of examples, Castañeda argues that this principle, when combined with methods fulfilling condition (V), can lead either to contradictions or to results militating against the very spirit of utilitarianism, and must therefore be rejected ([3], 266ff.). This would mean that simple utilitarian conditions cannot in general be necessary for obligatoriness. I shall render but the essentials of his arguments, and discuss them subsequently.

Argument IV. Suppose that in certain circumstances the agent ought to do action A. Then, by $(U_\alpha N)$, there is a set α_h of α-alternatives, to which A belongs, such that the value of A is greater than that of any other member of α_h. Consider a case where there are just three basic alternatives A, B, C with values interrelated as $V(A) \gtrsim V(B) \gg V(C)$, which case is undoubtedly possible. Given this case and a particular function F fulfilling condition (V), it may well turn out that $V(B) \geqslant V(A \vee C)$. (This relation will hold quite generally when method (V.c) is adopted, while it cannot hold when method (V.a) is used.) Since the set consisting of B and $A \vee C$ is the only set of α-alternatives to which $A \vee C$ belongs, we find that there is no set α_k with $A \vee C$ as one of its members such that the value of $A \vee C$ is greater than that of any other member. Hence, by the contrapositive of $(U_\alpha N)$, action $A \vee C$ is not obligatory. On the other hand, the fact that A is obligatory entails, by principle (DR_1) or theorem

(D_1), that $A \vee C$ is obligatory, in contradiction to the result just obtained.

How can a contradiction of this kind be evaded? One may think of doing so by distinguishing two types of obligatoriness: one, to be designated by 'O_U', for which the utilitarian condition of principle (U_α) is necessary, and one for which it is not. Only the latter, a neutral type of obligatoriness, will be supposed to obey the principles of deontic logic; it will again be designated by 'O'. In addition, one can adopt a principle to the effect that $O_U(A)$ implies $O(A)$. If we now presuppose that A is obligatory in the utilitarian sense and go on arguing along the lines of argument IV, we obtain, on the one hand, $\sim O_U(A \vee C)$. On the other hand, we still have $O(A \vee C)$, which, however, does not contradict $\sim O_U(A \vee C)$.

While a contradiction is thus avoided, the proposed modifications amount to nothing else but the idea that the utilitarian condition of (U_α) is not generally necessary for obligatoriness. It was precisely this point which argument IV was meant to establish. However, if this proposal is accepted, one will, from the very outset, not expect utilitarian theses like (U_α) or (U_μ) to validate principles of deontic logic, for it means that utilitarianism and deontic logic are not concerned with obligatoriness in the same sense. (Note that Castañeda's final formulation of a complex and troublefree act ought-utilitarianism contains practically the same distinction between obligatoriness in the utilitarian sense and that in the neutral sense ([3], 274).)

There are ways of evading the contradiction in argument IV which leave assumption $(U_\alpha N)$ untouched. The method referred to in this argument of valuing disjunctive actions may be replaced by a method which will not entail $V(B) \geqslant V(A \vee C)$. Indeed, the couple of assumptions $(V'.1)$ and $(V'.2)$ does not entail any definite relationship between $V(B)$ and $V(A \vee C)$. Principle $(U_\alpha N)$, when combined with these assumptions, will therefore not lead to a contradiction of the above kind. Since comparisons according to methods (V') do not lead to definite results in all cases, it is clear that utilitarian principles combined with these methods cannot validate principles of deontic logic *in general*, but do at least not interfere with them. Note that here, in contrast to the modifications discussed above, we do not allow for two senses of 'obligatoriness'.

As was parenthetically indicated in argument II, method $(V.a)$ will also ensure that $V(B) \geqslant V(A \vee C)$ does not hold. On adopting this method, we have $V(A \vee C) = V(A)$, hence $V(A \vee C) > V(B)$; and again no contradiction of the above kind arises. We simply find, by means of $(U_\alpha N)$, that now action B cannot be obligatory. However, using method (V.a) seems to be an act of force for the sole purpose of preventing any incompatiblity between the principle $(U_\alpha N)$ and rule (DR_1) or, more particularly, theorem (D_1). When method (V.a) is employed, value considerations become almost irrelevant, because it implies that $V(A \vee X) = V(A)$ will indiscriminately hold for any X when A is the basic alternative of highest value. As indicated in the preceding section, adopting this method may be justifiable in particular cases. As long as an action A is open to the agent he can always perform any action $A \vee X$ in such a way as to bring about value $V(A)$, namely, by doing A. But if there is no such action open to him, method (V.a) can lead to results contravening the very spirit of utilitarianism, as Castañeda shows by means of another example.

Argument V. Suppose that in given circumstances there are three basic alternatives A, B, and C; that actions $A \vee C$ and B are open to the agent, but A and C themselves are not; that the values of the basic alternatives are related by $V(A) = V(B) \gg V(C)$. Using method (V.a) we find that $V(A \vee C)$ is not greater than the value of the α-alternatives to $A \vee C$ in any set α_h; and similarly for $V(B)$. Thus, in virtue of $(U_\alpha N)$, neither $A \vee C$ nor B is obligatory. Yet performing B would guarantee the largest amount of value, while performing $A \vee C$ may bring about the small or negative value $V(C)$. The result that B cannot be obligatory, therefore, appears to be at variance with the very ideal of utilitarianism, which is to bring about the greater good and avoid the greater evil. (Even if we assume $V(A) \gtrsim V(B) \gg V(C)$ instead of $V(A) = V(B) \gg V(C)$, we still can argue against the combination of $(U_\alpha N)$ and (V.a) in a similar way. In this case we find that B cannot be obligatory no matter how little value, or how great a catastrophe, might be brought about by a realization of C, and how little more value than through B might be gained by a realization of A.)

It is clear that argument V tells rather against the adoption of method (V.a) in the circumstances given than against principle $(U_\alpha N)$. As has been mentioned in the preceding section, a disjunctive action should not be assigned a value by method (V.a) when, as in the above example, it involves a risk as to its final outcome. No other method – be it (V'.1), or one complying with (V.b), let alone (V.c) – will entail that action B cannot be obligatory. Hence they will not lead to results militating against the spirit of utilitarianism.

The discussion of arguments IV and V suggests that the method of valuing disjunctive actions, or comparing them with other actions, should not be chosen independently of the circumstances considered. As Castañeda's arguments convincingly show, counter-examples can be found against all fixed combinations of principle $(U_\alpha N)$ and one of the methods (V.a) and (V.c), or any one complying with (V.b), i.e., against every variety of simple ought-utilitarianism in his sense. (Note that in his final formulation of an act ought-utiltarianism, Castañeda makes the method of valuing disjunctive actions dependent on whether the highest-valued basic alternative is open or not ([3], 274).) They do not show that merely maximizing value cannot be a necessary condition for obligatoriness when the method of valuing disjunctive actions is flexibly chosen. In particular, the difficulties pointed out by arguments IV and V will be avoided when assumptions (V'.1) and (V'.2) are chosen. To be sure, these assumptions might be deemed insufficient, because they do not in all cases lead to definite value relationships.

7. ARGUMENTS AGAINST $(U_\mu S)$

By means of another series of examples, Castañeda argues that principle $(U_\mu S)$, when combined with methods fulfilling condition (V), leads to contradictions ([3], 268f.). This principle reads explicitly:

> $(U_\mu S)$ If (Z_A) (if Z_A is μ-alternative to A then $V(A) > V(Z_A)$) then $O(A)$.

Again, I shall render but the essentials of his arguments.

Argument VI. Suppose circumstances are such that disjunctive actions built from four basic alternatives A, B, C, D are open to the agent, but neither of these four actions themselves. Thus, by (O-OP), none of the four actions is obligatory. Let the values of these actions be related as follows: $V(A) > V(B) > V(C) > V(D)$. The open action $A \vee B$ has only one open μ-alternative, viz., $C \vee D$; similarly, the only μ-alternative to $B \vee C$ is $A \vee D$. There are undoubtedly cases where, given the values of the four basic alternatives and a function F satisfying condition (V), the relations $V(A \vee B) > V(C \vee D)$ and $V(B \vee C) > V(A \vee D)$ hold. Thus, by principle $(U_\mu S)$, both $A \vee B$ and $B \vee C$ are obligatory. Hence, by principle (D_2), action $(A \vee B) \& (B \vee C)$ is also obligatory. Since this action is logically equivalent to B, it follows, by (DR_2) or (DR_1), that action B is obligatory. However, this result contradicts our previous finding that none of the actions A, B, C, D is obligatory. The argument remains essentially the same if one chooses the particular method (V.a). Of course in this case we have $V(A \vee D) > V(B \vee C)$ besides $V(A \vee B) > V(C \vee D)$. These relations make A obligatory, again in contradiction to our previous result.

There are only a few points which need to be discussed. As a rejection of utilitarian principles, argument VI is much weaker than argument IV, because principle $(U_\mu S)$ is used in a relatively inessential way. Consider the pairs of open μ-alternatives $\{A \vee B, C \vee D\}$, $\{B \vee C, A \vee D\}$, and $\{A \vee C, B \vee D\}$. (For the sake of completeness I have also listed the third pair, not used by argument VI.) It suffices to presuppose that any one member of at least two pairs is obligatory. Then it follows, along the lines of argument VI, either that one of the actions A, B, C, D is obligatory, which leads to the above contradiction, or that a contradictory action is obligatory, viz., a disjunction with all its disjuncts being conjunctions of incompatible actions. The only role value considerations and principle $(U_\mu S)$ can play is to provide a sufficient reason for taking two or three *particular* members as obligatory.

Except for these inessential value considerations argument VI is virtually the same as argument III. Thus, the contradiction of argument VI can be avoided through the revisions of deontic logic proposed in section 4, i.e., chiefly through a clarification of questions of openness. (In his final formulation of an act ought-utilitarianism, Castañeda includes an idea to the effect of the revised principle (DR_1') ([3], 274). Note that this is not done as a modification of deontic logic, but as one of utilitarianism.)

So far it has been accepted that several of the open disjunctive actions can be obligatory. This is justified as long as methods complying with condition (V) are used for valuing disjunctive actions. It is plain that argument VI would also break down if one disjunctive action were alone capable of being obligatory. This is actually the case when disjunctive actions are compared according to assumption (V'.3). Applying principles $(U_\mu S)$ and (V'.3) to the circumstances presupposed in argument VI, we find that only action $A \vee B$ is obligatory, which after all, appears to be a very natural conclusion.

There are then several ways of evading the contradiction derived in argument VI. In particular, this argument employs inconsistent assumptions concerning the openness of actions, as was shown in section 4. This is why, in contrast to our conclusion in the preceding section, argument VI does not even provide good grounds for rejecting *fixed* combinations of principle ($U_\mu S$) and one of the methods satisfying condition (V). Thus, Castañeda's arguments along the lines of argument VI fail to show that merely maximizing value cannot be a sufficient condition for obligatoriness.

8. Conclusion

We found that Castañeda's arguments do not conclusively establish that merely maximizing value is in general neither a necessary nor a sufficient condition for the obligatoriness of an action. His first series of arguments does, however, show that no form of what he calls simple ought-utilitarianism, i.e., fixed combinations of principle (U_α) or (U_μ) and any method satisfying condition (V) for valuing disjunctive actions, will generally provide a *necessary* condition for obligatoriness. But there is a way of comparing disjunctive actions with other actions which, when combined with these principles, yields utilitarian theses which are as simple as those examined by him, yet are immune to his arguments. His second series of arguments fails even to show that those forms of simple ought-utilitarianism do not generally provide a *sufficient* condition for obligatoriness.

I pointed out various modifications of, or changes in, the assumptions on which Castañeda's arguments are based. As indicated, several of these are incorporated into his final formulation of a complex act ought-utilitarianism. They include making the choice of the method for valuing disjunctive actions dependent on matters of openness, and making implication relationships between obligations contingent on the openness of actions. Castañeda makes a modification of the latter kind part of his final version of utilitarianism, while I have suggested modifying deontic logic instead. Aside from elaborating on all these modifications, I specified a method of merely *comparing* disjunctive actions with other actions. This method, referred to above, can be used in place of Castañeda's methods which are designed *for valuing* disjunctive actions.

Because of the troublesome and ambiguous nature of disjunctive actions one may feel inclined to discard them altogether, thus eliminating most of the problems discussed in the foregoing. Yet it makes perfect sense to say that the agent ought to post the letter or deliver it himself, while neither posting the letter nor delivering it personally is obligatory. The disjunctive prescription as a whole is then to be regarded as an alternative, e.g., to burning the letter. Only it would seem that we normally use disjunctive prescriptions in this way when the relevant consequences of the actions corresponding to the disjuncts are the same and when all of these actions are open to the agent. It is plain that under these conditions valuing disjunctive actions presents no difficulties. It is only when these conditions are not fulfilled that disjunctive prescriptions can become troublesome and ambiguous. Castañeda's conception of an action machine is an attempt to make sense of disjunctive prescriptions in all cases. For his purpose of questioning the general viability of utilitarian theses, this machine is without doubt realistic enough. We found that it is also useful for pointing out the different kinds of actions – some involving a risk as to their eventual course, others not – which can, depending on the circumstances, correspond to one disjunctive prescription. This latter fact suggested that one should not insist on a one-to-one correspondence between prescriptions and actions when the formation of disjunctive prescriptions is generally permitted.

If disjunctive actions without risk are represented by prescriptions $G \vee H$, then those involving risk had better not be represented by the same prescriptions. They can be characterized as 'lotteries' in the utility-theoretic sense and be described by sets like $\{(V(G), P(G)), (V(H), P(H))\}$, where '$V(G)$' designates the value of the actual consequences of action G, and '$P(G)$' the probability that action G is performed (see [4]). It is clear that such sets or their members do no longer combine logically like propositions. It is questionable, however, whether utilitarianism should take lotteries into account. In the present context, utilitarian principles have been regarded as attempts to provide objective criteria for the obligatoriness of actions. If the risk involved in certain situations stems from the fact that the agent is partially ignorant of the eventual course of his actions, it need not be taken into account (see [8], 81f.; also [7], 26f.). However, there may be genuine chance elements as envisaged by Castañeda in his action machine. If we employ the method of merely comparing disjunctive actions with other actions, specified in section 5, in circumstances involving a risk of this objective kind, we find that no action may be obligatory. This method does not allow comparison in all cases, which can be regarded as a shortcoming. But why should we not find that in certain circumstances no action is obligatory? Using other methods, we still may want to point out one action as recommendable. Unless utilitarian principles are supposed to yield at least one obligatory action in all circumstances, they need, therefore, not cover situations involving chance or risk.

Apart from the particular problems mentioned so far, the task of wedding value considerations as specified by the forms of simple ought-utilitarianism to prescriptions in such a way that the implication relationships between obligations are safeguarded can also be of a more general interest. On the face of it, the task seems to be akin to measure-theoretic problems. In probability calculus, one defines a measure on a set of 'events' such that the measure ascribed to events harmonizes with their logical relationships, i.e., the algebraic structure of the set. There are attempts to cope with degrees of truth of propositions, where a truth function which takes on values between 0 and 1 is defined on propositions, one requirement being that the entailment relationships between propositions be recovered in case the values are 0 and 1. The present task is much more complicated. Not only deontic implication relationships will have to be accomodated but also relationships of the logic of prescriptions or actions that one may want to assume, as well as definite conceptions of alternativeness and openness of actions. It would seem that the problem of finding a value function under such conditions, which would lead to a genuine synthesis of utilitarian principles and deontic logic, is virtually incapable of a measure-theoretic solution. A detailed analysis of this problem is far beyond the scope of this paper. Several points discussed in this paper as well as Castañeda's final version of a utilitarian principle show that one can formulate utilitarianism and deontic logic in such a way that they at least do not interfere with one another.

ACKNOWLEDGEMEMT

The greater part of this paper was written while I was on a leave of absence from Wayne State University and had a grant from the Canada

Council. I should especially like to thank Prof. M. Bunge, director of the Foundations and Philosophy of Science Unit at McGill University for his hospitality. My indebtedness to Prof. H.-N. Castañeda, who introduced me to the problems touched on in this paper, should be manifest from the paper itself.

Monteith College,
Wayne State University

BIBLIOGRAPHY

[1] L. Åqvist, 'Improved Formulations of Act-Utilitarianism', *Nous* 3 (1969) 299–323.
[2] H.-N. Castañeda, 'Acts, the Logic of Obligation, and Deontic Calculi', *Philosophical Studies* 19 (1968) 13–26.
[3] H.-N. Castañeda, 'I. Ought, Value, and Utilitarianism', *American Philosophical Quarterly* 6 (1969) 257–274.
[4] H.-N. Castañeda, 'Open Action, Utility, and Utilitarianism', *Science, Decision and Value* (ed. by J. J. Leach, R. E. Butts, and G. Pearce), D. Reidel Publ. Comp., Dordrecht-Holland. 1973, pp. 128–147.
[5] H.-N. Castañeda, 'On the Semantics of the Ought-to-Do', *Synthese* 21 (1970) 449–468.
[6] B. Hansson, 'An Analysis of Some Deontic Logics', *Nous* 3 (1969) 373–398.
[7] D. Lyons, *Forms and Limits of Utilitarianism*, Clarendon, Oxford, 1967.
[8] G. E. Moore, *Ethics*, Oxford University Press, Oxford, 1912.
[9] A. Ross, 'Imperatives and Logic', *Theoria*, 7 (1941) 53–71.
[10] A. Ross, *Directives and Norms*, Routledge & Kegan Paul, London, 1968.

PART IX

METAPHYSICS

TOM SETTLE

HUMAN FREEDOM AND 1568 VERSIONS OF DETERMINISM AND INDETERMINISM

ABSTRACT. This paper marshals a case against some popular versions of determinism and in favour of partial indeterminism. First, a variety of versions of determinism and indeterminism is displayed, from which a few are selected for closer examination. Secondly, a clash is exposed between determinism and a necessary condition of the sort of freedom we might like to think we have. Thirdly, it is argued that several versions of partial indeterminism chime better nowadays with science than does determinism, which thus loses the underpinning it has enjoyed in the modern period.

1. INTRODUCTION: TOWARDS THE DEATH OF AN IDEA

From the point of view of a physicist trained since the 1920's it might seem as though the idea of determinism was dead. Einstein was almost alone in espousing the view in that period. Of course most scientists working with suitable material followed the maxim "Search for deterministic explanatory hypotheses!" But that is a far cry from the thoroughgoing (ontic) determinism of Laplace and Mill. And it would not be unreasonable for scientists to conclude the demise of determinism, given the exciting developments in physics in the second quarter of this century. Nonetheless, as far as philosophers are concerned, the idea is not dead. Old ideas like old soldiers, never die; and some fade away more slowly than others. In this paper I wish to contribute to the death of determinism – or at least to foster its faster fading.

First, I shall display a variety of versions of determinism and indeterminism, in order the better to focus upon the version I argue against. Whatever other defects previous discussions of human freedom, determinism and indeterminism may have had, they have not suffered from an overdetailed analysis of varieties. By contrast, I offer 1568 from which I shall pick a few for closer consideration.

Secondly, I try to characterize a necessary condition for the existence of a style of human freedom we think we have, a condition which clashes with many of the versions of determinism. Such a clash in itself constitutes an argument against determinism in its stricter form.

Thirdly, I shall try to strengthen the case against determinism by

M. Bunge (ed.), The Methodological Unity of Science, 245–264. All Rights Reserved.
Copyright © 1973 by D. Reidel Publishing Company, Dordrecht-Holland.

showing that several plausible versions of indeterminism chime better with how we presently understand the universe than does determinism. This argument has some special point, since the attractiveness of determinism in the modern period has rested to a considerable extent upon its compatibility with science. Such a foundation no longer obtains: indeed, the analogy now points the other way: science appears now to underpin indeterminism.

2. VARIETIES OF DETERMINISM AND INDETERMINISM

Let us use 5 distinguishing criteria, which I express as questions.

(A) *Is the universe law-abiding?* There are two importantly different sorts of descriptive laws used in science nowadays – leaving aside questions of any *prescriptive* law-abiding character the universe might have, else we would multiply uninteresting cases – namely, deterministic and statistical (or stochastic) where 'deterministically law-abiding' means, roughly, 'the hehaviour of the individuals in the population to which the law applies is uniquely determined by antecedent behaviour plus the law' and of 'statistically or stochastically law-abiding' means roughly 'whereas the behaviour of any individual in the population to which the law applies is not determined by antecedent behaviour, the states of an ensemble of individuals is determined by antecedent states of the ensemble.' I abbreviate the names of these two types of law-abiding characters thus: '*d-L*' and '*s-L*'.

I am not at all sure that I can conceive what it would be like to have a world which is neither deterministically nor statistically law-abiding. My inability by no means implies that there could not be such a world. I imagine that the Greek word '*chaos*' was supposed to point to what the universe was like before order was impressed upon it by, say, the *Logos*. The nearest the Hebrews came to the idea of chaos was the description '*tohu wabhohu*': 'like a desolation or ruin or wasteland'. Moreover all creation *myths* appear to assume a pre-creation stuff which is just there without being anything in particular, that is, without being ordered – unlike creation *doctrines* which may insist upon creation *ex nihilo*. Whatever one's success in imagining a completely haphazard world, there is little difficulty in imagining a *partially* haphazard world: It would be similar to how our actual world often seems. The phrase, 'it's just one of those things' and the notion of 'good luck' or 'bad luck' suggest the haphazard – incidentaliy, without implying that the haphazard is uncaused. The religious belief in miracles as interventions of the supernatural into natural order is a further example, from the point of view of the law-abiding character of the world, of partial haphazardism. I therefore include the theory that the universe is haphazard – 'H' – alongside d-L and s-L. Combinations of these three yield seven variants as answers to question A:

A (1)	d-L	A (5)	s-L & H
A (2)	s-L	A (6)	H & d-L
A (3)	H	A (7)	$(d$ & $s)$-L & H
A (4)	$(d$ & $s)$-L		

(B) *Does some power compel men's deeds to be just what they are?* It is unfashionable in some philosophical circles to take seriously the existence of either an external or an internal compelling power, but philosophers of religion, students of drama, Marxist interpreters of history, and others, use these notions. I here distinguish external necessity – the Christian Providential God, for instance – from internal necessity – like the self-destructivism of capitalism in Marxist theory or fate in Greek tragedy – because they seem to be interestingly and importantly different. Let 'P' stand for Providential (external) necessity and 'F' stand for Fate (internal necessity). Then there are four variants under this criterion (using the symbol '$\sim$' for 'not'):

B (1)	P & F	B (3)	$\sim P$ & F
B (2)	P & $\sim F$	B (4)	$\sim P$ & $\sim F$

(C) *Does God know the future?* I use the word 'God' to represent any possible being who is external to the universe and who may perhaps have knowledge of world events in advance of their occurrence. I have in mind knowing the future by a sort of clairvoyance or immediate knowledge rather than by a superb piece of calculation, because the case of God knowing the future by calculation is already covered by A (1): d-L If d-L, then God could know the future by calculation, if there were a God who could know the past, know the laws of nature and do the calculations. There are two variants under this third criterion:

C (1) K; C (2) $\sim K$ Where 'K' stands for 'divine knowledge'

(D) *Could a participator know precisely and accurately the future of what he takes part in?*
Clearly this is a different question from God's knowing, and also a different question from whether the universe is *d-L* – although the universe's being *d-L* is a necessary condition for the possibility of a participator knowing the future by calculation. I myself do not think the case of clairvoyance is interesting, but there are quite a few people devoting a lot of time and energy to studies in extra-sensory perception, which therefore perhaps deserves to be separated from 'mere' (machine-like) calculation of future states, given a statement of past states and appropriate calculating rules. There is of course some difficulty about a predicting device (human or engineered) predicting precisely its own future states. However, let '*Cv*' abbreviate 'clairvoyance' and '*Cal*' abbreviate 'calculation'. Then future-knowing by a participator in the universe may be by:

$$D (1) \quad Cv \ \& \ Cal$$
$$D (2) \quad Cv \ \& \sim Cal$$
$$D (3) \quad \sim Cv \ \& \ Cal$$

or not at all

$$D (4) \quad \sim Cv \ \& \sim Cal$$

(E) *What is the status of answers to the above questions?*
Parmenides long ago drew our attention to a possible gulf between reality and appearances. But his characterizations of reality were not illuminating and his denial of reality to what everybody judged to occupy public space was counter-intuitive. There's a certain danger in not living *as though* the appearances were for the most part real. The aim of the philosophers of science in the 17th and 18th centuries, notably Bacon, Descartes, Locke, Leibniz and Berkeley was to give some account of our competence at knowing reality. 'Why is our theoretical knowledge of the world true?' was the question. Hume rephrased that to 'What could possibly be the basis for our claim that our theoretical knowledge of the world is true?' Kant was shocked into wakefulness by Hume's skepticism, so he tells us. No one has, however, succeeded in giving an adequate answer to Hume's riddle of induction. Indeed, nowadays, we acclaim those who discover new forms for the riddle or even new riddles. Kant set himself to answer

the riddles and in the process opened up again the Parmenidean rift: only this time we learnt that reality cannot be known (Parmenides knew it too well!) while we may be certain of appearances, which after all we ourselves impress with a certain orderliness according to the functioning of our intellectual digestive system.

Many philosophers immediately after Kant accepted the rift as real, one group preferring to characterize unknowable reality in a latter day Parmenidean fashion, the other group sticking closely to the appearance of the appearances. This latter group, the positivists, could then by a simple shift, declare their reports of how things seem to be (which were clearly more reliable than anyone's theoretical, metaphysical guesses as to how things really are) to be descriptive of how things really are.

Meanwhile some scientists were still doing metaphysics, still guessing at theories deeper than appearances and still grappling with the difficult task of sharpening and tightening their speculations so as both to explain how things seem to be and to ready their ideas for empirical criticism. Could one call such guesswork 'knowledge'? *Unless knowledge be corrigible, there is not and never has been any scientific knowledge.*

Perhaps we may solve Kant's problem by claiming that theories proper in science (not simply empirical laws) are conjectures aimed to characterize reality, chiefly by the postulation of occult (hypothetical) entities and their modes of behaviour. With the aid of suitable additional hypotheses we aim also to explain how the postulated reality gives rise to phenomena such as we experience.

Let me put it this way:

The *real* world (world 'peopled' by things in themselves) is not open to empirical (sensual) inspection in the sense that sense reports are reports of the real world. *Metaphysics* may be viewed as speculation about such a world. The world of *appearances* (the public space and objects of common sense perception) is 'open to' empirical inspection or, rather, is judged to be the world after digestion of sensory signals. Positivism is the study of such a world.

Let us assume a link: Let us assume that sense signals originate in the real world.

Science conceived non-positivistically is the mesh of *metaphysics with physics* in which speculation as to an orderly model of the real world is

controlled to an extent by empirical criticism and empirical research is
directed by speculation!

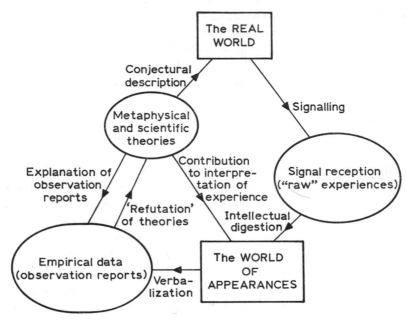

Fig. 1.

We may now distinguish determinism (or indeterminism) as an *ontic*
claim, a claim about the real world – hence speculative – from determinism (or indeterminism) as an *epistemic* claim, a claim about the state
of our knowledge, a claim that the world as characterized by scientific
laws is deterministic (or indeterministic). Both may be distinguished from
methodological or entolic determinism (entolé = precept), equivalent to
the maxim, 'search for deterministic laws'. Various combinations of
ontic (O), epistemic (E) and methodological (M) claims (O, OE, OM,
etc.) give seven variants.

Taking one variant at a time under each criterion gives us $7 \times 4 \times 2 \times 4 \times$
$\times 7$ different combinations. 1568 versions of determinism or indeterminism (of course, some of the versions are inconsistent, e.g. any combination of *Cal* with *H*; and many others are false; but most are not
without interest.) It is not germane to my argument in this paper to

pursue discussion related to all these variants, despite the interest which a number of them excite. I want to draw especial attention to the 49 variants achieved by taking criteria A and E together. B, C, and D will have to wait for another essay.

	O	E	M	OE	EM	MO	OEM
d-L	1.1	1.2	1.3	1.4	1.5	1.6	1.7
s-L	2.1	2.2	2.3	2.4	2.5	2.6	2.7
H	3.1	3.2	3.3	3.4	3.5	3.6	3.7
(d & s)-L	4.1	4.2	4.3	4.4	4.5	4.6	4.7
s-L & H	5.1	5.2	5.3	5.4	5.5	5.6	5.7
H & d-L	6.1	6.2	6.3	6.4	6.5	6.6	6.7
(d & s)-L & H	7.1	7.2	7.3	7.4	7.5	7.6	7.7

Fig. 2

3. THE UNIVERSE AS AT LEAST PARTIALLY DETERMINISTIC

While I think some of these forty-nine positions should be rejected, for reasons I shall give later, I do not think that there are many that are redundant (in the sense that no one in his right mind would want to take seriously the view in question), with the possible exception of numbers 3.1–3.7 (haphazardism). Furthermore, I think a number of very interesting differences are indicated by the distinctions I have drawn. We may, for example, contrast 1.6 with 2.2. or 2.4 and see the Einstein-versus-Bohr dispute about whether the universe was *d-L* at rock-bottom or not. Einstein held to determinism both as an ontic claim and as a maxim despite the fact that as far as we then knew (or know now) there was an element of the irreducibly statistical in the universe. Or one may contrast any square from 2.1–2.7 with the corresponding square in row 4 and find the issue whether the deterministic character of laws at some levels is an irreducible fact of life. There was a tendency prior to the 1920's to regard the universe as thoroughgoingly deterministic. This tendency was exhibited not only by atheists and agnostics but by such eminent believers as Spinoza and Leibniz. Furthermore, the central positions of Protestant theology had been occupied by troops loyal to the orders of Schleiermacher, a determinist, according to whom miracles were not to be regarded as nonnatural events; they were, rather, to be regarded as natural events which were extraordinarily revelatory: any event may be seen as a miracle to the religious man. (Paul Tillich subsequently organized this view of miracle within a more conventional theological frame than Schleiermacher's, in his post-post-Liberal theology.) Only d-L was taken seriously. The haphazard was not allowed to take place, and statistical laws were regarded as a stop-gap because of our temporary ignorance of causes. The discovery that a very powerful and fundamental theory (quantum theory) was thoroughly statistical was a shock. There were three variants in interpretation almost from the outset:

(i) If we pressed hard enough in the right direction we should, given time, find the deterministic laws that lay beneath the statistical laws (Einstein).

(ii) The rock-bottom of the universe had been reached: it was statistical (Bohr).

(iii) The laws do not refer to the real world at all but only to our measurements, which cannot be made sufficiently precise to give us deterministic laws (Bridgman).

More recently, other variants have been discovered which correct the swing of the pendulum from d-L to s-L:

(iv) Perhaps the universe is many-layered and does not have a 'rock-bottom' (Bohm).

(v) Statistical laws are true at some levels of analysis and deterministic laws are true at other levels and neither can be reduced to the other without loss (Bunge).

Further, one may contrast views in which at least partial H is permitted, with those in which it is not. Take the question, does the pursuit of science require a denial of the haphazard, and if so on what grounds? One interesting answer here requires us to notice that scientists take, not *every* event, but only recurring phenomena as tasks for explanation: the more the uniqueness of an event is stressed, the less easy it is to explain or to repeat; just those features of events which recur are what scientific theories explain. On this view, haphazard events, or the haphazardness of any event, are not tasks for scientific explanation. Leibniz, long ago, noticed that a scientist could not be satisfied with a miracle (or the haphazard or magical) as an explanation for an event; the pursuit of truth in science seemed to require the rule that no event be treated as an exception to the laws that pertain to the rest of the universe. Popper even suggested that metaphysical principles like the uniformity of nature could be replaced by methodological rules such as: treat no event as an exception to the laws of nature. I am sympathetic to this view, hence I think we should reject all versions which include haphazardism as a methodological component (3.3, 3.5–3.7; 5.3, 5.5–5.7; 6.3, 6.5–6.7; 7.3, 7.5–7.7). Now to some further rejections. In my view we should reject *s-L* (row 2). I think the view is falsified by the existence of deterministic laws which, as far as we know, are true. The best known of these laws refer to ordinary-size life. Some of them to be sure are hedged with provisos which protect them from refutation (such as classical mechanics which breaks down with the very small, the very large or the very fast moving). But not all: we know that zinc will release hydrogen from hydrochloric acid every time; we know impacts and diseased states through which human beings cannot survive; we know enough to shoot with astounding accuracy at the moon and, more astounding still, to get back what we shot. At least *partial d-L* means that we can to a very large extent and in a wide variety of areas control what happens in the world with considerable accuracy. *A fortiori*, we should reject *H* (row 3) and *s-L & H* (row 5). Now see Figure 3.

	O	E	M	OE	EM	MO	OEM
d-L							
s-L	///	///	///	///	///	///	///
H	///	///	///	///	///	///	///
(d&s)-L							
s-L&H	///	///	///	///	///	///	///
H&d-L			///		///	///	///
(d&s)-L&H			///		///	///	///

Fig. 3

4. HARD VERSUS SOFT DETERMINISM

Old fashioned determinism was what we may call *hard* determinism. It did not shrink from such words as fatality, bondage of the will, necessitation, and the like. Nowadays, we have a *soft* determinism which abhors harsh words and... says its real name is freedom; for freedom is only necessity understood, and bondage to the highest is identical with true freedom. ... all this is a quagmire of evasion under which the real issue of fact has been entirely smothered (William James, 1884).

My aim in this section is to analyse a necessary condition of what we call freedom in such a fashion as to make sharp the clash between freedom and determinism. This will incidentally show why I reject the approach of Hume, Mill, Schlick, Hobart and others to the freedom-determinism problem, for their solution is to adopt soft determinism (or a vacuous theory of freedom or both).

It is not my purpose here to say just exactly what freedom is, although I may, incidentally, make a few suggestions that could perhaps be helpful in framing a theory of human freedom. Rather, I have the much less ambitious task of characterizing or delineating a necessary condition of freedom, a condition, that is to say, which has to be satisfied if human freedom is to exist.

At first, I am going to try to capture the sense of the phrase 'x is a free deed' by capturing a variety of senses in which a deed x is not a free deed but rather is a compelled deed. I do this because I think it is easier to define compulsion rather than freedom from first principles. I talk about deeds and a doer rather than acts and an agent because I think my terms are more neutral and I wish not to sidetrack my readers by using loaded terms. For my purposes, I need six primitive concepts, which I introduce immediately:

PC (1) A set of alternative deeds, 'X', such that for any $x, y \in X$, $x \neq y$, and doing x does not entail doing y, and *vice versa*.

PC (2) The operation of doing $x \in X$: 'D'. 'Dx' reads 'the doer does x'.

PC (3) The attitude of the doer, towards a deed, of wishing to do it or wanting to do it or liking to do it or not minding doing it: 'W'. 'Wx' reads 'the doer wishes to do x'.

Notice that $(Wx \lor \sim Wx)$ exhausts the possibilities; indifference, not minding whether or not he does x, is included in Wx.

PC (4) The preference relation 'P' between two deeds $x, y \in X$, such that

'Pxy' means 'In the prevailing circumstances, the agent prefers doing x to doing y'.

I have used the phrase 'In the prevailing circumstances' instead of the (different) *ceteris paribus* phrase that might have been expected, for two reasons. First, I do not wish to assume *consistency* on the part of my doer, that is I do not wish to assume that given the same crucial features of circumstance again he would make the same choice. Secondly, I do not wish to assume any type of decision procedure beyond assuming that there are situations such that doers can prefer one deed to another. My phrase assumes that preferences *may* be circumstance-dependent but does not oblige any particular sort of dependence.

PC (5)   The relation between a deed $x \in X$, on the one hand, and the make-up of the doer, on the other hand, such that the make-up of the doer permits him to perform x: 'M'. 'Mx' reads 'the make-up of the doer permits x'.

This is an important primitive notion, but not, I think, contentious. It is widely accepted that there are restrictions on a person's physical powers – there are speeds he cannot run at, weights he cannot lift –, or his intellectual powers – puzzles he cannot solve, things he cannot learn – as well as inhibitions or other hang-overs from his upbringing. For any doer there is a wide variety of things he *can* do within these limits. Some of the things he can normally do, within these limits, may, however, not be permitted in some circumstances. When he is tired, his performance at many tasks is lower. When he is drunk or angry or 'in a mood' there are things he cannot do that he normally could. In view of these considerations, the formula:

$$(\exists x)\,(\sim Mx)$$

(where '$\exists$' is the existential quantifier and '$\sim$' represents negation) will be seen to be applicable not only to those deeds, 'x', which normally lie outside the doer's powers but also to those deeds which at a particular moment, for whatever reason or cause, he was not able to do. For example, the man who, despite encountering severely adverse conditions on a mission, correctly says of himself "I could not go back", is referring to a state of mind, a part of his make-up, which prohibits him from taking the decision to go back; he would not usually be referring to any *external* compulsion to proceed.

PC (6)   The relation between a deed $x \in X$ and the physical environment of the doer such that it is possible for x to be performed
by the doer: 'E'. 'Ex' reads 'The physical environment permits
the performance of x'.

The sense of 'permits' here resembles the sense in which equations in mathematics may permit of several solutions. Using these primitives, I want to try to capture, by various definitions, some different senses of the expression 'x is a compelled deed': 'Cx'. First, the type of compulsion involved when the deed is not deliberately chosen or perhaps when it is internally forced. Psychiatrists could provide us with many examples (if not a whole taxonomy) of mental disorders leading to what we term 'compulsive' behaviour – for example, kleptomania. And we all know that a sane person may do things on a reflex or involuntarily or in his sleep. I think these cases are all captured by:

Def.(1) $C_1 x =_{df} (!\exists x)\,(Mx\,\&\,Dx)$

This reads: 'x is a compelled deed, in sense number one, if and only if there is exactly one deed such that the doer's make-up permits it, that deed is x, and the doer does x'.

It may be stretching the sense of 'deed' somewhat to call say free fall in a gravitational field a 'deed', but, for the sake of the symmetry, I want to give:

Def.(2) $C_2 x =_{df} (!\exists x)\,(Ex)\,\&\,Dx$

This reads: 'x is a compelled deed, in sense number two, if and only if there is exactly one deed such that the physical environment permits it, that deed is x, and the doer does x'. $C_2 x$ covers those deeds which the doer is physically compelled to do by, say, having his hands moved for him. For example, an exasperated mother forcing her infant to feed himself by holding his hand over the spoon, scooping up, and putting it in his mouth, would make the deed of feeding himself a compelled deed for the child in sense number two.

A slightly weaker sense than either of the above is captured by:

Def.(3) $C_3 x =_{df} (!\exists x)\,(Mx\,\&\,Ex)\,\&\,Dx$

This captures such situations as those expressed by 'There was another course of action open to me but I could not bring myself to take it', or by 'I could think of all sorts of things I could have done, had the circumstances allowed'.

The fourth definition is of a form of compulsion which is weaker still, but it represents by far the most frequent usage. Most often when we say we are compelled to do something we mean that we choose to do that deed rather than any alternative open to us because perhaps we think the consequences of the alternative would be worse than the consequences of what we choose to do. It does not make sense (I think this is an uncontentious claim) to say that we choose to do what we do not prefer in the circumstances, but it *does* make sense to say we choose to do what we do not wish to do. The fourth definition tries to capture the notion of compulsion in circumstances where there *is* an alternative, but it is not taken.

Def.(4) $C_4x =_{df} (\exists x) (Mx \& Ex \& \sim Wx) \& (\exists y) (x \neq y : My \& Ey \& (y) (x \neq y : My \& Ey \supset Pxy) \& Dx$

This reads 'x is a compelled deed, in sense number four, if and only if there is a deed, 'x', which is permitted by both environment and make-up, but which the doer does not wish to do, and there is at least one alternative deed, 'y', which is permitted by both environment and make-up, but for all such deeds, y, the doer prefers doing x to doing y, and he does x'. And so on.

We could go some way to indicating what is meant by 'x is a free deed': Fx, simply by negating the various types of compulsion. Thus we could say, if i were to run over the values 1, 2, 3, etc.:

Def.(5) $F_ix =_{df} \sim C_ix$

Taking this step would expose what is often neglected, namely that there are numerous senses of freedom so that it is not contradictory to say 'I was free, in one sense, to do x, but in another sense, I had to do x'. I make no pretensions to having exhausted all the senses of 'compelled' and thus I have not exhausted all the senses of 'free' but I have at least taken some steps along the way towards the definition I have in mind for my necessary condition. The sort of freedom I am interested in is not preserved unless free acts of a particular sort are possible for human beings at least part of the time. To avoid complication and to be forthright, I offer a definition of the *sort of freedom we might like to have*: A choice between two desired options.

Def.(6) $F^*x =_{df} (\exists x) (Mx \& Ex \& Wx)$
$\& (\exists y) (y \neq x; My \& Ey \& Wy)$
$\& (y) (y \neq x; My \& Ey \& Wy \supset Pxy)$
$\& Dx$

This reads '*x* is a free deed in this desirable sense if and only if there are at least two deeds *x* and *y* which are both permitted by both environment and make-up and which are both wished-for deeds and such that *x* is preferred and *x* is done'. But this definition is too strong as a basis for a necessary condition for freedom because I think we can talk sensibly of people being free in an acceptable sense of 'free' even though none of the deeds open to them are such that they wish to do them. Wartime, for example, supplies us with many cases of individuals who for very long periods of time are in situations where there is no chance to do anything they wish to do: their choices are restricted to deeds that are all unpleasant. Furthermore, normative ethics has its more interesting problems when discussing what is the 'right' thing to do in cases where the only possible things to do are all clearly 'wrong'. Therefore, I think, the crucial sense of 'free' is captured better in my next definition, in which the wishes of the doer are not taken into account (although, of course, his preferences are: a deed is free only if the doer does what he prefers).

Def.(7) $F^+x =_{df} (\exists x) (Mx \& Ex) \& (\exists y) (y \neq x; My \& Ey) \& (y)$
$(y \neq x; My \& Ey \supset Pxy) \& Dx$

This reads '*x* is a free deed if and only if there is at least one alternative open to the doer but the doer prefers *x* to all open alternatives and does *x*'. Of course, a deed may be free in this sense but compelled in sense number four.

I am now in a position to state clearly the necessary condition I have in mind and distinguish it from the condition usually required by soft determinists.

NC   A man is a free man only if there are sufficiently numerous occasions in his life when alternative courses of action are open to him to follow.

I am not concerned to specify how numerous is sufficiently numerous

That is a side-issue to my present concern. The distinction between my position and the usual soft determinist position lies, as far as I can tell, in the sense we give to the concept of openness. Soft determinists usually say a man could do otherwise than he does, that is, alternatives are open, if and only if he would have done otherwise had he wanted to. This could perhaps be captured, in symbols, by:

Def.(8) $F_{sd}x =_{df} (\exists x)\,(Mx\;\&\;Ex\;\&\;Dx)\;\&\;(\exists y)\,(y \neq x;\;Pyx \supset (Dy\;\&\;\&\;Dx))$

However doing y entails that both the environment and the doer's make-up permit y:

$$Dy \supset My\;\&\;Ey;$$

and thus the claim that the doer would do y if he wanted to – in symbols:

$$Pyx \supset Dy,$$

this claim smothers the questions whether My and whether Ey, which are issues of fact, even if not the ones James had in mind. On my view:

$$F^{+}x \text{ only if } My\;\&\;Ey$$

Let us consider a doer deliberating at some time, 't_2', whether to do x or to do y at a subsequent time, 't_3'. As far as he knows, there are no hindrances to his doing either. Perhaps he is trying to decide which he prefers, Dx or Dy. Then, let us consider the state of affairs at some other time, 't_1', prior to t_3. We may make t_1 as distant from t_3 as we like – for example we may put it before the birth of the doer.

Now if it is the case that there is a set of deterministic laws such that material objects invariably move and exchange energy in accordance with these laws, then the configuration, at time t_1, of all material objects capable of causally influencing an event at time t_3, uniquely determines that event.

The unique determination may be mediated causally through the environment or the make-up of the doer, or both. In any case, there will be exactly one deed (let us say x) which both the environment and the make-up of the doer jointly permit. Any other deed (say y) would be inconsistent with the conjunction of the set of deterministic laws and the configuration of causally relevant objects at time t_1.

On the soft determinist view, the doing of y instead of x would require the universe to be uniquely consistent with Dy and inconsistent with Dx. Thus whatever possibilities, y, z, w, a doer might *consider*, his serious consideration of them as deeds he might do, is predicated upon his ignorance of what he *must in fact do*, the history of the universe being what it is. Otherwise: he is simply imagining what he might have done, if only world history had been different. On my view, whether a doer, free to do x or y, is going to do x rather than y might not be determined prior to his decision to do x. I want to claim that the mental-cerebral process of deciding to do x (assuming Ex & Mx) might be what picks out x rather than y and that y might have been picked even with world history as it is up to the decision process.

I claim that freedom is vacuous unless y remains open at least until the decision to do x is made.

Since we think we have the freedom characterized in part by my necessary condition, there is here a strong argument against ontic determinism. Ontic determinism should be retained as a doctrine, only if a good case can be made for it. Until recently, our belief in freedom was seriously threatened because of the existence of a strong argument in favour of determinism, an argument based on the state of knowledge in science. I propose now to try to show how what was, as far as I know, the strongest argument for ontic determinism has lost its strength.

5. THE COLLAPSE OF ONTIC DETERMINISM'S CASE

The quasi-epistemic claim, 'For all we know, the universe is thoroughgoingly deterministic' is equivalent to the claim that there is no conclusive evidence for an indisputable acceptance or rejection of *d-L*. This is an uncontentious claim. But the epistemic claim 'As far as we know, the universe is thoroughgoingly deterministic' is, I think false. Its falsity follows from the following 2 premises.

Premise (1): *As far as we know, we cannot reduce laws at one level to laws at another level without loss* – except, rarely, where explicit definitions are available. Mostly in quasi-reduction we use bridging hypotheses, themselves empirical conjectures which, taken together with the laws at the level to which the reduction has been made, will imply the laws that have been reduced. The statistical element in the universe is not eliminated by uncovering 'lower' deterministic levels.

Premise (2): *As far as we know, some statistical laws are true of the world* – for example, quantum theory.

It used to be the case, that, as far as was known to scientists, all laws of science were deterministic. Determinism was a universally acceptable attitude: the believers in God thought it vindicated their faith in divine Providence and the unbelievers thought it made belief in God redundant. Interestingly enough, in the early days of the theory that the universe was deterministically law-abiding, some believers were against it. For example, Pascal thought he could never forgive Descartes for rendering God redundant; and Clarke argued vehemently against Leibniz to retain the right of discretionary intervention for God. But by the nineteenth century, most believers had learnt from Spinoza and Leibniz how to use determinism as an argument *for* divine Providence.

Leaving questions of Providence aside, the argument in favour of thoroughgoing determinism could be put somewhat as follows:

A1.　　Given boundary (or initial) conditions, known scientific theories are successful in predicting, more or less precisely, states of the systems to which they apply.

A2.　　There are no good reasons for supposing that there are limitations in principle (as distinct from well-known limitations in practice) to the precision with which states of a system may be specified.

A3.　　By analogy with known laws, unknown laws are deterministic. The universe is, at rock-bottom, orderly, thus:
(i) Nothing comes out of nothing or goes into nothing – (Epicurus) and (ii) there is a finite, consistent set of true non-stochastic laws of nature which comprehensively explain the universe.

Conclusion: The states of the universe are exhaustively and precisely predictable in principle, given one complete state-description, and the set of true laws of nature.

This argument or one like it must have seemed good to Laplace and to Mill.

Nowadays, instead, the thrust of analogical argument goes the other way: the argument from the falsity of the epistemic claim for thorough-going determinism to the falsity of the ontic claim for thoroughgoing determinism, is strong. To overcome it, an argument *for* determinism must be stronger and I do not think there is one. It is not just "that as a total thesis determinism simply remains to be proved" as one critic recently put it. Rather it is that the good argument against determinism remains to be refuted or outweighed, while what used to seem to be a good argument to support determinism is now seen to be weak. Here are three ways in which this erstwhile seemingly good argument has recently been weakened:

(a) The rejection of the notion of cosmic simultaneity (though not of local simultaneity) as a consequence of Relativity Theory makes the notion of a "complete state-description of the universe at one time" somewhat incoherent.

(b) The proof – due to Gödel – that all finite, consistent axiomatic systems, rich enough to include arithmetic, are incomplete raises doubts as to whether the systematization of physical experience could ever be both consistent and complete.

(c) There are limits to the precision with which the states of a system are specifiable. This is a realist, theoretical objection, not simply an instrumentalist or operationalist objection. Whichever way one looks at quantum theory, precision of specification is restricted by the Indeterminacy Principle:

$$\Delta p \Delta q \geqslant h/2\pi$$

that is to say, there is a lower bound on the numerical value of the product of the scatters of 'momentum' and 'position' of an elementary 'particle'. It is well-known that an operationalist or instrumentalist or subjectivist interpretation of this principle – which is a 'theorem' in quantum mechanics – leads to indeterminism. The positivist move is to claim that the *physical* meaning of quantum theory is captured by discussion of measurements (=what we can know); hence epistemic indeterminism: but what is observable is what is so – hence ontic indeterminism. What is perhaps not so wellknown is that a thoroughgoing realist or objectivist account may lead to the same result, notwithstanding attempts to find perhaps deterministic levels below quantum level. For example, I refer to Bunge's axiomatization of quantum mechanics in which Δp and Δq are not measures of our uncertainty but actual spreads of value of objective qualities, which he calls 'quosition' and 'quomentum'.

In view of these weakeners, the case *for* thoroughgoing determinism may reasonably be considered to have foundered. Despite rejection of *d-L* as an ontic or as an epistemic claim (and thus the deletion of row 1 except for 1.3), I think it advantageous to keep it as a maxim.

Because I have rejected *d-L* (at least partially) on the grounds that as far as we know the universe is at least partially *s-L*, I should also reject *d-L & H*. The eleven remaining solutions are shown in Figure 4.

	O	E	M	OE	EM	MO	OEM
d-L	▨	▨		▨	▨	▨	▨
s-L	▨	▨	▨	▨	▨	▨	▨
H·	▨	▨	▨	▨	▨	▨	▨
(d&s)-L							
s-L&H	▨	▨	▨	▨	▨	▨	▨
H&d-L	▨	▨	▨	▨	▨	▨	▨
(d&s)-L&H			▨	▨	▨	▨	▨

Fig. 4

6. UPSHOT

It might well be asked why anyone should want to hold an ontic determinist view, anyway. What problems does *d-L* solve that are not solved as well or better by an alternative view? I cannot myself think of one except, perhaps the problem of the intolerability of all behaviour being random, disorderly, or unpredictable which might be supposed to be the case if determinism were false. Indeed, frequently, I find determinists argue that if determinism is false all is sheer chance. This seems to me patently false.

I want to stress that rationality, normal behaviour, moral responsibility, and so on, are not necessarily undermined by an element of indeterminism that is introduced by the rejection of thoroughgoing determinism.

Statistical or chance like behaviour at the neuron level of our brains is not inconsistent with orderly or even logical thinking if we allow that a mental event like thinking of an argument or taking a decision would be associated with (if not identical to) a rather complex cerebral process involving, perhaps millions of neurons. So the denial of thoroughgoing determinism need not lead to mental chaos. We do not know in the strong sense that the partial indeterminism I am arguing for is consistent with or guarantees rational, responsible behaviour in human beings. As a matter of fact, it does not seem always to lead to rational behaviour, though insanity and creative ingenuity are minority phenomena: most of the time most human beings do not make epoch-making decisions or discoveries or do anything very surprising or novel or weird. This is what would be expected if the stochastic processes in the brain were well integrated into the overall cerebral processes and governed such that there was no amplification of wild excesses. 'Snap' decisions are not amplifications of single synaptic 'decisions'. Such an arrangement would be analogous to, and compatible with, the general intricate homeostatic (cybernetic) control which the body has over its parts. Only a minority of individuals in the species have rather poor 'control': some of them are called 'insane' while others with more highly prized abnormalities are called geniuses. *The balanced mind is normal.*

In sum I claim that a consideration of the above should lead balanced minds to reject determinism in favour of one or other version of partial indeterminism. If nothing else, partial indeterminism makes life less dull even for the gods!

Department of Philosophy,
University of Guelph

THEORY AND DECISION LIBRARY

An International Series in the Philosophy and Methodology
of the Social and Behavioral Sciences

Editors:

GERALD EBERLEIN, *Universität des Saarlandes*
WERNER LEINFELLNER, *University of Nebraska*